The Courage of Conviction

The
Courage
of Conviction

Edited with an Introduction by
Phillip L. Berman

Dodd, Mead & Company
New York

All royalties from the sale of this book go to the Center for the Study of Contemporary Belief, the organization established by Phillip Berman, M.T.S., to promote the study of belief and to foster cross-cultural, interdenominational, and interracial tolerance and understanding. Contributions to further this work are tax-deductible and may be sent to the Center for the Study of Contemporary Belief, P.O. Box 4728, Santa Barbara, California 93140, U.S.A.

3 4 5 6 7 8 9 10

Library of Congress Cataloging in Publication Data

Main entry under title:

Courage of conviction.

1. Life—Addresses, essays, lectures. I. Berman, Phil.
BD431.C69 1985   190   85-13014
ISBN 0-396-08622-5

Contents

In Loving Memory of
Moses A. Berman
1927–1974

We stand on a mountain pass in the midst of whirling snow and blinding mist, through which we get glimpses now and then of paths which may be deceptive. If we stand still we shall be frozen to death. If we take the wrong road we shall be dashed to pieces. We do not certainly know whether there is any right one. What must we do? Be strong and of good courage. Act for the best, hope for the best, and take what comes . . . If death ends all, we cannot meet death better.

Fitz James Stephen

Acknowledgments

I am especially grateful to my assistant, agent, and lawyer, Linda Dubroof. Working without pay, hours on end, she gave her unflagging support and boundless enthusiasm, which were a constant source of inspiration during recurrent moments of self-doubt.

In the early stages of this book, Tim Schilz, then my editorial assistant, was more than an associate. His advice, support, and editorial expertise are evident in these pages.

Without the financial and emotional support of Steven Murray, this book would not be. He provided me with flexible employment during the first two years of its creation (hiring me to write or ghostwrite several books for his firm) and with a word processor as well. His belief made a difference.

Douglas Brooks deserves special credit. Working closely with Tempa Tsering (assistant to H.H. the Dalai Lama), his understanding of the intricacies of Buddhist thought added greatly to the quality of His Holiness' contribution. On top of that, his ready humor sustained my spirits throughout.

For friendship, advice, and love I am keenly aware of the impact Steven Gilbar has had upon these pages. His crisp prose style is also evident here. The biographies to these essays are in large part a product of his pen. Working with him has been a joy.

For editorial advice and support I am grateful to Charles Egan, Dan Sorrenson, and James Lochtefeld. Allen Klots, my editor at Dodd, Mead, deserves a special note of thanks. He found an early draft of this book, read it, liked it, and supported me warmly as I sought to complete it.

I especially wish to thank friends and relatives who cared enough to listen, offer advice, urge me on: Saul Ash, Mitch and Chris Berman, Mindy Berman, Sheridan Blau, Evon Borges, Walter and Lois Capps, Eric Dengler, Wilbur Fridell, Marion Gass (my ever-loving mother), Steven and Inga Gilbar, Robert and Kate McCutchan, Alfred and Anita Painter, Paul Ramirez, Debra Sills, Briar Todd, and Gregory and Sonia Walters.

For help and generosity of one sort or another I am grateful to John Akers (assistant to Billy Graham), Jean Anderson (assistant to Norman Cousins), Lark Bateau, Ayalla Dollinger (who did an excellent job translating Lech Walesa's contribution), Lois Dupre, Jeanne Ferrari (assistant to Hugh Downs), Sharon Joy (assistant to Elisabeth Kubler-Ross), Nancy Lutzow (assistant to Joan Baez), Melinda McGee (assistant to Jane Goodall), Ann Emmons Mintz (assistant to R. Buckminster Fuller, who passed away before he was able to compose his contribution), Margaret Murphy at Lescher & Lescher (literary agents for Benjamin Spock and Madeleine L'Engle), H.Y. Prasad (assistant to Indira Gandhi, who was assassinated before she was able to finish her contribution), Steven Short (assistant to Leo Buscaglia), Eric Swenson, Jolanta Skrzynska, and Tempa Tsering (assistant to H.H. the Dalai Lama).

To those of you who delivered my invitation and essay guidelines to Lech Walesa, and who also found a way to get his contribution out of Poland, you have my heart. During the three years in which I have had the pleasure to work with you, having never seen your faces or heard your voices, you have sustained and enriched me. I pray for but a portion of your courage.

This book would not have been possible without the assistance of thousands of postal workers throughout the world. Closer to home, I want to thank Don Monical, Leo Schummaker, and Nell Cambell at the Santa Barbara Post Office for service with a smile.

Finally, my deepest thanks go to the men and women who graciously stopped to share a part of themselves here. Your honesty and kindness was immense. You have all, in one way or another, increased my faith in life.

Phillip L. Berman
Santa Barbara

Introduction

In part, this book grows from a personal quest for meaning, which began in 1974 when I lost my father to cancer during my senior year of high school. During the less than six months in which I watched my father die, I came to accept both the shortness of life and the finality of death. But at seventeen, ready to embark on a life of my own, an acceptance of death was hardly enough. I was convinced that a career decision would have to be postponed until I answered to my satisfaction the same questions Billy Graham had posed to himself as a teenager: "Who am I? Why am I here? Where did I come from and where am I going?"

Initially, I felt an unsettling urgency for answers. But as I worked my way through college, majoring in philosophy and comparative religions, urgency gradually gave way to a growing, quiet joy in the study of life's mysteries. By discarding the notion that I needed to be certain about what I believed, I decided that William James's advice to "steer safely between the opposite dangers of believing too little or of believing too much" was the best and most difficult advice to follow.

I decided to compile this book because I have faith in the wisdom of James's advice, and because I believe that we live in a time when a number of people are hungry for meaning but have not the courage to seek it. Frightened by the demanding and often paradoxical nature of decision making in a world of uncertainties, millions today are either burying their heads in the sand or holding them up but wandering aimlessly, looking for meaning but unsure if it exists or in what direction it might be found. The recent, widespread cries for a "return to traditional values," the increased incidence of drug abuse in all sectors of society, the fact that depression now outnumbers all other medical symptoms put together—these seem undeniable signs that ours is a society out of balance, in need of new directions, revived hopes, greater courage. Some of the reasons for this are obvious: large-scale disappointment with modern science to bring us greater meaning with each new laboratory breakthrough; anguish over Vietnam; the failed quest of the excessively inward, psychological narcissism of the later 70s and early 80s; a growing fear of nuclear war; the frustration of young people facing the future in a rapidly changing technological society; and finally, more recently, the endless pursuit of personal financial success, which has greatly contributed to a further erosion of family, church, and community commitment. Seldom has there been a time when an examination of one's beliefs and a sense of values seem more needed.

With these concerns in mind, I founded the Center for the Study of Contemporary Belief in 1982 to encourage the study of personal values outside the walls of the university so as to promote intellectual and spiritual growth in the lives of the community and to promote tolerance on a cross-cultural, interdenominational, and interracial basis. In pursuing these aims, I hold two fervent beliefs: Tolerance is the one, absolutely necessary condition for the preservation of meaningful human existence, and for it to succeed, there must be open forums of expression. *The Courage of Conviction* was created to provide such a forum.

The plan for this book was simple. I invited prominent men and women from all walks of life to answer the questions "What do you believe?" and "How, emphasizing your occupation(s), have you put those beliefs into action?" Older readers may recall that similar books were produced in the late 1940s and early 1950s, most notably Clifton Fadiman's *I Believe*, and Edward R. Murrow's extremely popular "This I Believe" series. But *The Courage of Conviction* differs from these books in that contributors are asked to show how their beliefs actually exert an influence on their daily lives. I suppose it was only natural that an editor who graduated from high school during the waning days of the Nixon administration would be especially wary of hypocrisy. I felt it necessary that contributors examine their lives to see if they really had lived up to their beliefs—that they be faced, in other words, with the exceedingly difficult task of having to question their own integrity. Do their actions speak louder than their words? Or do their words speak louder than their actions?

I realized the dangers of this format. There was the danger that some contributors might use this book as a chance to justify some of their more questionable acts, or as an opportunity to promote their own brand of intolerance. And then there was also the danger that some would appear merely pompous. But I placed my faith in the reader's ability to judge the sincerity of these responses by the tone and manner of expression used by each contributor. I felt confident that the majority of contributors would be honest and sincere and that those who were not would drown themselves in the pool of reflection.

If these contributors share anything in common it is that they have spoken with honesty and humility. During the three years it has taken to complete this book, I have learned that for most of them talking about themselves proved tremendously difficult. Many have said that this was one of the most difficult assignments they have ever had. Some of them have spent months writing and rewriting their essays in an effort to know themselves better and to share what they know. For the nonprofessional writers, this task proved even more difficult. Yet none of them turned to ghost writers. Each recognized that this was too personal a subject to turn over to someone else.

The factors that account for what we call our personal philosophy are difficult if not impossible to chart. Where and when we were born, how we were reared, the type of early religious indoctrination we received, the degree of success, luck, or lack of luck we have had in weathering the storms of life—these all play a part. But it is how we choose to assess the unique experiences of our life that ultimately determines what we believe. "In this sense," says Norman Cousins, "each human being is a process—a filtering process of retention or rejection, absorption or loss. The process defines individuality." A genuine person's beliefs, then, are the outcome of a single complex personality that cannot be transferred. No two individuals, if sincere, can hold identical beliefs. Or, as Lech Walesa puts it, "Each person's belief and, accordingly, faith, is a little bit different, just as each one of us is different and goes through various, distinct experiences."

With the above in mind, the contributions to this book were arranged alphabetically, resulting in some striking seating assignments—accidents of chance, yes, but somehow as accurate a means of depicting the unique character of humanity as any form of categorization I know. And so you will find Benjamin Spock and Edward Teller seated together, each with equal passion seeking peace, but with strikingly different views as to how it can be achieved. Hugh Downs, Israel Goldstein, and Jane Goodall seem, on the other hand, more sympathetically joined. Each believes in what Mr. Downs calls the "uncaused cause," or in what Rabbi Goldstein describes as "God, the guiding force behind creative evolution." Mario Cuomo, a Catholic, finds himself beside H.H. the Dalai Lama, a Buddhist. And yet, for all the differences between them, both have chosen to live their lives in service—

believing passionately, in His Holiness' words, that their "own happiness depends not on seeking something for themselves but in helping others."

Much of the discussions in these essays centers on early parental influence and the impact it had on the formation of these contributors' beliefs. Leo Buscaglia, Joan Baez, Jane Goodall, Petra Kelly, Fazlur Rahman, Benjamin Spock, and Lech Walesa all viewed their early parental training as overwhelmingly positive, contributing significantly to their present-day beliefs. Sidney Hook, on the other hand, found it necessary to reject his parents' teachings, while for Robert Coles the contrast between his mother's religious faith and his father's scientific humanism presented him with a struggle of accommodation that persists to this day. In his deeply moving contribution, artist Jules Olitski recounts a decidedly more agonizing youth: "The evil I experienced in the cold bosom of my family was really of a low level: petty, sadistic acts accompanied with mocking laughter . . . day in, day out, I was told I looked like a freak, had the mind of an idiot, and would die in the gutter if not in the electric chair." That he would in later life overcome his bouts with alcoholism and be able to say that he was "fortunate from the start . . . that there was always someone or something to endure" is as powerful a testimony to the resiliency and potential courage of the human spirit as any I know.

God is discussed a great deal in these pages—his existence, nonexistence, or whereabouts. Over half of the contributors to this book express a belief in God. Yet it is clear that their views of the deity vary. For some, God is but the prime mover: He who set the universe in motion and who is, as Steve Allen puts it, "quite content to leave the necessary work of improvement to his human agents." Others believe that God takes a more active role in guiding the course of history. Israel Goldstein, Billy Graham, Andrew Greeley—all of them would likely agree with Fazlur Rahman's belief that "God . . . responds to prayers, guides men individually and collectively, and intervenes in history." For Rabbi Harold Kushner, God's existence is primarily dependent upon our willingness to seek him through relationships: "When people are loving, brave, truthful, charitable, God is present." Sidney Hook, Edward Teller, Irving Wallace, and E. O. Wilson consider such talk wish fulfillment at best. Each of them would likely feel comfortable with Dr. Wilson's description of himself as "someone who believes in humility toward other people but not toward the Gods."

Purpose, and whether or not there is any, is a frequent topic of discussion in these pages. For Colin Wilson and Andrew Greeley, the necessity for purpose is deeply felt. In Reverend Greeley's words, "Either there is a plan and purpose—and that plan and purpose can best be described by the words life and love—or we live in a cruel, arbitrary, and deceptive cosmos in which our lives are a brief transition between two oblivions." Irving Wallace, on the other hand, is unable to believe in purpose—although he would like to: "I would like to believe that my life has meaning in the history of the universe and that there is a plan to it in which I have a part, but I am simply unable to hold this view with rational dignity. In short, I believe in nothingness." Norman Cousins' view: "Nature rejects nothingness."

When society rather than the universe is under scrutiny, passion in these testimonies runs high. Socialists will likely agree with Benjamin Spock that "the United States is an imperialist nation, that our government responds to the desires of industry more than the needs of the people." Non-Socialists may disagree, but they will surely find his views worth considering. For those of a more conservative political temperament, the views of Edward Teller and Sidney Hook will prove more appealing. Political centrists, on the other hand, will take comfort in pondering the words of Elliot L. Richardson and Mario Cuomo. Certainly Democrats will sympathize with Governor Cuomo's dismay with "the so-called conservative idea, that, when it comes to government's redistributive function, God helps those whom God has helped, and if He's left you out, who are we to presume on His will?" Feminist readers will take fire from Petra K. Kelly's passionately written contribution in which she expresses her belief that "man's domination of women . . . remains a constant feature within every system of oppression." But who among us would find it possible to deny the sentiments that prompted His Holiness the Dalai Lama to write that "Without kindness for others we cannot survive, and the enemy of kindness is anger and hatred"?

Rita Mae Brown believes that "people are like teabags; you never know how strong they'll be until they're in hot water." Many of these contributors have been in hot water, have suffered for their beliefs. Benjamin Spock's indictment by the Johnson Administration on the charge of "aiding and abetting resistance to the military draft"; Rita Mae Brown's scrutiny by the C.I.A. for her early feminist and antiwar activities; Edward Teller's refusal to deny his "beliefs and understandings," which caused him to lose what he "wished to retain: friendly fellowship with my fellow scientists"; Lech Walesa's imprisonment for his refusal to compromise what he felt to be true—these are all vivid examples of men and women who have had the courage of conviction.

But courage can also be acted out more quietly. Robert Coles' efforts to wrestle constantly with what he calls "the devil that is pride" is as valid a means of putting belief into action as the raising of the mightiest temple. Similarly, William Barrett's decision to return to the Church so as not to "go on in self-denial forever," Edward O. Wilson's inward struggle to "reconcile evolution by natural selection," or Michael York's and Jane Alexander's attempts to, in Mr. York's words, "find some essential truth of character with which an audience could identify," are also instances of this quieter kind of courage; a courage evident throughout these pages. From Deborah Hyde Rowan's struggles to become a neurosurgeon against tremendous odds, to Elisabeth Kubler-Ross's efforts on behalf of the dying; Ashley Montagu's attempts to prove that "human nature isn't something that is fixed and inexorable" to Madeleine L'Engle's quest for human "connections," these pages are filled with examples of men and women who have had the courage to reflect on their lives and to act on the fruits of those reflections.

I do not propose that you choose between these various beliefs. Rather, I would hope that each of these essays can be of some assistance to you in formulating or strengthening your own credo, confirming convictions or generating questions, inspiring hope or stimulating self-discovery. Neither do I propose that adopting any of the beliefs in this book will make you a success, at least not as that word is generally thought of. In a world where things are all too often deified, it seems important to bear in mind that it is entirely possible to be wealthy with things and yet, at the same time, intellectually and spiritually impoverished. If you define success as the realization of your fullest humanity, however, or as following God's will, or as living productively and acting in accordance with the good, then *The Courage of Conviction* may well prove useful to you. Certainly if it occasions a new consideration of your beliefs and actions and helps you to appreciate the many ways in which it is possible to live fruitfully and with integrity in the world, then it has achieved its purpose.

Phillip L. Berman

The
Courage
of Conviction

Jane Alexander
b. 1939

Jane Alexander is one of the most versatile actresses working today. She has won both Emmy and Tony awards and has been nominated four times for the Academy Award, most recently for her performance in Testament, *a devastating film about the aftermath of a nuclear war.*

The Boston-based actress attended Sarah Lawrence College for two years before embarking on a New York theater career in the early 1960s. She has since appeared in numerous Broadway, off-Broadway, and regional productions. Her first major success came in The Great White Hope *in 1968, winning her a Tony Award. She went on to make her film debut in the movie version of the play, for which she received her first Academy Award nomination.*

Ms. Alexander is active on the boards of the National Stroke Association, Project Greenhope, Women's Action for Nuclear Disarmament, and Wildlife Conservation International.

My brother watched his first-born emerge into the world and greet it with a small wail—she was tiny, exquisite and very vulnerable—and he told me he knew suddenly for the first time in his forty-two years what the meaning of life was. There is no denying the miracle, the overwhelming feeling of gratitude and emotion with which we're infused when we witness the arrival of a newborn. It is peak experiences such as this that have informed my life and shaped my beliefs. All other memories pale and, indeed, have almost faded totally in my mind, but those moments that have overwhelmed my senses and emotions live with me and are recreated at will. They are moments in which I experience a feeling of oneness with the universe, of living in and of the world, rather than on it; a feeling of all in one and one in all, that I am everything and everything is me. A more Eastern way of perceiving things, yes, but Eastern is simply the label I now attach to beliefs I've somehow held from a very early age.

I remember, for example, experiencing this wholeness in my mother's arms when I was a baby: a sense of roundness and grace. And as a teenager I felt it when one night gazing at the stars I suddenly perceived them all in three dimensions, globes of light distanced from one another but inextricably bound to each other, and myself to them, by some awesome force. Since then, in moments of great passion or exhilaration, or when the natural world suddenly reveals itself in flashes of total color, sound, touch, or smell, I am similarly enveloped in a feeling of being one with others and with the universe.

These times barely last a moment, but because they live with me so profoundly they actually last forever. They occur infrequently, but are so stimulating I would not wish them to happen more often. If I had never had these experiences, however, I might try to induce them through religious disciplines or by taking consciousness-expanding drugs.

Psychic experiences have played a large part, too, in shaping my perception of the world. When I was quite young, I recall remarking to my parents or friends about events that were for me *déjà vu*. I was also able to occasionally predict events that were going to happen in the future. I called this my intuition, and it heightened as I grew older, culminating in my late teens in an out-of-body experience, which frightened me greatly. Early one evening I found myself spontaneously traveling a long, dark tunnel in my mind, from which I emerged out of my own body and looked down at myself. I thought I was going mad, so from then on I resolved to spend less time in my imagination and more time in the "real" world.

Being an actress is the perfect vocation for me, for it is in direct correlation to my beliefs. I wanted to be an actress since the age of six. Acting involves exploring and exposing obscure corners of the soul. My mind was already doing the exploring, so it made great sense to me to put it to use in this way. What is more, acting involves my senses and feelings, which I trust a great deal more than my intellect, in that the peak experiences in my life mean more to me than anything else. For me, they are God made manifest. This primary relationship with God is the basis and reaffirmation of my existence; and vice versa. Although I have journeyed through many organized religions, it has never been otherwise for me.

In Protestantism it was the hymns, the close, protected nature of the church itself, and the beauty of the story of Christ which attracted me. In Catholicism it was the ritual, the mystery of the Holy Ghost and the grandeur of it all that excited me. In Taoism I discovered the words that translated my perception of the world: the concept of yin and yang, of the passive and active principles of the universe, always contrasting yet complementary. In Buddhism I learned of nirvana, of all things being random and of nothing being random at all.

I no longer participate in organized religions. I am fearful of groups because in congregations of people there are always those who seek to dominate others, impose on others their rules for living. This squelches spontaneity and creative thought. It also fosters ill will. I believe that human beings are basically benign and loving, but when they undergo repression they become hateful. This is not to say that some group experiences are not extraordinary, indeed sublime. The June 12 Nuclear Disarmament Rally in New York City in 1982 was such an experience. Over a million people participated, and in my twenty years of marching and demonstrating I cannot recall a more compassionate day. Everyone there seemed infused with lightness and good will, including the New York City police. But for the most part, my group experiences (political, social, athletic, or religious) have been repressive and unrewarding.

The great exception for me is the collaborative experience of performing a play or making a film. Acting is a highly personal art, and yet a totally cooperative one, too. I am a kind of catalyst for the writer who wishes some truth of his or hers to be expressed. To perform in a vacuum without fellow performers or without an audience is to risk madness; practiced in context it is deeply fulfilling.

Acting is not difficult for me. Some roles are immensely challenging, but because I believe in a universal soul I feel that there is within me a deep well of human experience to draw upon. Sometimes it takes a lot of cajoling, patience, and despair before the right emotion or state of mind reveals itself, but I know it is there, and when I am truthful in my work it strikes a responsive chord within the audience.

" 'Beauty is truth, truth beauty,'—that is all/ Ye know on earth, and all ye need to know," said Keats. I, too, hold this as my precept. "Nothing human is alien to me," said the ancient Roman, and that also is my precept.

Through my work as an actress I believe I am able to reach other human beings on a one-to-one basis. Since I am often performing before thousands or even millions (in film), this may sound strange. But because I believe that we all share, or are capable of sharing, the same universal soul, I am conscious of performing for only one person. Perhaps this is the reason I've never been interested in the pursuit of fame or recognition for its own sake—reaching the masses has not been a goal of mine, nor has any sort of proselytizing. I do believe that acting is a powerful medium, quite capable of effecting change in the minds and hearts of those whose emotions have been stirred by it. I do not take this power lightly. I feel a responsibility to be true to myself, and through me to others.

The truth speaks for itself, and if and when I am able to express it through the work of a gifted writer, with the insight of a wise director, and the help of many skilled technicians, and an elusive event called luck, acting is for me a most fruitful way of life.

Steve Allen
b. 1921

"TV's Renaissance Man" is one of the terms often used to describe the multi-talented Steve Allen. At one moment he can be blurting out a hilarious off-the-cuff one-liner; at another he can be decrying the plight of the downtrodden. His lucid and open mind enables him to move easily from the most complex subjects to zany comedy. He uses it like a mine on a twenty-four-hour-a-day digging schedule, finding ideas literally awake or asleep. Always ready to extract them, he has small tape recorders everywhere: in his pockets, by his bed, in his car. This system supplies the raw material for the numerous Allen activities.

It is sometimes difficult to get the man in focus. He is, for example, a television comedian of thirty-five years' standing who has written a scholarly treatise on migratory farm labor, a volume on white-collar crime, and a study on China. The actor who has starred in plays and films is the same man whose poems have appeared in The Atlantic Monthly *and* Saturday Review. *Steve Allen, the composer of more than 4,000 songs, is the same man who is the author of twenty-seven published books.*

In 1977, the Public Broadcasting System presented the first season of Allen's "ultimate talk show": the award-winning series Meeting of Minds. *Created, written, and hosted by Allen, the witty and wise programs (as well as their book versions) brought together famed historical personages for stimulating conversations.*

When asked how he can turn from comedy to the serious problems of life, he responds, "I was a human being and a citizen before I was a comedian. And it is in those primary capacities that I take an interest in important social questions."

Much of my professional and private activity during the last thirty-five years has been motivated by the awareness—dim at first, but coming gradually into sharper focus—that there is no natural justice in the universe. There is justice in the conduct of our affairs, though not nearly enough of it, but such as it is, it is all created by human beings.

To state this truth in even simpler terms, life is unfair. I first felt this in a personal sense because I enjoyed far more than my proper share of good fortune. My health has been generally good, my fellow creatures have, for the most part, treated me very kindly, my work has been generously received, and I have been well compensated for my efforts. But all about me there are thousands I see—and distant millions I shall never see—who enjoy no such luck. Some are doomed physically at the moment of conception by genetic accident. Others are injured while in the womb. Still others are crippled while undergoing the process of birth. Millions more are struck by injury, disease, or death while still young. And always, all about us are the poor, the very old, the ill, the brain-damaged, the insane, the blind, the hungry, the countless hordes who suffer in places where the heat is crushing or the cold painful. Much of their suffering is caused by no human agency, though humans, by such institutionalized forms of cruelty as war and terror, add greatly to it.

I consider it foolish to believe that such tragedies are imposed by a vengeful deity. Such beliefs are an insult to God, rather than a way of paying proper respect to Him. And if portions of the more ancient Scriptures assert—as they do—that God is bent on bloody revenge and violence, so much the worse for the Scriptures.

But if all this is so, then every human is obliged to oppose it. Every one of us is absolutely required to do what pitifully little we, as individuals, can to set the scales of justice in better balance. This means, in part, that insofar as we are able to control our actions, we ought never to harm another human being, which conforms to Cardinal Newman's definition of a gentleman.

It is easy enough to recommend ideals, whether of modern or ancient creation, but some of us, observing that ideals are rarely achieved, proceed to the error of considering them worthless. Such an error is greatly harmful. True North cannot be reached either, since it is an abstraction, but it is of enormous importance, as all the world's travelers can attest. Even though we shall never be perfectly virtuous, we should still strive to be more virtuous. Even though we can never be perfectly courageous, we should strive to be more so. Even though we cannot be faultlessly compassionate, we should persevere as far on the road to that ideal as our moral frailties permit.

Another common error in thinking about morality concerns the timeless question as to whether there is an all-knowing, all-loving, all-powerful God. This, of course, is the inconsistent triad referred to in philosophy. Affirm any one, and it holds that one or the other divine attributes is false or limited. The question itself, obviously, has never been resolved to the satisfaction of the world jury, nor is it the case that only virtuous people believe in the deity and only sinful individuals do not. Most of the world's crimes are committed by people who accept the existence of God. But some, the faith of their childhood having been weakened, assume that if there is no personal, conscious God, there is no particular reason for persisting in our efforts to lead moral lives.

Dostoevsky, for example, believed that if there is no God then anything is permitted. He was mistaken. The debate on the point need not be continued in the abstract for we have evidence of two of the largest societies of all time—those of the Soviet Union and China—

which are officially atheistic. Despite their widespread assumption of the nonexistence of a personal God, we observe that it is simply not the case that everything is permitted in these two nations. But the truth goes farther than that, for, in fact, much less is permitted than in societies that are free and largely democratic.

In any event, if there is a God, holding all power, then He can certainly do a great deal to increase virtue and diminish suffering in the world. But if there is no God, or His power is limited, then the entire task is up to human beings. And even if God does exist, it should be clear by now, after hundreds of thousands of years, that he is quite content to leave the necessary work of improvement to his human agents. The deity has never yet miraculously introduced into the human drama a hospital, orphanage, convent, church, synagogue, temple, cancer research institute, or any other helpful social institution. He leaves that to the more compassionate of his creatures. May their tribe increase!

I believe in mystery, not in any dark-shadows-and-incense way, but as a matter of fact. The world seems to me absolutely based on mystery. The three most important philosophical questions—those concerning God, Time, and Space—remain questions, which is to say no answer to them has ever been proposed that convinces all interested parties. Each has, or seems to have, aspects of either-or-ness. The difficulty arises from the fact that these three pairs of alternatives, the six individual answers, are essentially preposterous, so much so that it is easy to think of objections to them.

For example, if there is no God, then we are left with a profound puzzle as to how the fantastically massive and intricate machinery of the universe came to exist. But if there is a God, a thousand and one troubling questions at once present themselves, since the vale of tears we live in is hardly consistent with the premise of an all-loving, all-knowing, all-wise creator with his eye on every sparrow. In reality, all sparrows suffer and die. The creatures of nature survive largely by eating each other alive.

As for Time, either it began one morning, say, at 9:27—which is obviously ridiculous—or it never began, which appears equally ridiculous.

As for Space, either one can go out to the end of it—which is absurd—or it has no end, which is equally absurd.

It is possible to do what millions have done, with varying degrees of satisfaction: accept one prepackaged philosophy or another and try to live by its precepts. A few individuals, over the centuries, have led edifying and productive lives by such means. But all the saints who ever lived could convene in one meeting hall of modest dimensions. And no philosophy, sadly, has all the answers. No matter how assured we may be about certain aspects of our belief, there are always painful inconsistencies, exceptions, and contradictions. This is as true in religion as it is in politics, and is self-evident to all except fanatics and the naive.

As for the fanatics, whose number is legion in our time, we might be advised to leave them to heaven. They will not, unfortunately, do us the same courtesy. They attack us and each other, and whatever their protestations to peaceful intent, the bloody record of history makes clear that they are easily disposed to resort to the sword.

My own belief in God, then, is just that—a matter of belief, not of knowledge. My respect for Jesus Christ arises from the fact that He seems to have been the most virtuous inhabitant of Planet Earth. But even well-educated Christians are frustrated in their thirst for certainty about the beloved figure of Jesus because of the undeniable ambiguity of the scriptural record. Such ambiguity is not apparent to children or fanatics, but every recognized Bible scholar is perfectly aware of it. Some Christians, alas, resort to formal lying to obscure such reality.

But if we are forever doomed to a state of less-than-perfect knowledge, if many of our beliefs are, in fact, only assumptions, none of this justifies a resort to either anarchy or apathy. Just as we say, in the context of modern science, that it is not necessary to reinvent the wheel, it is equally not necessary to reinvent or rediscover the classic ideals. The greatest minds of the ages have concentrated their attentions on such questions. The tragedy is that most of us go to our graves without ever having been exposed, however fleetingly, to the wisdom of the philosophers, saints, and seers around whose heads at least some helpful illumination has shone.

Having said all this, I should certainly not want to give the impression that I am an especially virtuous individual. I am, in fact, more impressed by my failings, ignorance, and sins than my pitifully few moral achievements. I can, nevertheless, refer to a few instances when I have practiced what I preached. One was the creation of the twenty-four programs of the *Meeting of Minds* television series, which a critic has called the ultimate TV talk show, whose guests were such as Thomas Aquinas, St. Augustine, Martin Luther, Socrates, Plato, Aristotle,

Francis Bacon, Adam Smith, Mohandas Gandhi, Susan B. Anthony, Florence Nightingale, and Thomas Jefferson. Such individuals' ideas and labors have greatly influenced our world. I thought that by expressing their views in conversational form I could provide an example of the sort of rational and informed dialogue that is in lamentably short supply in the modern world, except among scholars. Even though these visitors from the past were misguided in many of their views— as in the cases of Karl Marx, Machiavelli, the Marquis de Sade, or Attila the Hun—I felt it was necessary to become familiar with their teachings simply because they are still so influential in the world.

Because I had long argued that our society should undertake a formal commitment to reason, and nurture a respect for wisdom rather than attaching so much credit to blind belief, I wrote and produced a record album for children called *How To Think* (distributed by the *Gifted Children Newsletter*), as well as the thinking game, *Strange Bedfellows* (with educator Robert Allen).

I hoped, by those practical examples, as well as a good many lectures and published articles, to suggest the primacy of intellect and the moral sense. Man was not, after all, put on this earth primarily to buy philosophical merchandise before examining it, just as he was not put here to turn out hit record albums, or to be utterly irresistible to the opposite sex, to use cocaine, or to wear the tightest possible jeans.

From lecture platforms and in personal contacts, and even in speaking on television, I have taken every opportunity to defend rationality and to discourage the idea that it can be achieved with a minimum of effort.

We should not be deluded that all that is needed is a return to good old-fashioned common sense. While no one would deny the shortage of common sense, we need more than that.

I have tried to be specific in encouraging respect for reason, by pointing out, for example, the crucial difference between conclusive and consistent evidence. Consistent evidence argues only that we are still on the right track. Conclusive evidence shows we have reached the terminal of that particular track.

I have also attempted to arouse educators and parents to add a fourth "R" to our formal process of early education. The four would be readin', 'ritin', 'rithmetic, and reasoning. It might be objected that you cannot introduce a six-year-old child to logical thinking of a subtle and sophisticated nature. Indeed you cannot. By the same token you cannot introduce a six-year-old child to calculus or advanced geometry. But no one ever uses that fact to argue that we ought not introduce young children to arithmetic.

As I argued in *Beloved Son*, a book about my son Brian and the subject of religious communes and cults, one result of proper early instruction in the methods of rational thought will be to make sudden mindless conversions—to anything—less likely. Brian now realizes this and has, after eleven years, left the sect he was associated with. The problem is that once the untrained mind has made a formal commitment to a religious philosophy—and it does not matter whether that philosophy is generally reasonable and high-minded or utterly bizarre and irrational—the powers of reason are surprisingly ineffective in changing the believer's mind. We must acknowledge that the factual record is inconsistent with a significant part of religious belief, though not with morality. If we arbitrarily limit our historical research to the last five hundred years and examine the particulars of every factual argument that pitted the church against science, we find that science has represented the more reasonable and correct side of the debate. Consider the Pope's recent apology to Galileo.

But formal instruction in the techniques of reason, beginning at the kindergarten level, is only half the solution because the inability to reason is only half the problem. The other half is the deterioration of the American family, the soil from which each new generation grows. I recommend that from the same early point our schools, churches, and other social institutions provide instruction on personal human relationships. They ought to teach how to love, as well as how to reason. Just as there are millions who do not think very well, so there are millions who do not love well. They may constitute the majority.

I believe it is not merely enough to preach formally the supremacy of love, as the Christian and other religious traditions have done for thousands of years. Such abstract recommendations accomplish nothing. Indeed, they may achieve the opposite of their purpose in that those who hear such lessons may nod in philosophical agreement, assume that our acquiescence automatically puts us on the side of the angels, and then leave our churches and lecture halls only to resume our spiteful or vengeful activities. We must never forget that the monstrous atrocities committed by the Germans under Hitler were perpetrated by a populace overwhelmingly Christian. Nor must we forget that the Germans at that time were the best-educated people in Europe. Despite their frequent church attendance, scholarly studies, and interest in the arts, they succumbed to the appeal of hatred disguised as patriotism. This did not happen because they were German; it happened because they were human.

It can hardly be argued that such sadistic policies and acts were the result of either education or religious indoctrination, but they certainly were the result of the wrong kind of religious and secular instruction.

Since we Christians have slaughtered each other regularly for the last two thousand years, it can hardly be historically surprising that we would slaughter the Jews; and indeed, Hitler could at least claim that he did not invent such an outrage. A philosophy is necessary within which reason and religion reinforce each other and in which not merely nominal belief—in either God or science—would suffice, but in which the results of belief are emphasized. This, by logical necessity, leads to an emphasis on practice, which is to say, morality. That this is quite difficult to work out, I know from personal experience, and again I do not lecture my fellow humans from any position of moral superiority.

I believe that we cannot, in any event, learn about love in isolation, as we might take up other studies in solitude. Almost all religions preach that love is the supreme virtue. A few spiritual teachers, perceiving that we are all gifted at loving what pleases us, teach that the highest, most edifying forms, which might ultimately save the world, involve our regard for those it is difficult to love, some of whom are our enemies.

We have assumed that the ability to love is naturally nurtured in the home, and the home continues to be the ideal place for teaching it. But the American home, I repeat, is now a partly failed institution.

It is tragic that we train young people for practically everything except the two most difficult assignments they will ever face: marriage and parenthood. We train them in reading, mathematics, science; we train them to type, work machinery, pull teeth, maim, and kill—to perform a remarkable variety of manual and intellectual tasks. But for marriage and love, a complex, troublesome, and perplexing business for all its rewards, we prepare them practically not at all.

I am hardly the first to recommend formal courses to ready young people for the roles of husband, wife, father, and mother. But preparing fifteen-year-old boys or girls for marriage is starting at least ten years too late. Better late than never, assuredly, but the sooner we can get such courses into our schools and churches, the better.

I would not presume to suggest the specific content of such instruction. Specialists know what should be taught, and they have already perceived the wisdom of demanding the support of the church, legislators, and educators.

This will require the preparation of suitable texts. If a four- or five-year-old can be taught to read "See the dog. See the dog chase the ball. See the ball bounce," why could he not learn reading and loving at the same time, from a book that would say, "See the dog playing with the little boy. See the dog lick the boy's face. The dog loves the boy. The boy loves the dog. See the boy run with his father. The mother gives the boy a new toy and hugs him because she loves him"?

Human nature has grounds for hope, because love, in a sense, is inexhaustible. I expressed this insight once, years ago, in a poem.

> *God is love, you said. Or God is*
> *electricity.*
> *I do not know what God is. All I hope*
> *Is that He knows what I am. Electric force*
> *can be both measured and diminished.*
> *Love cannot, at least not in that way.*
> *When the first child was born, I*
> *loved it.*
> *But when the second child was born I found I*
> *loved*
> *Not half as much but just as much.*
> *And when the third arrived, he, too, received*
> *full share. So love's a magic force that*
> *Knows no laws, a well without a bottom,*
> *a purse that's never empty. Use your*
> *own cliché*
> *Just so you get the point.*
>
> *And one point more remains to make:*
> *that like*
> *The other faculties, the physical,*
> *The musical, the social, and the rest,*
> *Love swells in action. Will sets it*
> *aflame;*
> *It grows in height, direction, depth,*
> *and kind.*
> *It is the wise and wholly just investment.*

David Montgomery

Joan Baez
b. 1941

It is not only the purity of her voice and the power of her songs, but her commitment to human rights, that have won Joan Baez an international following since she first burst upon the scene at the 1959 Newport (Rhode Island) Folk Festival. At the zenith of her popularity in the 1960s, she served as a role model for a generation of students who appreciated her idealism, sincerity, and compassion. The Baez trademarks—long hair, informal dress, and guitar—became a uniform of the young rebel. For the student activists of the period who relied on violence, however, she had no sympathy. Her radicalism was firmly grounded in nonviolence, stemming from her traditional pacifistic beliefs. Over the years she has experimented with every possible alternative to violence (including serving time in prison for civil disobedience) while lending her voice to the civil rights and the antiwar movements and to the causes of American farm workers and prisoners, Cambodian refugees, Latin American desaparecidos, and disarmament.

In 1979, she founded Humanitas International to address human-rights violations. Under its aegis she continues to travel throughout the world, singing and advocating nonviolence like one of the warriors of the sun, "fighting postwar battles that somehow never got won."

When my son Gabriel was about nine, and we were sitting on the back porch watching the sunset, he asked me if I believed in God. I went on a long spiel about how Quakers say that there is that of God in every man and maybe the best way to translate that is that of "good"—I said it sounds like God—and he said, "But do you believe in God?" So I asked him, "Do you mean the man in the long robe and the white beard?" and he said, "Yeah." That's what he understood to be God, and he wanted to know if that is what I understood as well. "No," I told him, "I don't believe in that." And I tried to explain to him that what I do believe in is a force, a spiritual force, something that guides me.

Now this force does permit me to make choices. I can choose whether I'm going to do a wise thing, or something really stupid. But at some point it doesn't give me a choice. And occasionally I reach that point. I don't think that the events of my life are preordained, but they're definitely guided. I *hope* they're guided because I'd have a hell of a time trying to figure it out all by myself!

When I was ten and living in the Middle East, I spent a lot of time looking at the sky. The houses were all flat and it was so hot that we just automatically slept on the roof. I remember thinking at night about the universality of things. I would look at the Big Dipper and think, "God, that Big Dipper is going to be over California by morning," and things like that began to haunt me. Somewhere around eighth or ninth grade we had to write an essay on "The World"—a chance to explain how we saw the world. I had the very clear image of the world as a sphere with little dots all over it and the little dots were people and—probably partly because of my experience in the

Middle East—I knew that a lot of those little dots were going to bed hungry, and that I was privileged. I was a privileged little dot—for all my weird childhood fears and neuroses and problems, I still had a mom and dad who loved me and provided three meals a day and a cozy place to go to bed.

And then, at around the same time, I had what amounted to somewhat of a mystical experience. I was in my parents' car, looking out at a train, which was traveling parallel to us at about the same rate of speed, and I saw a little girl who was about the same age as I, and I was smitten as if struck by lightening by this thought: if she tried to walk from one car to the next and stubbed her toe, why wouldn't I feel her pain? And that had a monumental effect on me. I just thought about it and thought about it. I didn't know whether I wanted to take her pain for her or even if I could. It presented something to me that I just couldn't understand. But even looking back on that incident, what I see is a real desire to be connected in a constructive way with other people's pain.

For me, there is no separation between my spiritual and metaphysical beliefs and my ideological and political beliefs. When I'm trying to decide what direction to take in my life, for example, I go to a Quaker meeting and wait for direction—or perhaps it would be better to say search for direction. And I do the same thing at home. I've taught myself to slow down enough in the mind, because the methodical process of thinking doesn't get me there. Plotting and planning and thinking have never gotten me anywhere. If I've had a good idea, it's been an inspiration that has come at the end of a great deal of plotting and planning and thinking, but usually the inspiration has had absolutely nothing to do with all the thoughts that I had. Whether it is political action or artistic creation, it must be the same process. It seems to me that of those songs that have been any good, I have not had much to do with the writing of them. The words have just crawled down my sleeve and come out on the page.

I really do think that if we can use the word God to describe this source of inspiration, and I'd be happy to, it must be the power of love, it must have something to do with love and caring that wins out over all of our craziness and jumbled thoughts and ill intentions and neuroses and all the rest. If you can care on top of all that stuff or through that stuff, then that is what keeps you engaged in the outside world and not just turned in on yourself and unaware of other people. It has to do with passion for love and life.

What's more important to me is maintaining a connection between myself and the things that I do to bring about a better world. That seems to be what I was put here for. For instance, at those times that I've tried doing music without politics—politics meaning my involvement with people and social change—the music has lost its glow. I've done lots of things in my lifetime, and I know that I am least happy when I am least involved in social action. But when I seem to be on the track that's really mine, it has been because my activities were closest to pure Gandhian nonviolent action. I have rarely felt as content, as energized, as satisfied, or as fulfilled personally as when I marched with Dr. Martin Luther King, Jr., in Grenada, Mississippi, took the hands of little black kids and walked with them to their school, and confronted the white cops who viewed us hatefully as we tried to make contact with them as feeling, individual human beings.

The attachment to nonviolent action is spiritual—coming out of an old-fashioned Quaker heritage. What people do in Quaker Meeting is sit around as a group listening for the word of God to guide them. Alone, I am nothing. That's why I can speak immodestly, but with total humility, about my voice, and about some of the things that I've done because I consider that when I achieved anything, it was the result of something speaking through me. You could say that I've been a conduit, and that, most of the time, whatever I have done, it was not my idea at all; it was something that happened and it has to do with being inspired. That something could be called God.

Somebody recently asked me if I had ever had any doubts about how I had lived my life, if I had ever thought to myself, "I'm uncertain about everything that I've done before in my life; I don't know about everything that I've believed before in my life." I had never thought about that before, but when I reflected on it, I realized that I had never had any doubts because I don't think I ever believed anything. I've just done it. I haven't had a belief system except for a faith in nonviolence. I've had faith in it, I've done it, and what I have done, I have seen work.

Of course, I have seen places where it was impossible for nonviolent action to work because the situation had gone beyond the point where it could work. It hasn't made me turn against it, because I'm not about to take up armed struggle. It's just been kind of disheartening, knowing that what we've created in this world is a situation in which nonviolence as a social and political tool barely has a chance even to be planted, let alone flower. But if, looking back over the years, I ask myself if I think that I should have done it another way, or if I did the wrong thing, or if maybe I've got it all wrong and that human life is not important after all and killing each other is all in the natural order of things, the answer is no. I've never had that sort of cataclysmic disillusionment. Sometimes I think whales are nicer and kinder and more tolerant and brighter than people and I might wonder why I didn't spend any time for the last twenty years trying to save the whales. But I have priorities. Whales sing better than I do anyway, so I'd probably be jealous.

I wish I belonged to a church. My life would be a whole lot easier if I had the pattern of an organized religion. I don't have enough faith. I wish that, somehow or other, it had been arranged that I had more of a structure to lean on. I mean, even symbols would be nice. It would be easier for me to ground myself. Of all the structures I've tried, Quaker Meeting makes the most sense to me. It's something resembling a structure. And I like what happens there. At Quaker Meeting you can be and feel whatever you want. But I have had to discipline myself in whatever I've done all my life because I have not taken to other people's disciplines. I guess what I'm saying is that if something could force a discipline on me and I liked it, it would just make life easier—that's all.

As it is, I have to find the answers on my own. But as long as one keeps searching, the answers come. And to me that search has a great deal to do with nonviolence—with the things that are worth caring for: human life and respect for human life. This leads me automatically to the basic and most important rule: Thou shalt not kill. And so you spend your life looking for ways to work out conflict and to put that commandment into practice on a wide and practical scale.

Ira Allen

William Barrett

b. 1913

*During the 1940s and 1950s, William Barrett was an associate editor
of one of America's leading literary and political journals,* Partisan
Review, *which boasted such regular contributors as Delmore Schwartz,
Mary McCarthy, Dwight Macdonald, and Hannah Arendt. His "adventures" among New York's leftist intellectuals during those years
are incisively chronicled in his highly praised memoir* The Truants
(1982). But it is not only for his involvement in Partisan *politics that
Dr. Barrett is known; he is also a philosopher, the author of the
classic introductory text to existentialism,* Irrational Man *(1958), and*
What is Existentialism? *(1964). He has also written studies of modern
literature, including* Time of Need: Forms of Imagination in the
Twentieth Century *(1972) and a study of man's quest for dominance
over nature,* The Illusion of Technique *(1978).*

*After receiving his Ph.D. in philosophy from Columbia University
in 1938, he taught for a few years at Brown University, before serving in World War II. He did not return to teaching until 1950, when*

he joined the faculty of New York University, where he taught for over twenty-five years. During this time he edited, with D. T. Suzuki, Zen Buddhism (1956) and, with Henry Aiken, Philosophy in the Twentieth Century (1962).

I am afraid I will not have anything interesting to say on the subject of religion. Perhaps the religious, as Kierkegaard suggested, is the sphere of our human existence where "interesting" ideas no longer matter. In any case, one reaches a certain age where "interesting" ideas no longer engage one.

I was raised as a Catholic. But very early on—about the time of my confirmation, somewhere around twelve—I had become a precocious doubter, though I kept the doubts from my family. By the time of adolescence, my connection with the Church had withered away.

Yet even then, as I look back, there was a strange division in my disbelief. This was the Catholic Church before Vatican II, and the Mass was celebrated in Latin. I had fallen in love with this Latin, and I could intone to myself passages in exaltation even while my disbelieving mind might be chattering its cacophonies. Also, I learned Italian at an early age and read Dante—an experience that permanently shaped my sensibility more deeply, I realize now, than I grasped at the time.

So I issued from the troubled years of youth as a divided-self, a nay-sayer who was not quite godless. Then I became a professor of philosophy and spent many years wrestling with the arguments. In my classes I tried to keep the issue alive and open, ascribing to the dogmatism of neither side. I suppose I have become a Kantian of sorts. In these matters, I believe, there are no proofs, not proofs anyway in the strict sense. In the nature of the case there cannot be, since proof, in the strict sense, can only take place where there are very definite and sharply delimited concepts, and this requirement cannot be met when we are talking about God. By the same token, of course, disproof is also impossible.

Nevertheless, I have become aware more and more over the years that I personally cannot be godless. A matter of temperament perhaps, but in the end one has to become what one is. The dogmatist's statement of atheism strikes me as flat and uninviting. And beneath all the conflicting clamor of my ideas, over the years there has been deep down the growing hunger to worship. There are some intellectuals I know and respect for whom this need seems never to be felt. But I have to follow my own need; I cannot go on in self-denial forever.

So I have returned to the Church. I would not attempt to justify this choice by intellectual arguments. Had my background and my early shaping been different, I might very well be a Jew or a Protestant or a Mohammedan. I do not feel that my particular mode of worship separates me from the human souls who follow other sects and denominations. Rather, the act of worship seems to join us all together, and backward into the past to the whole life of humankind upon this earth.

In a sense, then, I do not know why I am going to church. Perhaps it will be clearer to me as I go on. Every now and then, however, I seem to catch a glimmer of what one part of that goal might be: to awaken to joy in the sheer fact, the wondrous miracle, of life itself. I am not there yet, I have to keep going on.

Roger Ressmeyer

Rita Mae Brown

b. 1944

Born an orphan in Pennsylvania, Rita Mae Brown moved to Florida with her adopted family when she was eleven, and ever since her heart "has been truly in the South." Good grades earned her a scholarship to the University of Florida; participation in civil-rights activities got her dismissed. She came north when New York University's Washington Square College offered her a scholarship. This time good grades earned her a B.A. and admittance into a doctoral program in political science at the Institute for Policy Studies in Washington, D.C. Although she was awarded the Ph.D. in 1976, she considered the process of acquiring it an "exercise in misery." During the seventies, she wrote, "I knocked around trying to learn to write fiction while working and organizing against the War in Vietnam, for women's and gay rights. I learned a good deal writing for all the underground newspapers during those days. Oftentimes, explosive social times are good times for writers. It isn't that one feels good but literature needs tension, conflict to work. I had a mess of it!"

Rita Mae Brown became a full-time writer when a friend convinced her to "get out of the fog of political rhetoric." The result was, at twenty-seven, her first novel, Rubyfruit Jungle. *Rejected by the major publishing houses, it was eventually brought out by a small feminist press and ultimately purchased by a major publisher in a mass-market paperback edition. Hailed by* The New York Times *as "the single most incendiary novel to have emerged from the women's movement," it has sold over 500,000 copies. The phenomenal success of the novel has enabled her to concentrate solely on writing fiction. Since* Rubyfruit Jungle, *five other novels have followed as well as numerous screenplays, two books of poetry, and a book of feminist essays. In 1982, she was nominated for an Emmy. She has also found the time to teach and to speak at colleges and universities across the country and to serve on the advisory board for the National Women's Political Caucus and to serve on the board of the Human Rights Campaign Fund.*

People are like teabags; you never know how strong they'll be until they're in hot water. In times of trouble, you not only discover what you truly believe but whether or not you can act on those beliefs. Much as I would like to put down a list of lovely, brave, and self-enhancing beliefs, I think I'd better stick to what's been tested. This will keep me to the particular as opposed to the ravishing abstract.

I believe you never hope more than you work. In action, this means I work ten to sixteen hours a day, usually seven days a week. Since I love my work, which is writing, this is a joy.

I believe you are your work. Don't trade the very stuff of your life, time, for nothing more than dollars. That's a rotten bargain. In my life I worked until I was thirty before I made enough money to go to the movies when I wanted to. Before that I existed on less than $5,000 a year and sometimes the figure dropped below $2,000. It takes a long time to develop into a writer. It takes about the same amount of time to develop into a neurosurgeon, but the young woman or man in medical school has an elaborate support system and a method of obtaining loans unavailable to the artist. For an artist it's sink or swim. I sanded floors, painted houses, refinished antiques, anything, to buy one hot meal a day and keep a dumpy roof over my head. I believed that learning my craft was worth this scramble. I'm sorry that our country and the people in it do not consider the arts as vital to our well-being as, say, medicine. Suffering is unnecessary. It doesn't make you a better artist; it only makes you a hungry one. However, to me the acquisition of the craft of writing was worth any amount of suffering. To have meaningful work is a tremendous happiness.

I believe the artist has an obligation to make his/her work accessible. This means that the style of the work must be simple, although the themes need not be. A clear, pure style is difficult to achieve. The simpler the style, the harder the author has to work to achieve it. This is important for another reason. To write in a tortured, "high-brow" style is a subtle form of insult to the reader. You're telling the reader that you're terribly intelligent, possibly more intelligent than s/he. I've always thought that if a person has to go out of their way to impress you with their intelligence, they probably aren't too smart. Or to put it in "high-brow" style: I distrust manifest knowledge.

I believe that piety is like garlic: a little goes a long way. In action, this means I have never inflicted my strongly held religious beliefs on anyone else.

I believe that monogamy is contrary to nature but necessary for the greater social good. In action I have not committed infidelities, but I'd be hurt if no one thought me capable of them.

I believe the true function of age is memory. I'm recording as fast as I can.

I believe that when all the dreams are dead, you're left only with yourself. You'd better like yourself a lot.

I believe that human sexuality is in a continual state of flux. For people in Western culture this, for some reason, is terrifying. One is either heterosexual or homosexual and thereby branded for life as though one had chosen a profession or committed a crime. I believe this is a very destructive attitude toward one's self and toward others, and the only action I can take against this attitude is to question it. I am no more afraid to be called a lesbian than I would be afraid to be called a wife.

I believe that our concept of romantic love is irrational, impossible to fulfill, and the cause of many broken homes. No human being can maintain that rarified atmosphere of "true love"—and we equate love with sex, another huge mistake. I'm not saying there is not loving sex nor long-term partnerships, but that our absurd emphasis on romance has created a nation of love junkies. Americans want to be passionately in love. I believe this is a sickness and I question it. In my personal life I act by taking the energy that most Americans reserve for their sex/love partner and pour it into my friendships. The result is that I have a host of people I truly love in this world, whereas the person who has reserved all their emotions for "The One and Only" is alone because "The One and Only" has a nasty habit of walking out on you—or you become bored with him/her. As to the partner in my life, I think of this individual as a friend with whom I share my body. I suppose I think of my partner as the Romans thought of the princeps, first among equals.

I believe it is my patriotic duty to question the actions of my government. I also believe that we deserve what we get. If you aren't willing to work for your political beliefs then you should have the good manners not to complain about the state of affairs in which you find yourself. In my youth, this meant working for civil rights: work that cost me my scholarship to the University of Florida. Fortunately, New York University at Washington Square College gave me one so I could continue my studies without fear of political reprisal. I had cursory contact with the antiwar movement. My attitude about Vietnam was different from that of many of the white, middle-class protestors. My cousin, who was like a brother to me, was in the Marine Corps. My thoughts were either we win the war or we pull out. As it became clear that we would not push to win but only to "contain" the North Vietnamese, I wanted out. I realized that many of my compatriots had deep moral reasons for being against the war, whereas I did not. I just didn't want my cousin blown to kingdom come for nothing.

In fact, I would have to say that my beliefs and actions are usually connected to something tangible. I do admire people who can become motivated by some large, abstract belief. Nevertheless, I am not one of them. I need to see a person, place, or thing before I feel anything, before I am willing to act.

It was this same simplicity, if you will, or earthiness, that encouraged me to help found the feminist movement. I wasn't compelled by a vast concept of female liberation, but rather by the fact that I had been pushed aside once too often. As we came together in the late sixties and the early seventies, I began to see that my individual experiences were not so individual. Only then was I able to go from the particular to the general. The mistakes I made in that political process were the mistakes of youth. I thought what made sense on paper would make sense with people. I have since been disabused of that notion.

These experiences taught me that actions have consequences. First, we were the only political movement that had a national image before we had a local base. Television cameras swooped upon us in our nascent protests, our excessive youthfulness, and our pictures were beamed across America. Suddenly, there was a women's movement. But if you wanted to find a women's center in Charlottesville, Virginia, there wasn't one. We looked half-baked in those days and we were. Consequently, I learned political organizing backward. Those lessons were extremely valuable. Whereas I had earlier distrusted government (and remember, it was the only sane thing to do in those days, to distrust Nixon) I now began to understand how disaster might result when the public scrutinizes a policy before it has been fully and properly formulated. I don't know how we strike the balance between the public's right to know and the government's right to create new policy.

These experiences taught me that most people enjoy the comfort of opinion without the discomfort of thought. As an example, child molesters are thought to be homosexual men, yet the statistics on child molesters show that over 95 percent of them are married men with two or more children. Still, can we dislodge the stereotype from this statistical reality? So it was with the feminist movement. Suddenly, I found myself freighted with instant stereotypes that had nothing to do with me or my work. When I pressed forward to gather gay people in their own political movement, this process of negative stereotyping became even more pronounced. The sadness of it is that many times the victims often think of themselves in such self-hating, negative terms.

My beliefs were severely tested. My actions brought unwanted consequences. The C.I.A. and F.B.I. kept a file on me, which I have secured through the Freedom of Information Act. I was disgusted that taxpayers' dollars were spent in watching the growing-up of a young woman whose only "sin" was that she asked questions. I have never advocated violence. I never will. I worship the Constitution of the United States. I am shocked that so few of our elected officials seem to care about it. I despise communism with a visceral passion. But I asked questions, and so I was watched, and even bugged, the whole nine yards. It didn't stop me from asking questions but it made me think about how fragile liberty really is. Those experiences were invaluable. They forced me to examine myself, my country, my generation. Those were bad times, and I do not wish to see them ever return. I hated being treated that way, but I wasn't shot or thrown in jail. In plenty of countries that would have been the price I paid. Still, you can't make gray look white by comparing it to black.

The behavior of our government toward its own citizens during those war years was reprehensible. Constant vigilance is required of each of us so that it never happens again.

I believe that it is the duty of every citizen to vote. I vote.

I believe each of us who is sane or partially sane, anyway, and physically healthy has a duty to watch out for others in our community. This applies to animals as well as to people. This is much easier for me than for those in big cities. My town has 45,000 inhabitants and there are another 45,000 in Albemarle County, Virginia. If someone suffers hardship I will know about it even if it isn't a close friend. Word gets around and our newspaper tells us. This is a good town because when disaster strikes, everyone who can chips in. I also help the S.P.C.A. when I can, too. I love animals.

I believe those who are in the mainstream have an extra obligation to consider the lives of those who are not. I am not in the mainstream. I was born, orphaned, adopted, raised with much love and practically no money. But I do have advantages. I am white. I am healthy. I secured my education, including a doctorate. So I think I must be on guard in those areas where I might be insensitive. On the issue of race, I marched, I sang, and voted. Now those times are gone and I do other things. I have instituted a small scholarship at Piedmont Community College to enable a student who is female and black to study literature. If my fortunes improve, so will the scholarship.

I believe that if you are heterosexual (meaning you have accepted your sexuality as fixed, you accept the cultural definition of static sexuality) then you have a responsibility to think seriously about homosexuality . . . not as a practice, but you should think about how it feels to belong to a misunderstood and despised minority. If you are a man, you should try to identify with women. And so on down the line. Even if you can't get yourself in gear to do anything about it, the very act of thinking about it, of putting yourself in another's shoes, is bound to give you some understanding, some compassion. That can only help us all.

Why am I putting the burden on the majority, on the mainstream? Because to fall into any minority group means you must learn to understand the majority in order to survive. A minority person knows much more about a majority person than vice versa. It's time we reverse this process.

I believe, passionately, that drugs, drink, and cigarettes are foolish. I do not drink, smoke, or take drugs. I never have. When I give speeches I beg people to give up this form of slow self-destruction. However, if you do it, that's your choice. It's your life. I only ask, then, that you contain your self-destructiveness. Why should I be forced to watch it?

I believe it takes courage to live. In action, this means I surrender myself to life. To try to control your life is the coward's way out. It means there are no adventures, surprises, or magical turning points. A controller doesn't trust his/her ability to live through the pain and chaos of life. There is no life without pain just as there is no art without first submitting to chaos. Stated another way: a neurotic solution is one that seeks to avoid legitimate suffering. You have to suffer; not every day, but as a consequence of time. Perhaps a five-year-old does not suffer (if the child is lucky enough to be in a good, loving home) but the rest of us must suffer at various times. You'll live through it. You can't control suffering because if you try to avoid it then you kill rapture and joy. The two are inextricably linked. Joy never comes without suffering and therefore demands courage. For myself that means that if something terrible happens to me, I say to myself what my mother used to say to me, "Worse things have happened to nicer people." You'd be amazed at how that works.

I believe the next great revolution will occur when human beings learn to politically organize without the concept of the outside enemy. Our entire foreign policy is built around ideological antagonism. So is the foreign policy of every other nation on earth and most individuals think the same way, i.e., that there is a person, group of people, religion, sex, or other country that is "the enemy." Their behavior is then crystallized around reaction to the enemy. How utterly perverse this is. It means your life is controlled by the very people you hate. A life of reaction is a life of slavery, intellectually and spiritually. One must fight for a life of action not reaction. Right now my only weapon in this struggle is my typewriter. The only thing I can do is introduce this concept and wonder if anyone will accept it, enlarge it, make it far better and sensible than my embryonic effort.

It was my mother who taught me to tell the truth and my father who taught me patience with those lands, people, and creatures entrusted to my care. I feel, whatever my personal failures, that I have lived up to my parents' teachings. How many times I have been encouraged, begged, and threatened to lie about what I believe concerning civil rights (back in the sixties), to downplay equal rights for women (back in the seventies), to back off from my criticisms of our defense octopus (today), and sadly, always, always, to lie about being gay. I cannot lie. I will not lie. I must not lie. You don't have to agree with me. You don't even have to like me. But you can rely on me. Ask me what I think and I'll tell you. I expect the same from you, whoever you are.

There you have it. I believe in you. I believe in myself. I believe in the majesty of the English language and I believe in the political system of the United States of America, flawed and infuriating though it sometimes is. But mostly I believe in you and I believe in me. We can change ourselves. We can change our communities. We have incredible spirit. We can brave life's pains and enjoy the triumphs. Generation after generation of human beings have walked this earth. They have known hunger, fear, ignorance and pestilence, war and rape. But they endured. You and I are here, thanks to them. They bequeathed to us the will to go forward. Whatever dragons we face, we can slay. Our dead mothers and fathers believed we would go forward. They did what they did with little hope of immediate reward but with a hope that life would be better for their children and their children's children. We are those children's children. We cannot fail.

Leo Buscaglia

b. 1926

The media, always quick to hang a catch name on a popular figure, have dubbed him "Dr. Love" or the "hug therapist," but to those who have heard him lecture he is simply ".Leo" or "Dr. Leo." A professor in the department of special education at the University of Southern California in his native Los Angeles, where he trains future teachers of handicapped children, Buscaglia has found the publicity that has accompanied his emergence as a national celebrity a little embarrassing and rather amusing. "I am a teacher, and I am not interested in having congregations or followers," he has said. "I am trying to be the very best Leo I can, and I hope that people who listen to me or read my books will be inspired to be themselves. . . . If people get excited, I hope they are excited about my message. I simply try to be a good person and a creative teacher."

And what is his message? In a word, love. "I have spent many years reviewing all of the literature and trying to find the essential commonalities on how we should live. They all have the same things in common with love as the central force. It's an interrelated point of view." His thoughts on the subject first saw print in his book Love *(1972), which grew out of the course of the same name that he taught for many years at USC. His subsequent books, among them such best sellers as* Living, Loving & Learning *(1982) and* Loving Each Other *(1984), expand on this theme of the transforming powers of love.*

To those who ridicule his idealism and denounce his message as simplistic, Buscaglia has replied: "I am merely offering an alternative that, it seems to me, is much needed." He has acknowledged that it is not the originality of his ideas, but, rather, the approach he takes—the very simple human, gut-level approach to communication—that is his contribution. "My hope is to be able to share ideas and interpret scholarly research in ways that Mrs. McGillicutty can understand when she's listening to me on the radio or TV while she's baking cookies for the kids she loves. Therein I hope lies the value of my work."

Over the entirety of a lifetime I have attempted to develop a clearer vision of the world. Circumstances have continually required me to expand that vision. As such, my beliefs reflect the limited knowledge, understanding, and experience I have accumulated to the present moment of my life. Psychiatrist Carl Jung suggested that existence is the rediscovery of our mythology and that through the search for and the demystification of this mythology we find our personal dream. So it has been with me. And so, I hope, it will continue to be until I have completed my life. I am my beliefs. My beliefs have formed my story.

My personal vision started with my parents who were Italian immigrants. They left their homeland, loved ones, and security to actualize a dream. They were not unusually adventuresome, tireless, or fearless; they were immensely human. They settled in Los Angeles with little more than a willingness to work hard, a spirit of adventure (or was it naiveté), and an unending sense of humor. They raised a family, acquired a small home and struggled to maintain an Italian-American culture in dignity, despite poverty and contending with strong anti-Italian prejudice. I remember our home as continually filled with the sounds of life, and too small for the myriad people moving through it. We seemed always to be living on the cusp between triumph and disaster, despair and celebration, tears and laughter, birth and death. Still, I never recall, even for a moment, fearing life or experiencing any sense of helplessness or hopelessness. Never did I question where, or if, I belonged.

It was in this environment that I learned much of what I still believe. Without ever defining the terms, I was taught love, responsibility, commitment, the dignity of work, and the import of laughter, song, dance, good food, and God.

I remember my parents best in their roles as nurturers: the menagerie of cats, birds, rabbits, along with outdoor gardens and indoor plants, which they attended with the utmost care. But my most vivid childhood memories still center mainly around the dinner table: colors, tastes, smells, mounds of *antipasto*, *risotto* with saffron and mushrooms, mounds of fresh *gnocchi* in tomato sauce, golden steaming *polenta* and *bagna calda* bubbling with garlic, anchovies and olive oil. Life was basic for us, and full. It always seemed a celebration.

Other loving individuals throughout my youth taught me to read, challenged my potential, taught me an awareness of the beautiful and the good, untied my tongue and encouraged me to speak. Later, in middle years, lovers around the world brought me in touch with the universality of all personkind. I learned that love was a common language and through it was released from the internal and external religious and cultural obstacles that artificially keep us separated. A Zen master encouraged my sense of humor and taught me to laugh. A Chinese scholar demystified the Tao and taught me to "flow." A Buddhist priest gave me the courage of my own "way." All together they released me from mind sets and the prison of my limited reality.

I was raised a devout Catholic. My understanding of God and the Church was a spiritual exercise to be felt intensely, not analyzed and explained. On Sundays, I was dressed in my best and with head bowed in silent reverence, I listened to the altar bells, smelled the incense, felt the organ vibrate through my body, and knew instinctively the rapture and the mystery. I have never lost this childlike feeling of sublimity. I have never required explanations. I remain overwhelmed by a very real presence, immense and immortal, to which I still attribute the name God. I feel this power both within and without. I need no longer participate in a ritual to find it. I have known it on mountain paths, on sandy beaches, as well as on busy city streets and in quiet temples around the world. Mine is still a nonintellectual approach to religion.

I believe instinctively, and have satisfactorily verified through my life and work, that love is the source of all things. I know that we are all born with love as a possibility and challenge, but know that it takes years of purposeful, volitional, acquired skill and practiced behavior to realize it in action.

I have always, even as a child, felt a deep responsibility to develop all that I am, not for myself alone, but also so that I could be more for everyone in my life. This deep desire led me to my chosen profession. There was never any doubt that I was to become a teacher. While other children in our neighborhood were pretending to be cowboys or ambulance drivers, I was gathering "students" in the garage (our classroom), where I was "teacher." No role, for me, could be grander.

I recall vividly, and rather sadly, my shock when I was discussing the results of my high school aptitude tests with my educational counselor. She started the interview by asking me about my professional goal. I answered without hesitation that I had always wanted to become a teacher. "A teacher!" she exclaimed, almost in horror. "Why would you choose to become a teacher when you have the aptitude to become a doctor, a dentist, or a lawyer?" I am certain that she meant well, but I was puzzled by the implication that a teacher did not have equal status with other professionals. It was not difficult for me to forgo the promise of becoming a doctor, a dentist, or lawyer. Even though I met this attitude many times over the years, I know I made the right decision. I became a teacher. I think I have been a good teacher over the past thirty-odd years. Through my classes at all levels of education, from elementary to graduate school, I have been able to touch the lives of thousands of individuals. I have tried to continue this through my public lecturing and my published works.

In a far less restrictive sense, I believe that we are all teachers. We teach with every act we perform, during each waking moment of life. We are in this way models of what we profess to believe. It is, therefore, the responsibility of all of us to create the environment in which we choose to live. If we select caring, responsibility, commitment and loving, then we must manifest this in daily action.

I attempt to be a bridge over which I encourage others to cross and go far beyond. I hope I have been more than an imparter of knowledge. I have tried to challenge and inspire. I attempt to do this by allowing my students to be free, for I am convinced that we can only learn, grow, create, and change in freedom. I also teach my students that freedom is not license, but entails the greatest responsibility and commitment. Albert Einstein once said that he was astonished that what we call formal education has not succeeded in strangling the holy curiosity of inquiry, for this delicate and exotic plant stood mainly in need of freedom, without which it would surely die.

I believe that within each of us there lies a unique and mainly unrealized potential. Since this has no equal, it is of inestimable value. If it is lost, it will be lost forever.

I know that we change our lives by altering our attitudes and perceptions of the world. This is accomplished each time we are given an opportunity to see, touch, taste, feel, or learn something new. So vast is the mystery that we can never know all that there is. As a teacher it has been my hope to help students to transcend continually and enthusiastically their reality. I take little comfort in just being. Hope lies only in becoming.

It is frightening to know that human behavior can be externally controlled and determined. As a result of this, if we are unable or ill equipped to lead our lives or make personal choices, someone will do it for us. History is a panorama of such tragedy and loss.

I believe that life was meant to be experienced in joy, love and tranquillity, and any deviation from this is due to personal maladjustment. We must not fear anxiety, pain, confusion, or despair, providing that they serve as symptoms of a life out of balance, and therefore provide an incentive to find new ways to move to happiness and a celebration of life. All of my books have had this as their singular goal.

We must be determined to share freely what we believe, and we have an obligation to do this despite the risk of being rebuffed, mocked, criticized and embarrassed.

Some of my most satisfying moments have occurred when I have risked being rejected or ridiculed, and performed some spontaneous act of loving. I have often seen people dining alone and asked them if they would rather have company. After the initial shock, I have been accepted far more often than rejected, and benefited greatly from the brief encounter. Being a food lover, I have taken the time to congratulate chefs, in gourmet restaurants as well as in truck stops on isolated highways, who presented me with an outstanding meal, or the person who served it with pleasure. I have gone out of my way to write a letter of commendation to airlines, phone companies, food chains, and theater box offices when simple consideration and kindness were shown.

These may appear to be small, unimportant things, but the cumulative effect seems to me to be well worth the small effort. We are most likely to repeat behavior that is positively reinforced. I have not in these acts changed the world. But this has never been my goal. I know that mass efforts of positive action are essential to overcome world poverty, famine, and violations of human rights. But there is also a great need to create and enhance our smaller environment, making it more conducive to hope, freedom, growth, and love.

Human history thus far has shown that we have made our share of mistakes. It has also suggested that many of us have refused to acknowledge and learn from them. Each generation seems determined to relive the past. Perhaps that is our human way. No matter. The wonder is that we continue to survive and even transcend. I am always exalted by our capacity to face extremes of pain, illness, death, with courage, hope, and a mystical determination to hold on to life.

I am optimistic. I have learned that often the most significant changes in our lives have been brought about through urgency and the threat of pain. Perhaps our having set the stage for total annihilation will cause us to seek alternatives to provincialism and isolation and bring us together (death is a great unifier) and stimulate new thinking about interrelatedness and love.

I hope that I, through the sharing of my beliefs, have played some small part in helping people to rid themselves of selfish egotism and petty behavior so that we might move, less fearfully, together. I am determined to keep encouraging the renewal, revival, and rebalancing of basic values like courage, concern, commitment, responsibility, and the positive experiences of joy, hope, and, of course, love. I am certain that these remain the major forces that will lead us from our present confusion to greater insight, to more personal and communal alternatives for living.

Robert Coles
b. 1929

One of the most influential research psychiatrists and psychoanalysts in America, Robert Coles is admired for his skill in making complex psychological and sociological subjects accessible to the lay reader. He first gained public attention with the publication of his award-winning book, Children of Crisis *(1967), a study of conflict and anxieties among black and white children in desegregated schools. An authoritative statement of the case for integrated schools, this book was to become the first part of a massive multivolume study of children in various stressful situations. He has also studied the children of the rich, reporting his findings in* The Privileged Ones *(1978) and, with his wife, Jane Hallowell Coles, published the oral histories of a group of working women in the two-volume* Women of Crisis *(1978–80).*

A member of the Harvard University faculty, Dr. Coles has attempted to combine a life of medicine and psychiatry with writing. He has written hundreds of articles on contemporary social issues in popular and scholarly magazines and literary studies on, among oth-

ers, two other physician-writers, poet William Carlos Williams and
novelist Walker Percy. Dr. Coles does not conceal the respect he holds
for novelists. He has said that "the wise people in our country are
novelists. When I see a President calling in Washington lawyers to
advise him, I wonder why he can't get together with a few people
like Saul Bellow, Eudora Welty and Walker Percy and have an ear-
nest conversation about what this country means," adding that he
wished somehow "that we could give sanction to people who have
some transcendent sense of why they're here and what they believe
in and what they're going to put themselves on the line for."

The word "pride" was my mother's constant verbal companion—ready
at all times, it seemed, for her summons. I have early memories,
indeed, of her voice offering that word again and again in the course
of particular family events. I remember once asking my mother to
define the word, to explain it, and she said: "It is the sin of sins—our
vanity." Well, what is "vanity," and why is it such a particularly
serious offense to God? I didn't quite come back to her, of course,
with such a phrasing for my inquiry, but I did want to know the
answer to that question—and at the age of seven or eight, even, and
maybe before then, too. Around that time I told my first-grade teacher,
Mrs. Velma Jones, "pride is the worst thing." Many years later when
I was in high school my mother told me what I had said to Mrs.
Jones. I asked my mother how she found out. She said Mrs. Jones
had reported it to my father, who had come to pick me up at the end
of the day, no doubt, in that 1936 Pontiac, red and with a radio and
a heater, that I can still remember, and that I can see anytime I want
in the thick photograph album my parents have.

My father had no great use for such religious talk. He was a scientist, and at times he registered his strong belief that we are accountable to rationality, to values that we ourselves carefully, thoughtfully
embrace—rather than to those handed down by God. As a young boy,
again, I didn't hear the matter as I have just phrased it—but I certainly recall this recurrent (every Sunday!) image: my father driving

my mother, brother, and me to the Episcopal Church, and staying inside that handsome, cozy Pontiac of his, while we got out and ascended "God's House," as my mother sometimes put it. When we returned, an hour or so later, he was still there, the Sunday papers strewn all over the front seat, with the particular section he was reading at rest on the broad, black steering wheel. He would often peer at us, over his reading glasses, and ask us this question, a faint smile on his face: "What did you boys learn this time?" My mother would manage her own thin smile in response to that inquiry and wait for one or both of us to come up with an answer, or at least a statement meant to justify the hour we'd just spent inside that (to my eyes, then) imposing building. I remember telling my father what song we'd sung, what piece of (Old Testament, New Testament) history we'd heard discussed, what moral lesson we'd been given. Not rarely I'd mention "pride" as a "big sin," and say to my attentive father that I hoped I'd not succumb to it "too much" during the week to follow. By then he'd have cleared the papers from the seat, put them on the floor, started the car. By then we'd be negotiating our way through a pleasant New England town's streets, homeward bound— and he would say (so many Sundays—the same words!): "When you locate that sin, pride, let me know, so I can put it under the microscope!"

He was kidding, of course, and we all laughed, my mother included. But he was making a point to us—reminding us, even as small children, that science has its own territory and authority, and that all the talk of "sin" we'd heard in church and would hear at home represented "a point of view," a phrase he often used. What was his "point of view"? We learned gradually the answer to that question— a faith in logic, in the research done by biologists and chemists and physicists, a faith in man's searching, exploring mind, and yes, a faith in the social and psychological consequences of such activity: in the words of the E.I. Dupont Company, used to announce its radio advertisements of decades ago, "better living through chemistry."

For my father such an assertion meant that we'd live "better" not only materially, but in the personal habits of everyday life. We'd be courteous and civil to one another, and (very important to him) we'd not try to impose our ideas or values on others in a forceful or self-righteous or imperious manner. He and my mother, after all, were already living witnesses to such a reality—her passionate, somewhat brooding Christianity, with its continual melancholic awareness of "pride" as a dark shadow over our daily lives, and his hopeful scientific rationalism, still well-muscled in the 1930s. They were happy together—a solid marriage; and indeed they are still alive as I write these words, in their eighties, and no less distinct in their differing views of the world, yet no less devoted to each other.

I mention the above because I realize how long and hard I have struggled to accommodate within myself both my mother's religious faith and my father's scientific mind, and especially, how strenuously, and not always with great success, I have tried to attend that oft uttered maternal remonstrance about "pride."

Now, needless to say, my own accusation is leveled against myself, and my kind, namely, members of the so-called "intelligentsia." I became a physician, a pediatrician, an adult psychiatrist, a child psychiatrist—a relentless pursuer of education, knowledge, and science, though not quite the physical sciences my father had mastered. But I also have been drawn to literature, to moral philosophy, and to theology, a response to my mother's interests. Moreover, I have a strong memory of what the Second World War meant to my father—the spectacle of so-called "civilized nations" that became murderous antagonists. With Hitler and Stalin and the nuclear bomb to contemplate, my father had become (by the middle 1940s, when I was an early adolescent) considerably less optimistic than he once had been—and more interested, I gradually realized, in my mother's view of life. I remember at sixteen hearing him say that "we are sinners."

He was mad at science harnessed to crematoria, at single atom bombs that could wipe out entire cities, and really, at the betrayal by others of the sunny optimism he'd for so long taken for granted. At the utterance of these ideas by my father, an awareness began to take root in my head that all secular, messianic faiths ought to be scrutinized with the utmost skepticism. No wonder I would eventually be so drawn to Reinhold Niebuhr's writing and would audit a course of his at Union Theological Seminary while I attended medical school. He, too, in *The Nature and Destiny of Man*, a book I've read and reread over the years, summons "pride" as a constant presence in our lives, an exceedingly tricky (and chameleonlike) antagonist. Yet, we can succumb to a strangely perverse kind of pride by letting a consciousness of it overwhelm us so that we end up doing all too little out of a sad apprehension of sin's continual hold upon us, no matter how our daily work or our supposedly idealistic pursuits unfold. I well remember Niebuhr cautioning us, as my mother did, lest we let pride get the better of us by emphasizing its power, and (in order to resist it) curbing prideful activities, assertions, endeavors. I remember so well hearing Niebuhr speak these words: "We risk pride all the time, and so we must, unless we choose to take no risks at all, and thereby give pride the greatest possible victory over us." I wrote those words in a notebook while listening to this great and wise man, and I ultimately typed them on a piece of paper, which I still keep on my desk: medicine for moments of pride, not to mention melancholy, with its attendant curb upon the mind's energy, its willfulness.

I fear I'd still be struggling with such ideas, such visions of what is or ought to be, had I not by chance ended up in the deep South during the late 1950s to take charge, under the old Doctor's Draft, of an Air Force neuropsychiatric service in a large military hospital. The civil-rights struggle was then fast gathering momentum, and I well remember leaving church on a particular Sunday and witnessing a swim-in (an effort of some Mississippi blacks to use a sandy stretch of the Gulf of Mexico). The result was a vicious assault on them—by the local police of all people. Soon thereafter I watched a small black child move past a terribly abusive mob in order to initiate school desegregation. I was on my way to a professional meeting. Since the streets were blocked, I sat and witnessed the event and wondered about not only this child, but myself. What should I do with my life, now that I was on the last leg of my training, my spell of fulfilling various obligations? The sight of those black people, being so badly beaten for trying to take a swim, and the sight of a lone dark girl of six walking with her head high past grown men and women who cursed her and screamed threats at her—these two moments affected me strongly. Even more important, my wife was not simply moved to thought or sadness or anger as I was, but to a determination that we somehow must act, commit our lives like that of, say, Ruby Bridges, whose early, mob-threatened education I have just described.

For my wife, doing is what matters. A school teacher, an outgoing and naturally active person, and not least, the great-granddaughter of a strong Yankee abolitionist who became a Union general in the Civil War, she would have no part of my temptation to ruminate morosely or angrily on the various sins of others or myself. Her inclination is to carve out a territory of moral action, and work it, work it, work it: the ground of one's particular life as a citizen of a country, as a worshipper of God. It was her ethical resolve that eventually (and not without a bit of struggle, I have to add) prompted me to abandon a conventional career. I stayed South, became involved full time in the civil-rights struggle, and carried on my studies of desegregation while acting with others for its achievement.

It is easy, I fear, for us to think about (and write about) our beliefs and actions without acknowledging the influence of someone else's beliefs and actions—one's wife's, one's friends'—on one's own. Yet, as I think back over the past twenty-five years I realize that even my wife's confident idealism, a constant, determining influence on me, has not caused me to overcome some of the moral anxieties I learned early in life. It is rather easy, these days, to emphasize the pervasive psychological conflicts in a given childhood while neglecting to take stock of childhood as a time of moral instruction and growth. For years I was reminded by my mother that egoism is a foe of sorts, constantly to be recognized and fought hard against; as I became involved in the civil rights struggle of the 1960s, as I did my work with families in various parts of the country, and more recently in other countries (South Africa, Northern Ireland), I began to realize how hard it is for all of us to struggle with that foe. There is the arrogance, the smugness, of the oppressor, but there is also the manipulative self-righteousness of those who fight oppressors—revolutionaries who themselves become oppressors. It is a long and sad story—the way people who take up arms in a decent cause often become all too full of themselves, all too self-centered, and self-assertive. Writers, social observers, and psychiatrists, people of my ilk, we can become as blindly self-satisfied and smug as those whose actions we hasten to criticize and deplore.

In *Middlemarch*, George Eliot used the phrase "unreflecting egoism" to characterize this seemingly inevitable inclination all of us have to be relentlessly (and sometimes deviously) taken with ourselves, so to speak—the sin of pride. Righteousness turns to self-righteousness. We become so thoroughly sure that we are correct, others mistaken, and often we fail to see the cost such egoism exacts not only on ourselves, but on others, and the hurt we do them as we come to our conclusions, pronounce our judgments. So it was that many blacks and whites of the early civil rights days turned on each other. And so it was, earlier in this century, that high socialist ideals were buried in Stalin's Gulag, and that Mao, the young and ardently compassionate rebel, became the old dictator responsible for so very much human misery. And so it is that many of us who are quick to denounce the greed or selfishness of others, fail to observe our own dangerously uncritical self-satisfaction.

I am a physician who has tried to learn how children live, make do, grow, turn into the particular people they are destined to become—Appalachian yeomen, black urban folk, migrant workers, members of our American upper bourgeosie, and so on. I try to work as thoroughly as I can, then write as accurately as I can about what I have witnessed. So doing, I find myself constantly wrestling with the doctor's pride, the writer's pride—with what my mother used to call "the devil that is pride." To wrestle every day with the temptation one feels of being all too sure of oneself, all too sure of one's beliefs, all too sure of the values of one's actions—that can be a life's worthy purpose. There can never be a definitive victory. To declare oneself humble, or hopeful of being humble, is to state one's persisting arrogance!

Sometimes, when I get low in spirit, I think of little Ruby going past those mobs in New Orleans, and yes, her praying for them: "Forgive them, Lord, because they don't know what they're doing." Her beliefs were put to unpretentious and honorable action. We can all only hope and pray that every once in a while such an occasion will arise for us, too—and meanwhile keep careful watch on our devilish pride, wrestle with it constantly, as we try to complete this life's journey.

Norman Cousins
b. 1912

There are two Norman Cousinses. The first is the eminent journalist who for more than thirty-five years edited the Saturday Review, *the prestigious weekly that was practically synonymous with his name. While guiding the magazine, the indefatigable editor found time to write more than a dozen books, lecture, accept Presidential assignments, and head organizations ranging in scope from the United World Federalists to the board of National Educational Television. For his efforts on behalf of disarmament and the nuclear test ban, he was given the Eleanor Roosevelt Peace Award and the United Nations Peace Medal.*

The other Norman Cousins emerged after his recovery from a paralyzing disease that struck him in the mid-sixties. Refusing to surrender, he entered into a partnership with his physician in which scientific and psychological resources combined to produce recovery. He explained his optimistic outlook in The Celebration of Life: A Dialogue on Immortality and Infinity *(1974) and his recovery in an article in* The New England Journal of Medicine, *later expanded and published as* Anatomy of an Illness *(1979), a best seller that served to introduce Cousins to a new generation of readers. Since then he has written* Human Options *(1980),* The Physician in Literature *(1982), and* The Healing Heart *(1983). He is a trustee of the Institute for the Advancement of Health, the American Institute of Stress, the Kettering Foundation, and a member of the Special Medical Advisory Group of the Veterans Administration. His main activity is as professor of the medical humanities on the faculty of the School of Medicine at the University of California, Los Angeles.*

Inevitably, the event during my lifetime that had the greatest impact on my thinking and, indeed, on the course of my life itself, was the atomic bombing of Hiroshima. I remember picking up *The New York Times* at about 7:45 A.M. the morning of August 6, 1945, and seeing the banner headline telling of the world's first nuclear weapon. Almost all at once, future history seemed to reveal itself.

Beginning that August morning, the editorial preoccupation of the *Saturday Review*, of which I was then editor, was a twin theme: the danger represented by nuclear weapons, and the inadequacy of absolute national sovereignty to deal with basic causes of war. An editorial I wrote that day entitled "Modern Man is Obsolete" attempted to anticipate the requirements of a world under law. It described the economic, ideological, sociological, and humanitarian arguments for world government. It recognized that the acceptance and implementation of world government was the largest order man had had to meet in his million or so years on earth, but noted that man himself had set up the conditions that made the order necessary. "Since man's survival on earth is now absolutely dependent on his ability to avoid a new war, he is faced with the so-far insoluble problem of eliminating the causes leading up to war . . . What does it matter, then, if war is not in the nature of man as long as man continues, through the expression of his nature, to be a viciously competitive animal?

The effect is the same, and therefore the result must be as conclusive—war being the effect, and complete obliteration of the human species being the result.''

If this reasoning was correct, then it followed that modern man was obsolete, a self-made anachronism, becoming more incongruous by the minute, who exalted change in everything but himself. It appeared, too, that we were left with a crisis in decision. The main test before us involved our will to change rather than our ability to change.

The quintessence of destruction as potentially represented by modern science had to be dramatized and kept in the forefront of public opinion. The full dimensions of the peril had to be seen and recognized. Then and only then would humans realize that the first order of business was the question of continued existence. Then and only then would we be prepared to make the decisions necessary to assure that survival.

I know it would be exhilarating, to say the least, if a shout were to go up all over the world for a human society under law. But this was not likely to happen overnight. What had to happen was the direct expression of raw concern.

There is primitive, colossal energy in the simply stated but insistent call by enough people for a situation of reasonable safety on earth, for an end to anarchy in the dealings among states, and for easier access by members of the human family to one another. It is therefore a matter of individual responsibility to take a hard look at one's own belief system and its broader implications. Such introspection, of course, is not a short-order affair.

One grows into one's philosophy. Year by year an individual is shaped by the sights, the sounds, the ideas around him. Consciously or not, we are forever adding to or subtracting from the sum total of our beliefs or attitudes or responses, or whatever it is we mean when we refer to our outlook on life. This is not to say that clearly defined religions and philosophies are inevitably subordinated to the total impact of individual experience. My purpose rather is to suggest that it is one of the prime glories of the human mind that the same idea or experience is never absorbed in precisely the same way by any two individuals who may be exposed to it.

In this sense, each human being is a process—a filtering process of retention or rejection, absorption or loss. The process defines individuality. It determines whether we justify the gift of human life or whether we live and die without having been affected by the beauty of wonder and the wonder of beauty, without having had any real awareness of kinship or human fulfillment.

There is a question, however, whether individuals are capable of recognizing and defining the essence of their own individuality. Can a camera photograph itself? In a mirror, perhaps; but even the mirror sees only the outside of the box. A mind that attempts to perceive itself uses the tools of language and logic. But the material with which it deals is beyond mere words or reason. The marrow of human thought or personality eludes its own product: human analysis—even with the same advanced scientific instrumentation.

The essential philosophical quest is for integration—which is to say, the need to bring together rational philosophy, spiritual belief, scientific knowledge, personal experience, and direct observation into an organic whole.

My own philosophical speculations, such as they are, perhaps belong to a trend of thought that could be called "consequentialism." By consequentialism I am thinking of the whole sequence of ideas by which we deal with cause and effect. Life is rich in its consequences. Consequences give reality to the struggle between good and evil, nobility and venality, altruism and selfishness. A human being fashions his consequences as surely as he fashions his goods or his dwellings. Nothing that he says, thinks, or does is without its consequences. Just as there is no loss of basic energy in the universe, so no thought or action is without its effects, present or ultimate, seen or unseen, felt or unfelt. Reality *is* consequences.

At every stop in life we are coping with the consequences of ideas and actions, most of them long since forgotten. These consequences or effects are the unseen factors in individual life and the affairs of man; they are imponderables only in the sense that they are not directly identified. But they are no less vital than that which is explicit and accessible in human experience. In short, life is of consequence—literally so. Wisdom consists of the anticipation of consequences.

Philosophically, of course, we also have to think of relationships—not just the relationship of individuals to one another and their collective life, but the relationship of human life to the cosmos. For all our lofty philosophical excursions, we are still earthbound. We are overly fond, perhaps, of applying concepts about size, direction, time, space, energy, to situations in which those concepts may be completely extraneous. We are measurement-minded. In fact, we have to be, because our plane of existence necessarily utilizes such concepts.

Yet there is a larger plane on which those approaches may have no validity.

We try to throw our arms around infinity and are left—not with the universe in our arms but with a closed and empty circle. The more we know about the discernible and the theoretical universe, the more confused we become. Boundlessness or endlessness at first fascinates us, then appalls us.

The concept of the Deity has been shaped by our earthbound preoccupations. We have a tendency to superimpose God on a design—in fact, to equate our speculations about infinity with God. This may be irrelevant—at least in the sense that we may be looking in the wrong direction. This universe and everything in it—our world, you and I and the rest of us—may actually be contained in a space that, in the context of infinity, may be smaller than the smallest part of an atom.

The universe, despite all the billions of galaxies, is still a vacuum. Its parts are so few in the context of infinity that it is closer to a perfect vacuum than any vacuum in our laboratories. But it is not a perfect vacuum. It is not perfect because nature will not admit nothingness. Nature rejects nothingness. It is not the enormousness or the scope or the grandeur of what results from the rejection of nothingness that is primarily significant here. What is most significant is that true nothingness is impossible. Infinity would swallow us up, but it cannot. Nothingness surrounds us, but it cannot claim us.

The proof of God, therefore, is in the rejection of nothingness. Not even science can conceive of pure nothingness; pure nothingness nowhere exists. The universe may be only a particle but it asserts itself, and the nothingness is kept from becoming absolute. Thus the universe is a vital particle. And there are vital particles inside it, the most vital of which is man.

The true contemplation of God, therefore, should proceed not out of manifest phenomena but out of a void. This is the final test of spiritual substance. If our spirituality proceeds out of awe, it loses substance as soon as awe is dissolved. God emerges in fullest glory, not when made to sit astride infinity or when regarded as an architect of cosmic spectacles, but when contemplated as the Ultimate Force that prevents the cosmic void from becoming absolute.

Whether the Great Design of Creation exists within a microcosm or macrocosm is unimportant; the vital particles inside it have order and purpose and they exist. And there is a place inside that order for humans, for consciousness, for conscience, for love. This is what is important. We are not children of relativity. We are children of God. And we are brothers. And we enjoy or suffer the consequences of our ideas, our acts, our hopes, and our fears.

These, then, are the articles of my faith:

I am a single cell in a body of four billion cells. The body is humankind.

I glory in the individuality of self, but my individuality does not separate me from my universal self—the oneness of man.

My memory is personal and finite, but my substance is boundless and infinite.

The portion of that substance that is mine was not devised; it was renewed. So long as the human bloodstream lives, I have life. Of this does my immortality consist.

I do not believe that humankind is an excrescence or a machine, or that myriads of solar systems and galaxies in the universe lack order or sanction. I may not embrace or command this universal order, but I can be at one with it, for I am of it.

I see no separation between the universal order and the moral order.

I believe that the expansion of knowledge makes for an expansion of faith, and the widening of the horizons of mind for a widening of belief. My reason nourishes my faith and my faith my reason.

I am diminished not by the growth of knowledge but by the denial of it.

I am not oppressed by, nor do I shrink before, the apparent boundaries in life or the lack of boundaries in cosmos.

I cannot affirm God if I fail to affirm man. If I deny the oneness of man, I deny the oneness of God. Therefore I affirm both. Without a belief in human unity I am hungry and incomplete.

Human unity is the fulfillment of diversity. It is the harmony of opposites. It is a many stranded texture, with color and depth.

The sense of human unity makes possible a reverence for life.

Reverence for life is more than solicitude or sensitivity for life. It is a sense of the whole, a capacity for inspired response, a respect for the intricate universe of individual life. It is the supreme awareness of awareness itself.

I am a single cell. My needs are individual but they are not unique.

I am interlocked with other human beings in the consequences of our thoughts, feelings, actions.

Together, we share the quest for a society of the whole equal to our needs, a society in which we neither have to kill or be killed, a society in which we need not live under our moral capacity, and in which justice has a life of its own.

Singly and together, we can live without dread and without help-lessness.

We are single cells in a body of four billion cells. The body is humankind.

Mario Cuomo
b. 1932

On January 1, 1983, Mario Cuomo was inaugurated as the fifty-second governor of the state of New York, an office that placed the Democrat from the borough of Queens in New York City at the fore-front of his party and made him a prominent national figure.

The son of Italian immigrants, his early passion and talent for baseball landed him a minor-league contract after high school. But his career was cut short by an injury, and he decided to complete his professional education instead. He attended St. John's University in Jamaica, Queens. After receiving his B.A., he attended law school there, graduating with top honors in 1956. While practicing law in Brooklyn during the 1960s he achieved public recognition for his work with community groups. In 1975, he was appointed by the Governor of New York, Hugh Carey, to the post of secretary of state. After an unsuccessful run for mayor of New York City in 1977, he was elected lieutenant governor of the state the following year.

A man of thought, he has acknowledged being influenced by the

French Jesuit Pierre Teilhard de Chardin, whose books emphasize the immanence of God. The governor has said he believes that, next to the religious vocation, politics is the highest because "the business of politics and government is to distribute the goods of the world in such ways as to improve the condition of people's lives."

Whatever one calls my political philosophy—whether traditional Democratic principles or a family kind of politics or progressive pragmatism—my commitment to it goes back a long way, well before I entered politics.

Some people become Democrats or Republicans the way they become Catholics or Jews or Protestants—they're born to it. I became a Catholic because at a stage in my life when I was too young to understand, my mother and father took me to church, had a priest pour holy water on my head and say words in Latin. I became a Democrat in about the same way. Although I was considerably older, the ritual was almost as automatic. I chose to register as a Democrat because all the people we knew in my neighborhood who voted had voted Democratic. And why not? Poor or struggling middle-class immigrants and the children of immigrants in the era of the Great Depression— one could hardly have been surprised at their choice.

But while affiliation was thrust on me in the one case and undertaken casually in the other, eventually both my religion and my politics became matters of conviction, and I have never felt that the two commitments were incompatible.

As I understand it, the so-called Christian ethic, while recognizing that we are too weak to do it perfectly, calls on us nevertheless to try to do good things for other people. Prudently, without ignoring our obligations to ourselves, realistically. But insistently. Trying always to arrange a package of justice, charity, and mercy, proffering it beyond the walls of our own homes, our own churches, our own lives.

More than thirty years ago, when I registered to vote, it seemed to me that despite many failures to live up to them, the traditional prin-

ciples of the Democratic party came closer to giving political content
to this ideal than the tenets of the Republicans. It seems so to me
now. The thrust of the "New Conservatism," as annunciated by Ronald Reagan in 1980, was that government's principal role should be to
help the strong flourish, in the hope that the force of their economic
ambition—or charity—would take care of the rest of us. It is, it seems
to me, a philosophy that is defensible only in the abstract. It depends
on the cynical assumption that those who do well will accept the sacrifice of others as the necessary price offered up for the commonweal—and the effects on human beings of the policies derived from it
are devastating.

If I believed that nothing could be done, that there was no answer,
I would not be in politics. But there is an answer, and it is not to
turn our back as a nation on any region, or, as the economic wagon
train moves on, to abandon those left behind. I agree that government
should allow the strong, the wealthy, the so-called producers to stay
strong, and even encourage them to grow stronger. But I also believe
that there are two major groups that deserve more of government's
attention than they are receiving at the moment. The first consists of
those who work for a living—not because a psychiatrist suggested to
them that it would be a good way to fill the tedious interval between
birth and eternity, but because they have to work. People not poor
enough to be on welfare but not rich enough to be worry-free. People
who labor, live modestly, ask little and get less than they deserve:
the so-called middle class. The second group is made up of those who
want to be in the first but haven't been able to make it: those who
want to work but can't because they're too old or too frail or because
there just isn't a job for them.

These are things I have said a thousand times in a hundred different ways beginning with my first campaign in 1974. If such views are
called "traditional Democratic principles," I find that perfectly acceptable.

Though the idea of family is the bedrock on which my political
philosophy rests, there are two other influences that are part of its
foundation: ideas I formed early about religion and the law.

For whatever combination of genetic, environmental, and educational reasons, I have always found it easier to discern a challenge
than to acknowledge success. Momma and Poppa, I suppose, had
something to do with that. So did the six o'clock Mass at St. Monica's
Church across the street from the cemetery. There on dark winter

mornings in cassock and surplice I would recite "Ad Deum, qui lae-
tificat" to begin my prayers as an altar boy. Then I would struggle
carefully, apprehensively, through the more difficult prayers—the
Confiteor and the Suscipiat—and the many intricate moves that, if
done perfectly, could earn a server the "big time," a solemn High
Mass on Sunday!

The whole religious experience of Catholics like myself in that time
and place painted for us a world of moral pitfalls that needed to be
avoided in order to earn an eternal peace. It was as though God had
created the world as a kind of hard passage to eternity. It was the
ultimate in the "carrot and stick" approach to religious philosophy,
with the stick being a lot more ominous than the carrot was appealing.

Of course that's not the way it was supposed to be. Those who
were learned enough or wise enough saw in our religion even forty
years ago the kind of joy and hope and affirmation that is apparent
now every Sunday morning at Mass. But for the simple folk of South
Jamaica, in Queens County, who came from behind the grocery stores
and from the tenements and from the little houses on Liverpool Street,
it was often a world of guilt and repentance and renewed effort to
avoid the final defeat. Seen that way, the greatest danger was forming
an attachment to the things of this world that would distract one from
the long-range—indeed, from the eternal—view.

I see things a little differently today. So do the modern young altar
boys who have been freed from having to stumble through the Suscipiat. But I am sure that I will never be totally free of the tentative-
ness, the concern—even, from time to time, the twinges of guilt—
that accompany anything I might be tempted to regard as material
success. Primary night, the general election, the inaugural, a thousand congratulations and embraces and even cheers: all of them create
a little discomfort that, if detected, might even be mistaken for ingra-
titude.

Self-interrogation about motive and direction and result is my fate.
Anyone who went to Father Eugene Erny for confession, and prayed
that the old German pastor wouldn't recognize the voice from the
darkened cubicle on the other side of the screen, will understand this
syndrome.

There was also a bright side to our old-fashioned religion, for those
disposed to see it. It was the joy of giving, as compared to the joy of
having. If you wanted to earn that carrot and avoid that stick, you

could do it by sharing, contributing, helping. That's why they called those marvelous, inscrutable women, those faces surrounded in starched white linen and flowing black, the Sisters of Charity. Their whole mission at St. Monica's and elsewhere was to teach that while you were suffering the pains of denying yourself temporary and superficial delights, you could also earn yourself an occasional moment of warmth and even, my God . . . self-satisfaction! You could do it by helping the sick, feeding the hungry, comforting the bereaved.

It is this part of my background that has always made it difficult for me to accept the so-called conservative idea that, when it comes to government's redistributive function, "God helps those whom God has helped, and if He's left you out, who are we to presume on His will?" And ten years of Vincentian training at St. John's Prep and St. John's University only reinforced my conviction that if St. Francis of Assisi were alive today, and reckless enough to get involved in politics, he would be fighting for some kind of progressivism that sought to help people improve their lives. I just can't see him arguing for the kind of social Darwinism that has been thrust upon us in recent years. (That some of the current believers in "survival of the fittest" were altar boys with me nearly forty years ago, or were my schoolmates, never ceases to surprise me.)

I suppose that to some extent the patterns of conduct and concern that are formed early in life don't really change a great deal, at least not fundamentally. Surely, some refinement of manner, some flourish, the ability to deal in nuances, may come with a few gray hairs at the temple. But the instincts born in the incense and the Baltimore catechism, amidst the groceries piled high in the back of the store, or while sitting alone in the backyard in the summer's heat lost in a book—those instincts operate through every campaign, every legislative session, even every decision on what words to write down for other people to read.

But this practically absolute ability to advocate raises questions about how the ability should be used by a public official.

Am I, as a Catholic governor who was elected to serve Protestants, Jews, Moslems, Sikhs, deists, animists, agnostics, and atheists, obliged to seek to legislate my particular morality, in all of its exquisite detail? And if I fail, am I then required to surrender stewardship rather than risk hypocrisy?

The question comes up frequently. The answer, I think, is found in the organic law on which our democracy is built, the Constitution.

The geniuses who wrote that instrument had the chance to select a specific religion or formal morality and make it an article of civic duty. They chose not to because that was precisely the condition in other parts of the world from which many of their forebears had fled. Instead—as I read this wonderful instrument—it says that no group has the right to insist that the rest of the community follow its religious views. It provides simply that where matters of private morality are involved—that is, belief or actions that don't impinge on other people or deprive them of their rights—the state has no right to intervene. I like the principle.

As a result of it, while the relationship between my private philosophical commitment and the law we make and enforce for the commonweal remains difficult to articulate, I have for the most part felt comfortable living with both of them simultaneously. My Church allows me to participate in a government that does not enforce adherence to all my Church's mandates; and my government regards my religion as irrelevant and will not permit itself to enforce religious mandates for fear of having to choose among many conflicting ones.

All of this, however, is not to say that our Constitution is simply an invitation to selfishness. In it is also embodied a central truth of the Judeo-Christian tradition—that is, a sense of the common good. The Constitution says to me, as the Gospel says to me, that freedom isn't license; that liberty creates responsibility; that we have been given freedom in order to encourage us to pursue that common good. And if the Constitution restricts the powers of the state in order to save us from the temptation to judge and persecute others, it does not thereby deny the necessity of the shared commitment to help one another—a shared commitment that is the basis for justice and mercy and human dignity and, therefore, the basis of any religion that believes in a loving God.

Seen that way, there is a perfect consistency between everything I believe privately and everything I am free to do publicly.

J. Treasure

His Holiness Tenzin Gyatso, 14th Dalai Lama of Tibet

b. 1935

The Dalai Lama of Tibet, as the spiritual and temporal head of the Tibetan people, is no mere figurehead. Since 1937, when at the age of two, Tenzin Gyatso was recognized in accordance with Tibetan tradition as the reincarnation of his predecessor, he has inspired respect and reverence amongst not only Tibetans, but the world at large, not only for the office he occupies, but for his distinction of mind and spirit. He has spent years studying in the rigorous academic tradition of the Buddhist universities, earning the Doctor's degree with highest honors at the age of twenty-five. In the midst of governmental and diplomatic affairs he has found time to teach and record in writing his insights in philosophy and the meaning of contemplative life in such books as Kindness, Clarity and Insight *(1984) and* Universal Responsibility and the Good Heart *(1982).*

In 1959, after ten years of Chinese military occupation in his country, His Holiness decided that his continued presence there would no longer help his people and might in fact precipitate violence against their occupiers. Since that time he has been in exile in India, living the simple life of a monk and executing his responsibilities for the welfare of his people. He has lectured widely abroad, where he has stressed the unity of mankind and the importance of regarding all people with love and compassion, without concern for conventional boundaries of any kind.

For the seeker of truth there are certain beliefs that must accompany every action: one should act without selfishness, cultivate compassion for all living things, and develop respect for others. I believe all religions carry this same message despite their differences in philosophy. Though there are differences of opinion in the various schools of Buddhist thought, all emphasize the value of a warm heart. This fundamental quality is not restricted to human beings. I believe all living creatures show some form of compassion. A life full of compassionate actions is at the very center of the Buddhist faith and the most important teaching of the Buddha. Compassionate intentions accompanying our actions help us to rise above selfish desires and in the lives of the Buddha we see many examples. In one such tale the Buddha, in a previous human birth, sacrifices his own life to a hungry tigress whose newborn cubs would otherwise perish without her nurturing care.

In human beings compassion is not merely a deep, emotional feeling but a part of ourselves that needs constant development and deep contemplation. A person can achieve true peace and happiness without becoming a monk or going to a lonely mountain cave but by remaining in the everyday world acting always with compassion. The greatest acts of asceticism are useless if they do not generate a warm heart. If one helps the needy, feeds the poor, or defends the helpless, then by their compassionate nature they move closer to the perfection of Buddhahood.

In Sanskrit, one of the languages of the Buddhist scriptures, the word "Karuna" is usually translated as compassion. On the emotional level I think all of us recognize the basic meaning of Karuna. All living creatures wish to avoid suffering and live happily. This is true despite the fact that most of us suffer tremendously and do not lead happy lives. In my own life I sometimes feel frustration because I cannot help everyone who needs it. The sufferings of my own Tibetan people are just one example, but I am certain that even in the face of such frustrations persistent and sincere efforts will eventually succeed. Compassionate action will, in the end, always triumph over ignorance and selfishness.

As Dalai Lama, if I do not seek to reduce the sufferings of others, then I am not worthy of the title and could not even call myself a Buddhist. So I must act to make a better life for my people who have suffered so much in the past twenty-five years. In India where I now live we have built schools and hospitals and have promoted the free practice of religion. I also try to influence others by traveling around the world, teaching the philosophy of a warm heart, and meeting with other spiritual leaders who seek world peace.

But there is also another deeper understanding of compassion, which draws a link to the concept Buddhists call dependent-arising. The notion of dependent-arising simply suggests that all things come into existence depending upon other things and that nothing ever stands apart from relationships. If we pause for a moment and think about this, we can see how dependent-arising is linked to compassion. We all depend upon one another in our present life, like a child depends upon its mother and father for its basic needs. Yet it is clear, even as we grow out of childhood, that as human beings we always need others to live and be happy. But the teaching of dependent-arising considers more than just our immediate living situation. As we broaden our perspectives we see that we are not only existing in dependence upon one another in our present lives, but that the past and the future are also dependently arising. Our very idea of *self* depends upon thinking "this is mine" and "I am so and so." As a Buddhist I believe that there can be no independent self distinct from relationships and that clinging to such a notion of ourselves as permanent, independent entities only causes us to act selfishly, eventually leading to suffering. When a person eliminates this false notion of an independent self, he or she is on the path of selfless action that leads to the deeper understanding of Karuna.

Thus it is by the wisdom of there existing no independent self that the deeper understanding of Karuna becomes possible. Let us consider this subtle understanding of compassion: The task of eliminating suffering cannot be directed merely toward one's own self since such a self does not exist apart or independent of relationships. If I am to eliminate my own sufferings, I must act in the knowledge that I exist in dependent relationships with other human beings and the whole of nature. My own happiness depends not on seeking something for myself but in helping others.

In Buddhism we believe that the more one cultivates the wisdom that all things are selfless, the closer one comes to pure compassionate action. The being who acts at all times responding to true selfless nature we call a *bodhisattva*. But the bodhisattva is also a practical person who realizes that it is convenient and even necessary to speak of one's self in order to effect selfless action. The Buddha's teaching is called the Middle Way because while it is necessary to deny false conceptions of persons and other phenomena, it is equally important to affirm meaningful action. We can say that the bodhisattva acts positively to bring about the alleviation of suffering because he or she has come to know the nature of the world as selfless in the sense that everything, though existing, is understood as being without inherent or independent existence. But one cannot begin to contemplate the fact that there is no independent self if the stomach aches with hunger. First we must attend to our most basic needs, and only then can we begin to control our desires and cultivate the deeper sense of Karuna.

I think it is clear that a bodhisattva can be a person of any religion, or even of no religion. Certainly anyone devoting his life's search to the elimination of suffering for all living beings can be called a bodhisattva.

The first step on the bodhisattva path is for each of us to try to gain inner mental peace. One must improve oneself, but one must then progress for the sake of others, for the very question of the survival of the world depends upon extending kindness and love to others. The leaders of the world must face these choices with more than greed or self-interest in mind; they must stop building more and more deadly weapons aimed at destruction and turn their resources to eliminating the sufferings of the living.

As a Buddhist I accept the powers of reason and agree with factual conclusions of science when there is no contravening evidence. But I must emphasize that the use of technology for the good of the world depends upon the spiritual progress and attitudes of humanity. Spiritual progress must go hand in hand with technology. In the present world, it seems technology has taken the upper hand, and this must be corrected. Technology, no matter what it benefits, cannot produce warm feelings for others; the good heart must come from within ourselves. It is not the product of science but of conscience. Western science has produced many advancements for the good of humanity while Buddhism offers a very deep examination of the mind and of human nature. Each can enrich the other, and I believe that each is needed to remove suffering and help the cause of peace in the world.

When I was a boy in Lhasa studying to be the Dalai Lama, I learned many things from my teachers, but the knowledge imparted to me was always balanced with the need to develop right attitudes and behavior. A child needs this sort of training right from the beginning. Now I realize that my education began not when I came to Lhasa but as a boy in the village with my mother and father. There must always be a balance in education between the development of skills and moral teachings. Today there are unhealthy degrees of competition, causing greed and anger. But competition itself it not bad so long as it is coupled with the cultivation of proper motivations.

As a person committed to the beliefs and practices of Buddhist tradition, their value in the modern world has been confirmed in my own experiences. From meditation and the practice of compassion many puzzling things become clear. In Tibetan tradition I am regarded as the reincarnation of previous Dalai Lamas, and in my own experience I have come to understand that I share a very special relationship with all the Dalai Lamas before me. This can only be known by meditative practice. Yet I feel I still have so much more to learn and so much more to travel along the spiritual path.

Since 1959, I have lived as a refugee and know that thousands of Tibetans have suffered as a result of the actions of the Chinese Communists. But the Chinese have been teachers for me, too. I must feel compassion for them because they have taught me to love my "enemies." Even though they have tried to destroy Buddhism in Tibet, I do not deny that they have also done some good things. The spirit of Buddhism is strong in the Tibetan people and I hope someday to return to Tibet, but only under the proper circumstances. Communism itself is not bad, nor is it incompatible with Buddhism. We must look closely at the true motivations of the persons involved. If the communist wishes to improve the welfare of the people, then the Buddhist agrees, but we must always look closely at motivations and prac-tices. Without kindness for others we cannot survive, and the enemy of kindness is anger and hatred. Through hatred and anger it is not possible to achieve world peace, and peace achieved through force will only be temporary. Lasting peace comes from inner mental peace and the proper motivations for action. This I have learned in my own experience as a refugee, and this is why I harbor no hatred for the Chinese Communists.

I believe we can see clearly that there are close connections between political actions and human welfare, as well as between technology and its uses. All these things are themselves dependent upon one an-other and all fundamentally depend upon our attitudes and motiva-tions. In Buddhism the development of proper motivation and com-passion depends upon each one of us, not on any absolute reality. The teaching of dependent-arising frees our minds from a selfish ego-ism and shows us that suffering is not irreversible or permanent. Compassionate action is the means through which we can alleviate suffering and dissolve our selfish desires.

I remain committed to these ideals not only as a Buddhist but sim-ply as one human being speaking to another. Our beliefs as well as our actions must come from our heart, for in our hearts the true wisdom that frees us and the path of compassion are inseparable.

Hugh Downs
b. 1921

Hugh Downs, one of American television's most visible personalities, became nationally known during the fifties as the announcer and intellectual-in-residence on the Jack Paar Tonight show. In the sixties he was anchorman on NBC's popular two-hour morning program, the Today show. Hosting the game show Concentration occupied his talents in the seventies, while in recent years viewers have seen him as host of the public television program Over Easy and of ABC's 20/20 news program. Over these four decades he has made himself a television tradition.

Downs's low-keyed, unflappable, erudite style accounts for his continued success. He radiates a sincerity and integrity that is rare on television. A man of wide-ranging interests—science, music, aviation, painting are but a few—he is able to share his curiosity and enthusiasm with his audience. He has written books, assembled his own telescope, composed an orchestral suite, contributed regularly to Science Digest, sailed a ketch across the Pacific Ocean, served as a mem-

ber of the Citizens Advisory Board on Mental Hospitals in New York State and as a consultant to the Center for the Study of Democratic Institutions, and taught at Arizona State University. He also somehow finds time just to read and tinker.

In recent years much of Mr. Downs's time and energy has been spent as chairman of the U.S. Committee for UNICEF, which he claims has given him the most satisfaction of all his avocations.

I remember wondering when I was about five years old, "Why is there anything?" "Why is there something instead of nothing?" as the philosophers phrase it. An answer very gradually emerged, amounting to the necessity of an uncreated creator, which I finally, as an adult, found no shame in calling God.

Current scientific belief holds that the universe had a beginning at a point in the finite past, somewhere between ten and twenty billion years ago. If this belief were to be swept away tomorrow, to be replaced with the idea that the universe has no beginning or end, the changeover would not effect my basic theology, for the following reason: Causation requires that everything, every condition, is caused by a condition or force that has preceded it. Either there must be a first cause, which itself has no cause, or the chain is infinite, in which case an uncaused cause must be responsible for the chain itself.

I believe God is the reason there is something instead of nothing. I believe that God created everything and probably supports its continuance either from moment to moment, or through physical laws set into the cosmos at its creation, causing mass and energy to behave in an organizing and enduring way.

I have exerted some effort to separate what I believe from what I hope or desire. I had little success in this until I was prepared to entertain seriously the proposition that there is no God. To come to this view with firmness—as a tenet of faith—was dogmatic, and my feelings are not generally compatible with dogma. Rather, a comfortable agnosticism allowed me to see what ideas entailing God could remain, once I was rid of wish. And the need for an uncaused cause kept reasserting itself.

Out of the study of physical science came the knowledge that my body is made of chemicals compounded of elements that were forged in the interiors of massive stars, which later exploded; that the stars themselves were formed from matter (hydrogen and helium clouds in gravitational collapse); that this matter had condensed out of a plasma that came from particles and forces, which in turn resulted from the laws that impel all behavior that has led, in a series of organizational thresholds of ever higher complexity, to the human brain and body.

These laws, even when incompletely understood or inelegantly stated, are (in the eye of this beholder) beautiful and of the substance of thought. And this is the second reason I believe I came from that first cause I call God. The awareness of a relation between the activity of conscious thinking and the deeply beautiful laws that are responsible not only for all of material existence, but for the urge to know, the thirst for the rationale behind what may seem merely absurd, the capacity to care, the inclination to wonder and to worship, produces a strong sense of kinship with the author of all this—whether or not that author remains unknowable to me.

If my beliefs or convictions about God in any way form a religion, however, then I must say, with Carlyle, "There is one true Church, of which at present I am the only member." This is because the sects of all religions I have encountered and examined embody dogma I cannot accept.

Most of my more solid beliefs formed slowly, but one came suddenly, in my early twenties, and it has never left me. I was reading about stoicism. Something in the meditations of Marcus Aurelius caused me to realize that hatred is never anything but fear—that if you feared no one, you would hate no one. At the same time, and partly through the same revelation, I came to know that no one ever does anything he doesn't want to do. The value of these ideas is that they almost immediately freed me from fear of anyone and hatred of anyone, and knowing I was responsible for my actions (and could not be forced to do anything I didn't want to) took the bitterness out of choices. Would I really rather lie in bed than go to work on time? If so, I could lie in bed. I was free to do this. If I went to work instead, it was because that's what I preferred and chose to do. The price of this freedom is responsibility, but it's a bargain, because freedom is priceless. All phrases such as "I had no choice," "They made me . . . ," "My schedule won't permit . . . ," "I was forced to act," etc., become hypocritical nonsense.

And somehow to be free of hatred causes the fear itself to melt away. This is truly liberating, and it came quite suddenly for me.

I believe that the mind is greater than its scaffolding of reason. The realm of feeling, ranging from esthetics to genuine caring for others, transcends reason, even though reason is an indispensable tool to be recruited in the service of important life issues.

And this leads to my most recently developed belief, which is so curiously self-referential it might at first glance appear to cancel itself out: I believe that belief is relatively unimportant, and that proper feeling and actions are what give meaning to life. It may be important to a Christian to believe Christ existed, to believe in His divinity, to believe that He taught what He taught, and to believe this teaching is powerfully true. But none of this, the Christian is often admonished, is worth anything unless the feeling of love for others is present and results in loving action.

Part of Christian doctrine (and Christianity has no monopoly on dealing mercifully with others—Hebrew and Buddhist scripture are full of this urging) acknowledges that counterfeiting the caring for others—behaving as though you cared, even if you don't—has value, in that it tends to ignite the genuine feelings somewhere along the line. The concept of *agape*—the practice of loving the unlovable—justifies "going through the motions" on these grounds. But unless you have charity you are merely an apprentice and have yet to reach the goal. The implication in this respect of Christian idealism is that the love itself is more important than the belief. When that kind of caring is at full flame, personal salvation becomes unimportant and it is at that point that salvation takes place. "He who would save his life must lose it."

So much for the personal credo. I have wished for the strength and size of soul to put into practice all these beliefs. But I can only claim beginnings. And I must be careful not to misinterpret certain things, like a tendency to be agreeable and compliant and sometimes generous that probably comes from an almost neurotic (and certainly selfish) desire to be well liked.

In my profession of broadcasting my activities provide some satisfactions that may have a degree of purity. A letter from someone whose life has been changed for the better by watching one of our program segments is a powerfully gratifying reward for the effort

that went into it. Not all the broadcasting I do is of such a service
nature that this kind of reward follows. Some of it is frivolous, some
perhaps only attention-getting. And it is, of course, the way I make
my living.

Among avocations, far and away my most rewarding is the work
on behalf of UNICEF. As of this writing 40,000 small children a day
die of disease and dehydration on this planet. To work toward cutting
down this appalling suffering is extremely important to those of us
engaged in it. UNICEF's Child Survival Revolution, initiated about
five years ago, is beginning to prove that these deaths can be cut in
half in another decade. The use of growth charts, oral rehydration
therapy, the encouragement of breast feeding (as opposed to powdered
milk formula), and the new immunization breakthroughs involving
heat-stable vaccines are moving the revolution forward. The work in
consciousness-raising and fund-raising is still urgent as drought and
famine seem to keep pace with humanitarian efforts.

I have to face the possibility that subconsciously I may be moved
in part to rack up brownie points for myself in some huge ledger
upstairs, but I know that the larger drive to action is that the loss of
these children is simply intolerable.

Puny as my own personal contributions may be compared to a
Mother Teresa or St. Francis (I haven't sold everything I own to get
food and medicine for these children), still, when I ask myself if there
is an integration of my beliefs into the daily actions of my life and if
my life is given more meaning by them, the answer comes back between mirrors, as it were.

Not only have my beliefs, implemented in my life, changed it, but
the finding of deeper feelings is constantly molding my beliefs—confirming the kinship with something infinite, and perhaps moving me
back toward some of the traditions, religious and otherwise, with which
I was brought up.

Strangely, the more resigned I become to failure in finding those
ultimate truths I thirst for, the more satisfaction I get from pursuing
them. It may be enough to quest. The landscape through which I
search is increasingly attractive. The little satisfactions become more
satisfying. Even the selfish ones: loving the ones I love, the creature
comforts of everyday life, the prosaic duties, the esthetic flavor of
secular rituals—these all become woven into the larger tapestry of
what is becoming a faith in the ultimate goodness of this awesome
universe.

This life, whether regarded as benefice or suffering, does seem to be a sort of exile. We come into it "trailing clouds of glory," and we go out of it freed of limitations and linear time. Perhaps nothing is ever lost: what has been, is, and if there is a sensed need to recapture it, to see again those we have loved and been parted from by death, this will somehow be provided for us. Billy Graham once answered a woman who asked him if her dog would be in heaven when she went there, by saying, "Whatever you need for your happiness will be in heaven." This is as reasonable and elegant as any scientific theory I know, and it violates no theory I hold to be true.

In the end, I expect to have what I need. If the good I try to do in the meantime is done because it pleases me, I can live with this selfishness. And if I see that I have done no harm and that some positive results have come about because I was given a role here I will be content.

Dr. J. Fishman

Israel Goldstein
b. 1896

My World as a Jew *is the apt title of Rabbi Israel Goldstein's memoirs, published in 1984. Reared in the ghetto of South Philadelphia, and, for a while, in a Lithuanian village, he attended the University of Pennsylvania. Upon graduating at the age of eighteen, he simultaneously enrolled at the Jewish Theological Seminary and Columbia University of New York City. In 1918, with an M.A. from Columbia and ordination from the Seminary, he was elected rabbi of Congregation B'nai Jeshurun, the second oldest Jewish congregation in New York. He remained there until his retirement in 1960.*

During those many years his ministry assumed ever-broadening proportions in Jewish, civic, and interfaith activities. He was one of the founders of the National Conference of Christians and Jews in 1928 and the founder of Brandeis University in 1946. He has served as president of the Jewish National Fund of America, the Jewish Conciliation Board of America, the Zionist Organization of America, the Synagogue Council of America, the American Jewish Congress, and

the World Confederation of United Zionists. The author of ten books,
he is the recipient of numerous accolades, including honorary docto-
rates from the University of Pennsylvania, New York University, and
Brandeis University. Chairs in Zionism at Hebrew University of Je-
rusalem and in practical theology at the Jewish Theological Seminary
have been named for him.

In 1960, he and his wife settled in Israel, where he served as world
chairman of the Keren Hayesod—United Israel Appeal, and as a
member of the Jewish Agency Executive and as a governor of the
Weizmann Institute of Science and Haifa University. Since his retire-
ment from active public office in 1971, he has devoted most of his
time to writing, to the Youth Village in Jerusalem bearing his name,
and to Israel's institutions of higher learning.

As I view it, life is not divided into neat, separate categories of belief
and action. The test of belief is action and the motivation of action is
belief. Indeed, the whole of cognitive living is belief in action.

Belief unaccompanied by action is sterile. Action that is not rooted
in belief is like a building without a firm foundation, in danger of
collapsing under the strains and stresses of life's experiences.

Ordinarily, men and women start out with beliefs and principles
imbibed from their rearing. Therefore, the home environment is the
earliest factor. Another factor is the environment outside the home.
Learning by experience is perhaps the most decisive factor of all.

Since I was reared in synagogue premises, my earliest conditioning
was religious and Zionist. My mother, who was rheumatic, decided
to go to a spa in Russia, combining it with a visit to the village where
her folks lived. I was only five years of age when she took me with
her. The visit turned out to last two years. These were formative
years in my childhood, when my exposure to the *heder**, to the Yid-

* Hebrew term, literally "room," applied to the old type of one-room Jewish religious elementary school.

dish vernacular, and to life in the *shtetl** impressed those influences
upon me.

There were no Christian playmates. The neighborhood of the Russian Orthodox church was avoided for fear of unpleasant encounters.

Several years ago, in Jerusalem, I had occasion once to refresh my
heder memories when the famous artist Chagall, responding to honors conferred upon him in the President's House by the Hebrew University and the Jerusalem Municipality, reminisced about his childhood years in Vitebsk. He recalled his *heder* school days when he
would come home in the dark winter afternoons, carrying a lantern
to light his way. "That lantern," he remarked, "has lighted up my
path in life." In my own lesser way, I am able to identify myself with
his reminiscence.

Upon my mother's return to Philadelphia, we went back to the
Jewish ghetto. It was contiguous to the Polish ghetto, clustered around
the Polish Catholic church and parochial school. There were occasional conflicts. A few blocks farther south, the black population was
concentrated. Their relationship with Jews was not strained. Yet, I
was already sensitive to their underprivileged status.

Our home was a Zionist home. It housed the blue and white box
of the Jewish National Fund, in which coins were deposited, especially
prior to the advent of the Sabbath, for the purchase of land in *Eretz
Israel* (Palestine) on which to establish Jewish settlements. When Dr.
Theodor Herzl, the founder of modern political Zionism, died on July
3, 1904, our home was among those plunged into mourning.

A casual incident in my youth strengthened the development of my
belief in action. It was a lecture delivered by the Rev. Russell H.
Conwell, founder of Temple University and of the Baptist Temple in
Philadelphia. Rumor had it that Temple University was founded and
funded by the proceeds earned from this lecture, "Acres of Diamonds," delivered before audiences throughout the United States. When
I went to hear it at the Academy of Music, it was a special occasion,
marking its two-thousandth delivery. The central theme of this lecture had to do with a man who, having failed in his quest for diamonds far and wide, found a diamond one day while digging in his
own garden. This lecture often reverberated in my mind.

One of my most memorable experiences dates back to July 1945.
The European phase of World War II was drawing to a close when I

* Yiddish word for the East European townlet.

visited concentration camp survivors in the American Zone of Germany. I came as president of the Zionist Organization of America and in other capacities, to bring a message of fellowship and encouragement to these Jewish survivors of the Holocaust.

I found camps in which Polish Jews and Polish Christians were herded together. It was distressing to see how the agony they had experienced together had not cured the Poles of their inbred anti-Semitism. My recommendation to General Eisenhower, that separate facilities be provided for the Jewish survivors, was heeded.

I came upon other manifestations, however, which were heartening. One such was my visit to Feldafing, a village facing the Bavarian Alps. Lieutenant Irving Smith, a Jewish boy from Indianapolis, was with the U.S. Army unit that liberated that area. They had found nearly eight hundred Jews herded into trains destined for the Auschwitz crematoria. Lieutenant Smith and his unit liberated them and, with the help of U.S. Chaplain Abraham Klausner, installed them in the comfort of what had been a Hitler Youth Camp.

In honor of my visit an evening concert was arranged, in which a woman singer, a contralto, and a male pianist participated. An improvised platform, a requisitioned piano, and requisitioned formal evening attire for the performing artists, together with stage lighting beamed from a U.S. Army truck, provided the appropriate setting.

The response of the audience can be imagined. They were part of civilization again. The reaction of the performing artists themselves cannot even be imagined. They were alive once more in their own field of artistic self-expression, bringing esthetic pleasure to fellow humans. These were unexpected diamonds in an unwonted garden. For me, it was an overwhelming experience to witness a kind of resurrection. How grateful every one of us, I thought, should be for his place, high or humble, in making life more livable for his fellow men!

On subsequent occasions, I underwent the harrowing experience of visiting the death camps of Auschwitz, Dachau, and Mauthausen. I can never forget the heap of children's shoes at Dachau, the steep precipice at Mauthausen from which Jews were forced to leap to their deaths, and the gas chambers and adjoining furnaces in Auschwitz-Birkenau.

Such experiences intensified my resolve to do what lay in my power to help rehabilitate the surviving remnant of the Holocaust, to help achieve the establishment of a Jewish State, *Medinat Yisrael*, to which all Jews could come as of right, and to strengthen its capacity to provide a viable future for them and for their children.

Facing me at my desk here in Jerusalem is a bas-relief carved in local Cyprus soapstone, the work of one Jewish survivor of the Holocaust who had been detained by the British on the way to Palestine in 1946. It depicts a column of Jews, men, women, and children, marching toward the death factory and surveyed by an armed Nazi to ensure their orderly procedure to annihilation.

Life is compounded of both disappointments and fulfillments. I have always been resentful of the racial and religious quota system in admissions to a number of American universities. A great fulfillment came to me therefore when, in 1946, I succeeded in founding Brandeis University at Waltham, Massachusetts. Named for Justice Louis D. Brandeis, a prominent American liberal and Zionist, it was meant to be—and has become—a successful, corporate contribution of American Jewry to higher learning, where racial and religious quotas are taboo.

In sum, I am profoundly grateful for the opportunities that have come my way to translate beliefs into actions, that my years have been cast in one of the momentous periods of history, and that occasions have arisen for contributing to the causes that have meant most to me.

My advice to young idealists is this: "Don't shy away from a big challenge; you may surprise yourself!"

An exhortation of the ancient rabbis comes to mind: "Be as careful in the performance of a light precept as in the performance of a difficult one."

In the closing phase of a long and active life, may I venture a summation, however inadequate, of the beliefs and principles that seem to have activated and guided me, sometimes consciously, sometimes subconsciously:

I believe in God, the guiding force behind creative evolution, the ultimate guarantee for the improvability of the human species. I believe that through a long process of trial and error, the human race is learning to respect the validity of the exhortations of its prophets touching individual and national behavior.

I believe in the power of regeneration, that it is a God-given capacity for making a new start. The Biblical story of Jacob, struggling with the angel and leaving the encounter limping but blessed, holds a lesson for all men.

I believe that the Jewish people, in the course of their history, have demonstrated a unique capacity for producing spiritual guidance, governing conduct between individuals and between nations, and that they have an ongoing special responsibility, as a group, to be ever a witness to their heritage.

I believe in the value of tradition, since it distills the experiences of past generations, but tradition must be coupled with progress, for otherwise it is stultifying.

I believe that restoration of their ancient homeland in the Land of Israel was an act of international and historic justice to the Jewish people, which, however, imposes a responsibility to be worthy of this opportunity for national self-renewal.

I also believe that the United States of America retains the principles of human freedom that underlie its founding, yet needs to be ever freshly reminded of them.

I believe that the future of mankind should be our number-one concern, since, in the atomic age, the line between survival and extinction is precariously thin. The exhortation, "Seek peace and pursue it" (Psalm 34:14), is the supreme imperative of belief in action.

I believe in the possibility and in the necessity of interfaith understanding and comity, communally, nationally, and internationally.

I believe that the deepest and most abiding satisfactions of life come not from receiving but from giving, that greatness is not synonymous with prominence, and that the most meaningful kind of earthly immortality is that of commitment to human enterprises that live on after us.

As mine is the tradition of Judaism, I consider it relevant to mention the *Chapters of the Fathers*, a 1,700-year-old compendium of ethical guides to conduct. More than a few are still usefully quotable: "If I am not for myself, who will be for me, and if I am only for myself, what am I, and if not now, when? . . . It does not devolve upon thee to complete the work, but neither art thou free to desist from it . . . Who is mighty? He who subdues his passions . . . Who is rich? He who rejoices in his portion."

The categorical imperative in my Jewish tradition can be found in the concluding paragraph of our daily prayer service: "To improve the world under the kingdom of God."

The ultimate validation of belief is action.

Jane Goodall

b. 1934

In 1960, when young Jane Goodall first ventured into the rugged beauty of Tanzania's Gombe Stream Game Reserve, the world knew little about the behavior of chimpanzees in the wild. It was the British ethologist's pioneering efforts that uncovered the truth about the manlike primates. Her observations of the great apes' behavior and, in particular, her discoveries that chimpanzees are crude toolmakers and not strict vegetarians, threw significant new light on the study of prehistoric man and his evolutionary development.

Dr. Goodall—she received her Ph.D. in ethology from Cambridge University in 1965, one of the few in the University's history allowed to work for a doctorate without first taking a B.A. degree—has described her work in scholarly journals and in the National Geographic, as well as in such books as My Friends the Wild Chimpanzees (1967) and In the Shadow of Man (1971). Her work has also been featured in films by the National Geographic Society.

According to Dr. Goodall, the chimpanzees seem to regard her as an inferior primate—on a level with the baboon—but a superior source of bananas. Humans, however, regard her as one to whom we look for continued guidance in preserving and protecting our natural environment. Her work has helped millions understand the importance of wildlife conservation to life on Earth. It has also aided us in understanding ourselves, for, as she wrote in In the Shadow of Man:

> It is only through a real understanding of the ways in which chimpanzees and men show similarities in behavior that we can reflect with meaning on the ways in which men and chimpanzees differ. And only then can we really begin to appreciate, in a biological and spiritual manner, the full extent of man's uniqueness.

When not working at Gombe or on the lecture circuit, she takes her pleasures in quiet things—reading and writing poetry, listening to classical music, or just being by herself in nature, away from people and the things of people.

Some years ago I visited Notre-Dame. By good fortune there were very few people about, and it was still and quiet inside. Just as I was gazing up where the sun made the great rose window glow, the whole cathedral, without warning, was filled with a huge volume of sound. As the organ thundered out Bach's Toccata and Fugue in D Minor, the music was alive. The moment, a suddenly captured moment of eternity, was perhaps the closest I have ever come to experiencing ecstasy, in the sense of the mystic. How could I believe that it was the chance gyrations of bits of primeval dust that had led up to that moment in time—the cathedral soaring to the sky, the collective inspiration and faith of those who caused it to be built, the advent of Bach himself, his brain that had translated truth into music, the mind that could, as mine did then, comprehend the whole inexorable progression of evolution in a split second? Since I could not, and cannot, believe that this was the result of chance, I have to admit anti-chance.

And so I believe in a guiding power in the universe—in other words, I believe in God.

We didn't talk much about religion in my family when I was growing up but we went to church fairly often, our values were Christian values, and the rules we had to obey were based on the Ten Commandments. One person outside my family who had a profound influence on my early beliefs was the parson with whom, when I was fifteen, I fell madly—and platonically—in love. Then, of course, there were never enough services for my liking! And, talking of belief in action, I remember when the text of one of his sermons was on the "second mile" how, for the next few weeks, I performed all my chores twice over. Two buckets of coal, two beds made—even two baths, one after the other! When I left home and faced the realities of the world, I put my thoughts of God in cold storage for a while, because I couldn't reconcile what I believed, deep inside, with what was going on around me. But that early period, when God was as real as the wind that blew from the sea through the pine trees in the garden, left me with an inner peace, which, as I grew older, swelled—until, perforce, I had to open my mind to God again. How did this happen?

I was taught always to believe that if you wanted something enough, and worked steadfastly toward that goal, you would probably be rewarded. Success came through effort and "the fault . . . lies not in our stars but in ourselves that we are underlings." I still believe that, but I have to admit that the "stars" played their part in the realization of my goal—Africa and animals. Certainly I worked hard to earn the money for my fare but the stars led me to Louis Leakey, who set me on my way to Gombe and the chimpanzees. And at Gombe I could wander in the timeless forest and touch the bark of ancient trees. I could sit on the beach and watch the moonlight glinting as the waves tumbled, one after the other, onto the sands. There I felt part of the harmony of all life, and that, for me, was to know God again. Against the backdrop of billions of years of evolution, the violence and misery around us can be divorced from "here and now" and viewed in perspective. Seen as part of the millions of years of human evolution, our troubled century is but a flash, finite like our bodies. Think of the millions of years before the first primates emerged amongst the dinosaurs, and the millions more during which, slowly but inexorably, evolution developed the anatomy and above all the brain of the creature that would become man. At last the vehicle was ready. At last cultural evolution could take over from genetic mutation. And if, as Lecomte du Noüy suggests, we are now in the throes of "moral evolution," we cannot expect this to be resolved in a trice.

It is my study of the chimpanzees that has crystallized my belief in an ultimate destiny toward which humans are still evolving. It is just because the chimpanzee, our closest living relative, shares so many behaviors with us, and shows the beginnings of the intellectual abilities that characterize the human mind, that we can see, so clearly, the ways in which we are different. Chimpanzees form enduring, affectionate, supportive bonds, mostly between family members. This, along with an understanding of the evolutionary theories of kin selection (you help your relatives so that, even if this causes your death, they live and perpetuate some of your genes—those that they share) helps us to map the pathway that has led to human compassion, self-sacrifice, and love. The chimpanzee is capable of violence and cruelty, but we cannot compare this with human brutality, warfare, and torture—for only man acts with full understanding of the suffering inflicted on his victims. The chimpanzee can be taught a simple symbolic language—but he has not developed one for himself; he cannot discuss ideas. From the chimpanzee we learn much that helps us to understand our biological heritage. Thus we can better appreciate the extent to which we can control our "animal" instincts and subjugate them to our will.

I believe that to some extent the success or failure of an individual to live up to his or her uniquely human potential depends on the family background. We know that major disasters in childhood—such as the death of the mother—can have lasting effects on human behavior. But what of lesser traumas—an infant dumped with different caretakers each day, thus disrupting that all-important mother-infant bond, or left alone and crying in the dark? Distressing at the time—can there be long-term effects too? For monkey infants the answer is yes. A two-week separation during the early months leaves an emotional scar still apparent during adolescence. We cannot assume that experiences leading to disturbances in monkeys will necessarily lead to disturbances in humans, but I feel it is desperately important that we find out. What causes one person to break down in a stressful situation while another weathers it? Many factors are involved, but one of them is probably differential rearing. And if it is true for humans, as I believe it is for chimpanzees, that childhood experience can influence the subsequent ability of an individual to form good personal relationships, then it is one of the most important research questions of our times. For surely it is through better relationships, greater understanding, and compassion that we shall move toward our final human destiny. On the other hand, humans have the ability to overcome the destructive effects of poor upbringing, provided there has been no physiological damage. For we can learn how we should behave. We all know at least one person who has "made good" despite a terrible childhood, even, perhaps, because of it—steeled and tempered by hardship, determined to prove him or herself.

How fortunate I was in my own childhood. It was such a happy one, filled with the exhilaration of discovery, with laughter and fun. My grandmother—a real, self-disciplined, iron-willed Victorian—ruled the house with supreme authority and a heart big enough to embrace all the starving children of the world. She counted her blessings every night. Her favorite text I took for my own: "As thy days, so shall thy strength be." We (my sister and I) had a wonderful mother who not only understood the importance of discipline (it is very important for chimpanzees, too, incidentally) but always explained why some things were strictly not allowed. Thus if we transgressed, the worst punishment was self-inflicted—the realization that we had caused hurt as well as earning displeasure (not that we worked it out quite like that at the time). My family environment was immensely supportive and immensely encouraging. It still is.

I tried to bring up my own son in the same way. I resolved that my work should not come first, especially when he was tiny, and it never did. For his first three years I never left him for a single day. After that he and I were together for at least half of every day until he was nine and went to school in England—and there he was with my mother. It was not only lucky for me that she was there, it was immeasurably lucky for him.

When I was seven years old I had a dramatic demonstration of the powers of the mind. It was wartime and we were on holiday. One day my mother suddenly decided to take a different route back to our little guest house—a very long way around that meant we would miss lunch. But she was determined. Ten minutes after we had set off, a German plane flew overhead on its way home and dropped a bomb. It made a deep crater halfway up the lane where we should have been. For me that was the most meaningful of all my mother's psychic experiences! And if, as some scientists argue, these things cannot be proved, then I have to suggest that science is not using the right tools.

I was lucky then; I have been lucky since. I was born at the right time and got to the right place to meet the right people. Chance? Perhaps, but at any rate, I have, as a result, been privileged to listen to the heartbeat of nature, to glimpse, on occasions, truth beyond experience. One such moment came at the end of a long day at Gombe. I had been following a chimpanzee family since dawn and, together, we had endured the buffeting of a fierce storm. Now we climbed onto a high place. Down below, the lake was dark and angry with white flecks where the waves broke, and rain clouds, which had drenched the mountain forests, were black in the south. To the north the sky was clear with only wisps of gray clouds still lingering. The chimpanzees climbed into a tree. In the soft sunlight their black coats were shot with coppery brown, the branches on which they sat were wet and dark as ebony, the young leaves a pale but brilliant green. Behind was the dramatic backcloth of the indigo black sky where lightning flickered and distant thunder growled and rumbled. I stopped recording. This was a precious moment in time when I and the chimpanzees, the earth and trees and air, seemed to merge, to become part of the mystery of life itself. There are many windows through which we humans, searching for meaning, can look out into the world around us. There are those carved out by Western science, their panes polished by a succession of brilliant minds. Through them we can see far and clearly, penetrating depths, which, until recently, were beyond human knowledge. Through such a window I had been observing the chimpanzees all day. There are other windows, used more often by philosophers and theologians—those through which the mystic seeks his vision of truth, through which the sage of the East gazes as he searches for the meaning of human existence. As I sat there, it was as though an unseen hand drew back the curtain from such a window, bidding me to look through and understand. All around us was a sense of timelessness and a quiet joy. Yet the joy was tinged with sadness, for with it came the knowledge of imperfection, of inadequacy, and a yearning for that which is, for most of us, unattainable in this life. Later, as I sat by my little fire, cooking my supper, I knew that I could never be content until the dark shadows that, for me, lay between the views from those windows were forever banished. Only then could I hope for an inkling of reality.

I know how fortunate I have been in my life, and I feel a strong compulsion to share, with as many as possible, something of the wonder, the peace, that I have found in the forest. And I want people to understand why animals are such a rich part of our human heritage and not only need, but deserve, our love and help. Perhaps it was to this end that I was given a gift—and a gift it certainly is for it was untaught: the ability to communicate. When I give a lecture, people listen; when I write, they read. And when they also understand, it is a real reward, as when a young woman came up and said: "I want to thank you for giving me the courage to enjoy my family and baby." An older person, with faraway eyes: "Listening to you talk of your chimps has made me think about myself and my family."

With this public exposure has come an increasing sense of responsibility. When youngsters write and ask how they should proceed to follow in my footsteps, I can give advice, though it is becoming more and more difficult to study animals in the wild. But when they write, "You are my heroine. I aim to be just like you," how am I to respond? God knows—and I say that advisedly—*I am no heroine*. But because my life at Gombe seems so unreal to people, they fantasize— not only as to what I do and how I live but also as to what I am. And so I am under pressure to try to live up to these unrealistic images of myself. The model their fantasy has created is the model I too must try to emulate. We are each as likely or unlikely to succeed.

The way in which my own life touches those of so many others, those I know and thousands of those I don't, has strengthened my belief that each human has his or her own unique place in the ocean of existence. Some make a great splash and the ripples spread far and wide. Others seem to sink without a stir but it is not so, for the currents of their passing move beneath the surface. And some, buried silently in contemporary mud, are dug up afterward with a great swirling of the waters. At all different levels the ripples and currents pass or mingle, and some merge inextricably. With each merging a new force is created, itself as unique as the two beings that forged it. What joys the world would have lost if some of these forces had never been created, and what pain in other cases would it have been spared. The merging of minds, not only teacher and pupil, parent and child, world leader and his people, but also seemingly casual encounters. Every time I talk with another human I wonder what will become of the mingling, whether it be prolonged discussion with a colleague or chance encounter on a plane. The merging of bodies; how many thousands of couplings it took to create a Beethoven, a Schweitzer— a Hitler. The blending of millions of unique strands can lead to one person so strong, for good or evil, that he can influence the lives of millions of others and change the course of world history.

For me, the very fact that one person can have such a tremendous impact is a source of hope. It means that *if* the right leader appears he—or she—could do so much to alleviate the desperate muddle and anguish of our troubled times. But there is another note of hope, too, for despite the despair and pessimism that surrounds us, man has, nevertheless, come a long way. Less than a hundred years ago, in our Western culture, children were sent down the mines and up the chimneys, and shivered with blue feet and rags in the snow. There were unspeakable slums, and slavery was accepted. The modern welfare state, for all its drawbacks, is certainly a step in the right direction. Our predecessors emerged triumphantly from the teeth of mighty *Tyrannosaurus rex*. God willing, we will also emerge from the dark menace of nuclear war. We do not (so far as we know) have any choice as to the circumstances of our birth and this has an overriding influence on the pattern of our lives. The son of a Russian peasant has very different opportunities from those of an American millionaire's child. But no matter in what position we find ourselves, we can exercise our human birthright—free will. Life offers a continual succession of choice points: Do this? or that? Speak? or keep silent? "To be? or not to be?"

Circumstances may indeed force us along paths we are reluctant to follow, but we are still free to proceed with rebellion or resignation, with a determination to make the best of things, to change the pattern if we can, sometimes with bitterness, hostility. Oftentimes a person labeled "lucky" is one who has seized, or quietly created, an opportunity to change his life.

And so, while I believe that God wills the ultimate destiny of the human race, I feel sure that the destiny of each of us as an individual lies in our own hands: to succeed or fail, love or hate, create or destroy, within our own particular circumstances. The trouble is that only a few people understand the importance of that most difficult choice of all—to sink comfortably deeper into the selfish materialism dictated by our biological instincts, or to struggle upward toward a way of life dictated by human values, following an ethical code of behavior we sincerely believe to be right.

I am aware of the importance, for myself, of this choice, yet I have traveled pitifully few steps along the upward trail. I have met a handful of people who have traveled far, who have crossed the bridge to a level of existence in which spirit dominates matter. They are easy to recognize for they have a special stillness, like a quiet smile, even in adversity. Mostly they, and their like through history, live apart, at peace in their vision. Only a few have tried to lead their fellow men across the gulf. For they know the price: disbelief, ridicule, contempt. The outstretched hand of the greatest of them was seized and pierced with nails. Today, more than ever before, we need their help.

> *The world has need of them, those who stand upon the bridge,*
> *Who know the pain in the singing of a bird*
> *And the beauty beyond a flower dying,*
> *Who have heard the crystal harmony*
> *Within the silence of a snow-peaked mountain—*
> *For who but they can bring life's meaning*
> *To the living dead?*
>
> *Oh, the world needs those standing on the bridge,*
> *For they know how eternity reaches to earth—*
> *In the wind that brings music to the leaves*
> *Of the forest, in the drops of rain that caress*
> *The sleeping life of the desert, in the sunbeams*
> *Of the first spring day in an alpine meadow.*
> *Only they can blow the dust from the seeing eyes*
> *Of those who are blind.*
>
> *Yet pity them! those who stand on the bridge.*
> *For they, having known utter peace*
> *Are moved by an ancient compassion*
> *To reach back to those who cry out*
> *From a world which has lost its meaning,*
> *A world where the atom—the clay of the Sculptor—*
> *Is torn apart, in the name of science,*
> *For the destruction of love.*
>
> *And so they stand there, on the bridge,*
> *Torn by the anguish of free will;*
> *Yearning, with tears like blood,*
> *To go back—to return*
> *To the starlight of their beginnings,*
> *To their nestled roots, deep down*
> *In the warm, dark heart of the earth.*
> *Yet only they can whisper songs of hope*
> *To those, helpless, who struggle toward light.*

Oh! Let them not desert us, those on the bridge,
Those who have known love in the freedom
Of the night sky, and know the meaning
Of the moon's existence beyond
Man's fumbling footsteps into space.
For they know the Eternal Power
That encompasses life's beginnings
And gathers up its endings,
And lays them, like Joseph's coat,
On the never changing, always moving canvas,
That stretches beyond the Universe
And is contained in the eye
Of a little frog.

Billy Graham Evangelistic Association

Billy Graham
b. 1918

Billy Graham is one of the best-known religious leaders in the world today. His dynamic radio and television messages, books, syndicated newspaper columns, and soul-saving crusades have reached millions of people on every continent. Indeed, he has preached the Gospel to more millions than anyone in history.

The son of a North Carolina dairy farmer, he was ordained as a Baptist minister in 1940 after graduating from the Florida Bible Institute. After earning his B.A. from Wheaton College in 1943, he went on the road to reach the people—very much in the great tradition of American revivalism. The burning sincerity of his conviction that came across so readily in his personal appearances and his Sunday night radio program, "The Hour of Decision," soon made him one of the most respected men in the country. He is regularly listed as one of the "Ten Most Admired Men in the World," and has appeared in the Gallup Poll more often than any other person—twenty-six times in the last twenty-seven years. With characteristic humility he has said that he is neither a theologian nor an intellectual, but simply one who proclaims the word of God.

Billy Graham's counsel has been sought by presidents and his appeal to both secular and non-secular worlds is shown by the wide range of groups that have honored him. These recognitions range from addressing the President's National Prayer Breakfast to the Gold Award of the George Washington Carver Memorial Institute in 1963, from the Speaker of the Year Award in 1964 to the Templeton Foundation Prize for Progress in Religion in 1982.

Is it really possible to know any answers to the basic questions of life—questions like, "Who am I? Why am I here? Where did I come from and where am I going? Does God exist, and if so does it make any difference? Can I know Him?"

There was a time in my life when I would have answered, "No. I'm not sure we can answer those questions. And frankly I don't care, because the only thing that matters to me is living life to the fullest right now." And if I had been pressed, I would have had to admit that I had never bothered to explore those questions very much. Yes, my parents were devout and made sure I was in church regularly. But as a teenager religion seemed to me to be dull and irrelevant. Besides that, it struck me as a bit smug or even arrogant to say that we could really know God. And some of the people I knew who claimed to be Christians were no different from some of the unbelievers I had met. Religion might be fine for some people, I reasoned, but I wanted to stand on my own two feet. Somehow it seemed like a sign of weakness to admit that you needed God.

In my late teens, however, all this changed. After a period of spiritual search and struggle, I made a conscious decision to become a Christian—to become a follower of Jesus Christ as my Savior and Lord. At first I did not feel particularly different, nor did my life change overnight. But down inside I sensed something important had happened to me, and as time went on I began to realize not only that those basic questions of life were important for me, but that they had answers.

It was only gradually, however, that I began to understand *why* these questions can have answers. It is not because Christians are necessarily better or brighter than other people, nor is it because they have an especially vivid imagination or indulge in wishful thinking about life. Instead it is because of a conviction that is at the heart of historic Christianity: *We can know God, because He has made Himself known.* We are not left to grope blindly in the dark, because God wants us to know Him and has taken the initiative to reveal Himself to us.

Christians acknowledge that God has revealed Himself in various ways. In the intricate world of nature, for example, the eye of faith can see something of God's power and wisdom. But that alone does not tell us if God actually is a loving God. Instead, God's love for the human race He has created is revealed by His actions within human history. The Old Testament tells of His selection of one nation, the Israelites, to be His channel to bring the knowledge of Himself to humanity. The New Testament tells us that God's plan to reveal Himself has reached its height in the person of Jesus Christ. That is why the Bible is so important to me. It is not a collection of ideas and teachings about God; it is instead the Word of God in written form. It tells us how God has acted to show Himself to us, what He is like, and how we are to respond to Him.

My faith is centered in Jesus Christ. The Bible declares that God has created us and stamped us with His image so we might have fellowship with Him. But the Bible also tells us that we have willfully turned our backs on God. In our pride we have thought we could get along without God, but every day our headlines tell us how wrong we are. Down inside we have a longing for God—what Pascal called "the vacuum which God has left behind." (Quoted in Emile Calliet, *Pascal: The Emergence of Genius*, Harper & Row, p. 102.) Only God can fill that vacuum, although we frantically fill our lives with substitutes for God, trying in vain to find peace and lasting happiness. Because man continues to sin and reject God, however, he stands under the judgment of God. His greatest need is to be reconciled to his Creator.

Why do Christians put Jesus at the center of their faith? They do it because of a very deeply held conviction: Jesus Christ was God incarnate. In a mystery we cannot fully fathom, the infinite God of the universe humbled Himself and assumed human flesh. As the late Professor C. S. Lewis of Cambridge has stated, "The central miracle asserted by Christians is the Incarnation. They say that God became Man. Every other miracle prepares the way for this, or exhibits this, or results from this." (C. S. Lewis, *Miracles*, Macmillan, p. 131.)

Jesus Christ was therefore totally unique, fully man and yet also fully God. We may not understand how God could become man, but from beginning to end the New Testament affirms that He did. If we take the New Testament seriously and examine Jesus' claims and actions objectively, we will realize that we cannot just categorize Jesus as another great moral teacher. To quote Professor Lewis again, "That is the one thing we must not say. A man who was merely a man and said the sort of things Jesus said would not be a great moral teacher. He would either be a lunatic—on the level with the man who says he is a poached egg—or else he would be the Devil of Hell. You must make your choice. Either this man was, and is, the Son of God: or else a madman or something worse." (C. S. Lewis, *Mere Christianity*, Macmillan, p. 56.)

Why did God do this? Why did He take the step of becoming man, a step that staggers our imagination?

He did it first of all to show us what He is like. "Anyone who has seen me has seen the Father," Jesus declared (John 14:9). We know God loves us, because we see that love in Jesus Christ. But God also did it so we could be reconciled to Himself. The New Testament declares that by His death on the cross Jesus Christ took upon Himself the judgment we deserve for our sins. God did for us what we could never do for ourselves: He destroyed the barrier between us, and now through faith in Christ we are forgiven by God's grace and reconciled to God. "God was reconciling the world to Himself in Christ, not counting men's sins against them" (2 Corinthians 5:19). We need no longer fear death and judgment, because by His death and resurrection Christ has conquered sin and death.

All over the world I have been privileged to see people respond in faith to the simple—yet profound—message of God's love in Jesus Christ. They have come from every conceivable social, racial, political, and ideological background, for Christ transcends the boundaries that divide us. And in Christ they have found the answer to their deepest spiritual longings. They have discovered the truth I discovered as a teenager, a truth affirmed by all who truly commit their lives to Christ and seek to follow Him: Jesus Christ will change our lives if we will let Him. He brings hope in the midst of despair, joy in the midst of sorrow, forgiveness in the midst of guilt, and peace in the midst of turmoil. "Therefore, if anyone is in Christ, he is a new creation; the old has gone, the new has come!" (2 Corinthians 5:17). This can be the experience of every person who humbly turns to Christ in repentance and faith.

Becoming a Christian can be the act of a moment; *being* a Christian is the act of a lifetime. I have grown to understand more fully what Jesus meant when He spoke of spiritual commitment and conversion as being "born again" (John 3:3). Physical birth is a process, moving from conception through the period of gestation to the miracle of the moment of birth. But birth is not only the end of one process—it is the beginning of another, the process of growth. The same should be true spiritually. My commitment to Christ was a "spiritual rebirth," but this was to be followed by spiritual growth.

Some of that growth has been in the area of beliefs. There are many convictions I hold much more firmly today than I did years ago, because I have come to understand the Bible more clearly. Likewise, there are some ideas and prejudices I once had that I have cast aside because I now see that they are inconsistent with the Bible's teaching.

But that growth has also been in the area of action. One of the most basic truths of the Bible is that faith in Christ is not just an intellectual idea, to be accepted and then stored in the back of our minds. True faith affects every aspect of our lives, for Jesus Christ is to be not only our Savior but our Lord and Master. "What good is it, my brothers, if a man claims to have faith but has no deeds? . . . . As the body without the spirit is dead, so faith without works is dead" (James 2:14,26).

Understanding the implications of my faith and putting it into action have been a constant challenge. I recall, for example, coming to realize that the traditional racial attitudes I had grown up with needed to be changed, because Christ's love extends to people of every race. I had grown up in the South long before the start of the civil-rights movement, and although some of my closest friends were blacks I was blind to many of the injustices they suffered. In time, however, I became deeply concerned about this and determined that my team and I would never hold a segregated meeting. In one southern city, years before the passage of the Civil Rights Act, I had to go through the auditorium personally before the service and remove the ropes that had been set up to segregate the races. Even in South Africa our public meetings were not segregated.

In recent years I have become increasingly concerned about the dangers that confront our world because of the unchecked development and deployment of nuclear and biochemical weapons of mass destruction. These weapons have an awesome capacity for destruction, threatening even the existence of civilization itself. But the arms race, I began to realize, already claims its victims daily because it consumes hundreds of billions of dollars every year—dollars that could have been used to fight starvation, poverty, and disease in many parts of the world. I am not a pacifist, nor do I favor unilateral disarmament. But the control of weapons of mass destruction is a moral and spiritual issue as well as a political one, and demands the concern of every Christian.

In 1982, I went to Moscow to be an observer and speaker at an international conference of religious leaders sponsored by Patriarch Pimen of the Russian Orthodox Church. Many urged me not to go, saying I would be manipulated by the Soviet government. I went, however, because of my deep conviction as a Christian that we must take risks and do whatever we can to solve this urgent problem of the arms race. In 1984, I returned to the Soviet Union to preach in a number of churches in four major cities.

Many issues and social problems concern me deeply today. Ultimately, however, I am convinced the only answer to these problems is Jesus Christ. In the midst of the turmoil and fear of our age, Christ can give us hope—hope in our world, and hope in our personal lives.

My basic calling remains what it has been for many years: to be an evangelist—one who declares the good news that Christ will forgive us and reconcile us to God and to each other if we will turn to Him in trust and faith. Jesus Christ has changed my life, and He will change the life of anyone who sincerely turns to Him in faith.

Andrew Greeley
b. 1928

For those who know Reverend Andrew Greeley only by his best-selling works of fiction, it may come as a surprise to learn he has published scores of books and articles that have earned him a reputation as one of the nation's leading authorities on the sociology of religion. His writings cover myriad topics, many of which deal with the role of religion in modern life, ethnicity, the family, death and dying, vocations, history, and the future.

Reverend Greeley now divides his time between the National Opinion Research Center at the University of Chicago, the institution that granted him his doctorate in sociology, and where he has been involved in social research since 1966, and the University of Arizona, where he holds a professorship. In 1984 he took royalties from his books and pledged $1.25 million to establish a chair in Catholic studies at the University of Chicago. Nineteen-eighty-four also saw the publication of his provacative HOW TO SAVE THE CATHOLIC CHURCH, written with his sister, theologian Mary Greeley Durkin.

I am a priest, a sociologist, and a novelist. My priestly concerns led me to the study of sociology twenty years ago. My sociological research on religion led me to write novels because the empirical evidence persuaded me that stories are the most effective way of talking about God. Oddly enough, writing fiction proved, in terms of the sheer numbers of positive reactions from readers, the most priestly work I have ever done. I'm sure I would have articulated my faith in different ways at different times in my life, not so much expressing a different faith, but using different rhetoric to express the same faith. At the present time, I would put it this way:

Because I am a Christian, I am committed to the notion that the universe is finally animated by a love so powerful and passionate that the most aroused of human loves is pallid by comparison. It seems to me that in the last analysis there are only two choices: Macbeth's contention that life is a tale told by an idiot, full of sound and fury and signifying nothing and Pierre Teilhard's "something is afoot in the universe, something that looks like gestation and birth." Either there is plan and purpose—and that plan and purpose can best be expressed by the words "life" and "love"—or we live in a cruel, arbitrary, and deceptive cosmos in which our lives are a brief transition between two oblivions. The data are inconclusive as to these two choices, at least if we look at the data from a rational, scientific standpoint. Neither position can claim such evidence as to mandate consent. Those who opt for a chaotic and absurd universe will insist that theirs is the hard-headed position and that the position of those who see purpose and plan is merely wishful thinking. But to dismiss any stand as "wishful thinking" is to beg the question. The question is not whether a belief is wishful, the question is whether it is true. The fact that we wish life to have a purpose and that that purpose be love does not mean we are wrong. If anything, it might more likely mean that we are right, that there is a wisdom in the collective conviction of the race, which cannot easily or quickly be dismissed. The critical question is, it seems to me, whether that hope from which we cannot escape even when we want to is deception or revelation, a cruel trick played on us by the evolutionary process or a hint of an explanation. Even those who insist that there are no grounds for hope (like Professor Lionel Tiger, who suggests that we cannot help but hope because of our genetic programming), nonetheless hope. Their very attempt to persuade us not to hope is evidence that minimally they hope to talk us out of our hopes.

Thus, I opt for hope, not as an irrational choice in the face of the facts, but as a leap of faith in the goodness I have experienced in my life—based indeed on the facts, but transcending them. To those who make the opposite choice, I can only say that they too leap beyond the facts and ignore the goodness in their lives, which hints that there is goodness. In the last analysis, faith is fundamentally an act of love, a response to an invitation to a love affair that one senses, intuits, feels, knows is what life is all about. Either we are caught up in a love affair or we have been badly tricked.

Jesus, I take it, came as a messenger from the Father (who is also a Mother) to tell us that we have not been tricked and that where the wildest human hopes end, where the most impossible human dreams cease, where the most fantastic of human fantasies fade away, that which God has prepared for those who love him/her only begins.

Such a view may very well be wrong, but I do not think any other view can be considered Christian. There isn't much doubt anymore, as a result of the most sophisticated modern New Testament research, that this is the Good News Jesus came to preach. One may not like it because it seems much too good to be true, but one must at least admit that it is what Jesus came to reveal—the generous love of the father of the prodigal son, of the good Samaritan for his enemy, and of the farmer who paid a full day's wage to the loafers who came into the field at the eleventh hour. These parables are not primarily moral lessons for our imitation. Rather, they are religious tales about the nature of God. The parables tell us that God is so hopelessly in love with His/Her creatures that S/He would be considered mad by human standards, as would be the father and the farmer and the Samaritan.

Because I am a Catholic Christian, I also believe that God is present in the world in such a way that I experience His loving grace in and through the events, objects, and persons of this life who are "sacraments" of God's grace for me. Unlike those who are committed to other branches of Yahwistic religions (Islamism, Judaism, Protestantism), I do not see the need for a monotheism so radical as to draw a sharp dividing line between God and world, a dividing line which calls into question my Catholic conviction of sacramentality—that is to say, a God lurking in the events of every day, a God who, in Richard Wilbur's words, can be seen in the branches of a tree as a "Cheshire smile which sets us fearfully free."

Moreover, because of my sacramental conviction, I am also committed to an "analogical imagination"; that is to say, I think it fair and proper to compare God to the graces that reveal Him/Her to me in this world. God is like a father, like a mother, like a friend, and especially, like a human lover. Obviously God is also very different from these human persons, but I feel the need to note this difference only after I have first of all rejoiced in the similarity. To say that Juliet is like the sun is first of all to compare her to the sun and second the sun to her. Only afterward need I add that of course the sun is much brighter than she is and she much warmer personally than the sun. Similarly, to say that Juliet is divine is to say that Juliet is like God, which may not bother anyone. It is also to say that God is like Juliet, which bothers a lot of people, but not those raised in the Catholic tradition. Unlike our brothers and sisters in the other religions of Yahweh, we are not afraid of anthropomorphism (perhaps we should be, but that's another matter). Therefore, I see this world and the people and the relations and the structures in it as basically good because they are basically grace-full; that is to say, they reflect God's grace for me. They are clearly imperfect and subject to weakness, frailty, corruption, and sin. There is the need for endless reform in the human condition, not because it is bad, but because it is good, though often deprived of the gracefulness it ought to have. Therefore, as a Catholic Christian, I must reject (and do cheerfully reject) the conviction of some of my brothers and sisters in other religious traditions that human nature and nature and society are fundamentally or totally depraved. They may be right and I may be wrong, but my point is that the Catholic position does not accept the depravity of human nature or human society.

As a Catholic, I also believe in stories with happy endings; I am committed to comedy rather than tragedy. The little boy in the manger grows up to be a great king. The good man who is put to death survives death. The great plot of fiction (boy meets girl, boy loses girl, boy finds girl) is but a reflection of the overarching religious story (God meets humans, God loses humans, God finds humans).

"Wherever the Catholic sun does shine/there is music and laughter and good red wine/at least I've found it so/*Benedicamus domino.*"

Alas, Hilaire Belloc's poem may not always be true. But it does represent what seems to me to be the essence of the Catholic celebratory position. In a world in which God discloses His/Her grace through the events, objects, and people in our lives, in which these things do really tell us what God is like, and in which we perceive God as being like our most passionate of human lovers, only more so, there is no room for endings that are ultimately tragic. Tomorrow, says the Catholic, will be different because we are loved, even when tomorrow is the day after the last day of life. So let us celebrate in advance the happy endings, which we know will ultimately win out over the tragic endings.

Finally, as a Catholic, I believe that I share my religious convictions and experiences and celebrations with a community that is a network of close relationships. In my Catholic conviction, the Church is not a mediator added on from the outside by theological doctrine, but an inevitable conclusion of my intuition that God's self-disclosure takes place through human relationships. I need others to respond to God because others have been the occasion of my coming to know God. I live as a human person in a social network. I do not and I cannot leave behind that network when I turn to religion. For I have met God in and through the network and I necessarily respond to Him/Her as part of a network. The institutional church, in its present form, may often be considerably less than a perfect network for encountering and responding to God, but it's the only one I have, the only one indeed that claims to be in the business of communal religious response.

I deliberately omit any discussion of specific doctrines because I believe the basic instincts of a religious heritage are prior to the doctrinal formulations and that the Catholic sensibility of sacramental experience, analogical imagination, comic stories, and organic community are the essence of what distinguishes me as a Catholic Christian from Protestants, Jews, and Muslims. They may be right in their different religious sensibilities, and I may be wrong. That is not the point. Rather, the point is that what I have described is, I am convinced, a fair summary of my religious heritage, the one in which I was born, and, to quote Belloc again, "the one in which I hope to die."

How has this faith affected my life? Obviously, I wouldn't be a priest unless I bought the whole package. Moreover, I would not have survived in the priesthood during the years of crisis since the Vatican Council without this faith, nor would I have survived the idiocies of Catholic leaders (like the current terrible financial scandals that are taking place in the Vatican) or the relentless envy of my fellow priests who bitterly resent any priest who does anything that others might deem "successful."

The other side of the coin is that the intellectual flexibility of Catholicism has made it relatively easy for me to continue to be Catholic in the mostly non-Catholic and occasionally anti-Catholic world of the secular academy. For a priest to venture into the world of the great university graduate school in the early sixties was, in the minds of both his parishioners and his faculty, to put his faith and his priesthood in jeopardy. Religious faith in those days was not normally attacked explicitly. Rather, it was viewed with amused disdain. How could anyone with intelligence and sophistication continue to be religious? It did not take me long to realize that the middle-class agnosticism of the university was as much a leap of faith as was my own commitment and that there was nothing in empirical social science that could constrain a religious answer one way or another.

Later on, my Catholic heritage provided me with the intellectual and religious underpinning to take the risk to turn to novel writing, which was almost certain to make me an outcast in both sociology and priesthood. If stories were the best way to communicate about religion, then I would write stories, no matter what the murmuring critics would say.

My conviction that the stories of our life finally have happy endings, though not always in this life, has sustained me in my role as the permanent pariah in my own city, rejected by the Church, the university, and the media. Even though I am forced to teach and to preach and to expect favorable notice for my work away from home, I realize that rejection is the lot of the Christian and that it does not last forever.

In particular, I do not relish being an outcast in my archdiocese. Yet, if the Cardinal and my fellow priests must assiduously pretend that I do not exist, then that is part of my story. I regret it, but my faith makes it possible to live with it. I understand that even though human nature is fundamentally good, there is still much weakness and sinfulness in the human condition, even among those who claim to serve God directly, and I realize that my own human nature has a long way to go before it begins to approach the ideals of the Gospel message.

None of what I am would I be if it were not for my Catholic Christian faith. I do not expect others to agree with this faith, and I can understand that many who were educated in the very narrow and rigid variety of Catholicism that existed in many places in this country before the Vatican Council will not think what I have described is Catholic. Nevertheless, the ground on which I stand is the central ground of the Catholic heritage and I intend to stand nowhere else.

Sidney Hook
b. 1902

On May 23, 1985, in a ceremony at the White House, President Ronald Reagan presented Professor Sidney Hook with the Medal of Freedom, the highest civilian honor bestowed by the U.S. government. It was a fitting tribute to the long career of the philosopher-educator so widely admired for his wisdom and humanity. Like Socrates, Professor Hook's gadfly attacks on the hypocrisies and contradictions of the reigning marketplace ideas have earned him numerous critics. Yet even they have rarely failed to appreciate his brilliance of thought and abiding moral concern.

Over a career that has spanned seven decades—from his days at the City College of New York, where he studied with Morris R. Cohen, and as a student of John Dewey at Columbia University, through his more than half-century tenure at New York University, and continuing through his present fellowship at the Hoover Institution—Professor Hook has had a profound influence on twentieth-century thinking. In his many books he has commented on most of the major *issues of the day. He is a leading exponent of the democratic philosophy and of secular humanism.*

It has been said that Professor Hook exemplifies the two key humanist virtues: critical intelligence and moral courage. Unlike so many of his contemporaries, his philosophy declares a confidence that human intelligence and optimism can help resolve the major problems of the world. This alone makes him a unique figure in American intellectual life.

As I write these words I am of an age older than most of those who have taught me, and of almost all of those who will read me. But although considered, and sometimes referred to, as an old man, I feel no different from the days when I set out on my career or from the earlier days when I resolved to add to the store of truth or beauty that inspired me when young. I have been mistaken about many things, some of great importance, and I have modified my views accordingly. But I am not aware of having abandoned any of the ideals that motivated me to run risks, to throw myself into the political movement of my time, to do some rash and foolish things from whose consequences I escaped I know not how, to endure long years of unpopularity, to pit myself against powers and movements that could have easily crushed me.

When I try to explain myself to myself I find one trait that may account in part for some of my beliefs. I have always been unduly sensitive to the sight and thought of human suffering. Sardonic critics may dismiss this as just a case of weak nerves. But I can endure prolonged physical suffering and pain and have had several occasions to do so. A few years ago when I lay at death's door in the throes of agony, drowning in a sea of slime, I asked my doctors to cut off my life-support services. I was skeptical about their judgment that my request was premature. I persisted in my request, in vain as it turned out, because of the thought that even if I recovered, the likelihood of going through the same or similar experience again, and imposing once more the burdens and grief of "the last days" on those I loved, could hardly be compensated for by the satisfactions of the uncertain period ahead. I had paid my dues to death. Once was enough. Long before this, the sight of hundreds of persons living on mattress graves in the home of the disabled and incurable in which my father took twenty-five years to die had made me a fervent believer in voluntary euthanasia.

I can reconcile myself to the sight of suffering and pain when they are necessary for treatment. One of my most gruesome memories is of the time when I held my three-year-old daughter in my arms when her wound, caused by the bite of an animal suspected of having rabies, was being cauterized with fuming sulphuric acid. But I cannot reconcile myself to cruelty—to the deliberate imposition of gratuitous suffering on sentient creatures, especially human beings. Cruelty has always enraged and sickened me. Some of my own actions, which have verged on the immoral, have been those in which I have reacted to cruelty in the spirit of Shakespeare's lines: "The villainy you teach me I shall execute. And it shall go hard: but I will better the instruction." I am no Christian, but I can honor and admire a man who can forgive someone who has abused and tortured him, who in his personal life can live by the Sermon on the Mount. But any man who can forgive, no less cherish or love, those who have abused or tortured others including his loved ones, must be more than man—or far less.

These autobiographical details may be considered irrelevant but in my case perhaps they throw some light on some of my basic beliefs with respect to religion and society. At the age of twelve I discovered the problem of evil—the age old problem of reconciling the existence of an all-powerful and all-loving God with a world He created and controlled in which so many of the innocent suffer and so many of the wicked prosper. I was unaware that theologians had choked over this problem from time immemorial and that the bone was still choking them. I refused to go through the ritual of confirmation—the Bar Mitzvah ceremony, when a Jewish child takes responsibility for his own sins. My rabbi was affronted, my parents distressed. In trying to persuade me, my father, an autodidact but an intelligent man, rediscovered Pascal's argument although he had never heard of Pascal. "What are we asking you to do?" he pleaded. "To say a few prayers, to attend the synagogue occasionally. Suppose it turns out there is no God. What will you have lost? A little time at most. But suppose there is a God, and you refuse to obey His Commandments? You will suffer forever in the fires of Gehenna. Why take the chance? You are investing a few hours to insure yourself against an eternity of pain." My mother, whose first-born child had been scalded to death in an accident, seemed more sympathetic to me but quietly said that if she could live with her pain and still have faith, I could try.

I had wit enough to retort to my father that if God did indeed exist and was all-knowing, he would hardly approve of the grounds of my piety or give me any credit for it. In the end I capitulated not because of any arguments but out of social consideration to avoid the scandal to my family of community disapproval. But my faith was gone, and I soon realized that to someone like myself there was not the problem of evil but only problems of evils—some remediable, some not. I could not accept any of the multiple explanations that I later read about. William James's view that God was finite in power and needed our help, a good angel, so to speak, summoning good men for the good fight, seemed quaint and charming. It made as much sense as to postulate the existence of a finite bad angel. Zoroastrianism was more consistent but no less credible. The Hindu views of *karma* and *samsara*, which taught that every evil or suffering experienced in this life was the justified punishment for an evil action committed in a previous life, and that no matter how desperate one's plight, there was the redeeming hope that one could advance in the scale of being by adhering strictly to the rules of the caste system in this existence— all these beliefs shattered on the elementary facts of the sciences. It was an illuminating explanation of why India, locked in the grip of these beliefs, had no genuine social revolution, as Karl Marx claimed, until the British came.

It has always amazed me that intelligent and sensitive thinkers could ever have convinced themselves that every case of evil or suffering in the world is a necessary part of the good of the whole. Since dissonance is sometimes a necessary element in the harmony of a whole symphony, the agony of a tortured child is a necessary part of the structure of existence. Since the *concept* of good has no meaning unless contrasted with the *concept* of evil, good *things* cannot exist unless evil *things* necessarily exist. All of these views seem to me to betray a willful refusal to accept the stark facts of unnecessary cruelty in nature and social life. Ultimately it presupposes the view that all is well with the world, that evil is an illusion of perception or perspective. To believe this seems to me an intellectual mask for cruelty.

I could never take Emerson seriously as a thinker after reading his essay on *Compensation* in which he argues that there is always a compensating good for any and every evil, that if a man loses his legs, the muscles of his arms, as a compensating blessing, become stronger, and if he loses his sight, his other senses become more acute. First of all, this is not always true; and secondly, even if true, it certainly is not a sufficient compensation. It is comparable to the Hebrew prayer in times of calamity, in which one thanks God, if he has been struck blind in one eye, that he has not been stricken blind in both. The last person or power to whom such a prayer should be addressed is the all-powerful architect of the universe—if there is one. The response of Job's wife to the gratuitous persecutions to which Job was subject seems more appropriate than his unwavering faith.

At the age of fourteen I read Heinrich Graetz's *History of the Jews*. I never recovered from the consequences. It left me reeling with horror at the periodic and prolonged waves of savage persecutions, which were visited on the unarmed, peaceful, and inoffensive communities of European Jews. There was not the slightest justification for the autos-da-fé, pogroms, exiles, tortures, and holocausts they suffered at the hands of their neighbors. My opposition to organized religion was rooted in the shock of that searing experience of reading Graetz, and it was reinforced in subsequent years by my reading of Lecky, Henry C. Lea, Gibbons, and Coulton. It built up in me the lasting impression that all peoples obsessed by fanatical dogmas are capable of lapsing into the unspeakable barbarities of the past.

Although as a secular humanist I reject all religious faiths, I nonetheless recognize and respect the role of religion in *personal* human experience. Religion is and should be a private matter. Freedom of worship (including not to worship) is central to our Bill of Rights. I would never dream of disputing or trying to deprive anyone of his or her religious faith. My arguments with religionists have been only with those theologians or representatives of organized churches who have attacked my views or who have sought to convert me or to invoke religious dogmas to support dubious social proposals. This they have every right to do, as I have to make a critical response to them.

Even in my salad days as a Marxist I realized that Marx's philosophy of religion was shallow compared to the profound views of Feuerbach from whom he had originally taken his point of departure. Both were unbelievers. Marx accepted Feuerbach's analysis that religious beliefs and emotions were projections of man's emotional needs. Yet he saw in the succession of religious ideologies and myths nothing but the systematic exploitation of human and emotional needs in order to keep the masses in subjection. By promising the masses enjoyment of a heavenly estate, religion kept them from rebelling against their miserable earthly estate. Feuerbach, on the other hand, anticipated Max Weber's insight that the great religions were interpretations that tried to make sense of the meaningless suffering in human life. He, too, believed in science and socialism and that man's moral vocation was, within the limits of his capacity, to remake and reform the world in the light of consciously held moral ideals whose appeal, as distinct from their validity, could be enhanced by symbols and rituals. He called atheism a religion—to the disgust of Marx and his followers. He believed religion had a sustaining and consolatory function in helping human beings to face evils that did not necessarily flow from economic deprivation but from the experiences of death, failure, and tragedy.

It may be hard to separate the existence of organized religion from personal religious experience, but it is possible to distinguish them. It is only the first with which I have been polemically involved. In a statement made long ago, which still expresses my considered view, I wrote:

> So long as religion is freed from authoritarian institutional forms, and conceived in personal terms, so long as overbeliefs are a source of innocent joy, a way of overcoming cosmic loneliness, a discipline of living with pain or evil, otherwise unendurable or irremediable, so long as what functions as a vital illusion, or poetic myth is not represented as a public truth to whose existence the once-born are blind, so long as religion does not paralyze the desire and the will to struggle against unnecessary cruelties of experience, it seems to me to fall in an area of choice, in which rational criticism may be suspended. In this sense a man's personal religion justifies itself to him in the way his love does. Why should he want to make a public cult of it? And why should we demand that he prove that the object of his love is, as he believes, the most beautiful creature in the world? Nonetheless, it still remains true that as a set of cognitive beliefs about the existence of God in any recognizable sense continuous with the great systems of the past, religious doctrines constitute a speculative hypothesis of an extremely low order of probability.

With such views about religion, it is not surprising that I immersed myself in the socialist movement in order to modify social and economic institutions and to improve the lot of the working masses. I never shared the Utopian illusions of many of my comrades who, having lost their traditional religious faith, found a substitute faith in the Socialist revolution that would solve all human problems, and introduce on earth a secular equivalent to the kingdom of heaven. To me socialism was a set of institutions, which I hoped would realize two things: the elimination of material want and the resultant suffering of all persons able and willing to work, and secondly, the extension of freedom of opportunity based on the acceptance of the moral equality of all members of the human community. Today I would sum it up as a commitment to democracy, in John Dewey's words, as "a way of life." The first approximation to democracy as a way of life is the establishment of a genuine welfare state free of the waywardness and abuses that infect some of its exemplifications at home and abroad. The transformation of the socialist dream into a totalitarian nightmare in the Soviet Union and other Communist countries does not invalidate the premises of a democratic welfare state.

One of the great and abiding problems of a democratic welfare state is to avoid the generation of a welfare *class*. The members of this class gradually lose the incentives to engage in the productive labor necessary to sustain growth. One must provide the means that enable the community to erect the safety net or minimum adequate standard of living beneath which human beings should not be permitted to sink. This should be one of the primary tasks of our educational system.

Certain misconceptions about the nature and place of equality in a democratic society sometimes have mischievous effects. A democratic society, indeed any society, cannot reasonably be based on the assumption that all its citizens are physically or intellectually equal or that they are equally gifted in every or any respect. It recognizes and cherishes individual differences that are the basis of the diversity of personalities that distinguish truly human communities from animal and insect societies. As we have said, in a free and open democratic society, citizens enjoy a *moral* and *legal* equality, and therefore, as far as the times and resources permit, the institutions of such a society should seek to provide an equal opportunity to all its citizens to develop themselves to their full potential.

There cannot, of course, be absolute equality of opportunities for all children since they are brought up by parents of different degrees of emotional and intellectual maturity in homes that reflect different levels of cultural achievement and appreciation. Nonetheless, despite this and all the drawbacks of the family system elaborated upon by thinkers from Plato to Freud, the compensations of family life more than make up for them. The family as a rule provides the emotional security and support obtainable in no other way. If the esteem and affection necessary for growth depended only on our beauty, intelligence, congeniality, or other virtues and talents, the world would be a cold place for most of us. The family accepts us and cherishes us for what we are regardless of our merit or achievement. Home is the place we return to after all and everyone has failed us.

The belief in moral equality does not require that all individuals be treated identically in every respect or that equal treatment entails, or can be measured by, equality of outcome or result. It requires that there should be no invidious discrimination against or in behalf of anyone on the basis of race, color, religion, sex, or national origin. For example, every citizen should have a right to equal access to an education appropriate to his talents, interests, and special needs. That does not mean that all persons necessarily will have the same education on every level or even that they should have the same amount of the same schooling regardless of their capacities. Equal access is no guarantee of equal achievement. Where resources make it possible, I believe that all citizens should have an equal right to health care and medical treatment. But only a quack or ideological fanatic would insist that all individuals should have the same medical regimen no matter what ails them. This would truly be putting all human beings in the bed of Procrustes.

It cannot be too strongly emphasized that moral equality is perfectly compatible with the intelligent recognition of human inequalities and relevant ways of treating these inequalities, without invidious discrimination, to further both the individual and common good. After all, intelligent and loving parents are equally concerned with the welfare of all their children. Yet precisely because they are concerned, they may take measures to provide different specific strategies in health care, education, environmental stimulus, and intellectual and psychological motivation, to elicit the best in all of them.

More broadly speaking, if all human beings able and willing to work receive adequate compensation for their labor, there is nothing morally wrong if some receive more, even much more, for their efforts. In other words, when everyone has enough, there is nothing wrong if some receive more than enough because of some service they perform. A great deal of nonsense is written by some philosophers who assert that a good society must make up for the injustices of nature or life. They hold that society must redress the imbalance resulting from the fact that some people are born more beautiful or more intelligent or more energetic or more musical and artistic than others, and that they, in virtue of their unearned gifts of nature, receive more than others. Hegel answered these philosophers with his tart observation that neither nature nor life can be unjust. Only human beings can be just or unjust to other human beings.

I have always maintained that a reliable sign of whether a human being has found life on the whole worth living is whether he or she would be willing to accept another incarnation—another chance to live—if it were in his or her power to make the decision. By this criterion I have had a life very well worth living. This is not the same as a desire for immortality. Extinction has no terror for me, and I can very well imagine a time at which I would tire of being myself.

Nonetheless, aside from one thing, I shall have a few regrets at leaving the world as it is presently constituted. I shall feel remiss in not being able to continue the struggle in defense of a free and open society. The fear that civilization will be destroyed in a nuclear holocaust, which is fed by horror stories in all the media, seems to me to be an expression of paranoia that weakens the will to resist aggressive and expanding totalitarian systems. There will be no world-wide nuclear war unless the Kremlin is certain to win it, and the Western world can easily keep a posture of deterrent defense that can keep its enemies guessing.

Even if Western Europe and North America survive as free communities, the remaining world will remain predominantly one of squalor and tyranny. In the relatively free areas of the world, eroding its vitality and the health of its institutions, we can observe the growing abandonment of the sense of moral responsibility, the proliferation of noisy demands for all kinds of rights and entitlements without the willingness to accept correlative duties and obligations. The quality of human relationships between the sexes has deteriorated. The obligation to help those who are weaker and more vulnerable is rooted in the fact of interdependence, in the recognition of the community and its traditions as the source and support of our intellectual achievements. We owe more to the heritage of the past than we can ever repay.

Not everyone can do everything well, and so long as individuals make uncoerced choices of careers and vocations they should be judged by their achievements and not by their race, religion, or sex. The woman who freely chooses to fulfill the role of wife and mother is as worthy as the woman who forswears that role for others hitherto pursued by men. The male chauvinist who decries the career woman and the militant feminist who scorns the housewife are equally miscreant proponents of the democratic ethics. The traditional chivalry of men toward weakness and vulnerability, both in men and women, has been undermined by false conceptions of equality that overlook biological differences that transcend social and cultural forces. Such a false view absolves many men of a sense of responsibility.

It is sheer sentimentalism to deny the fact that men, as a rule, are more brutal to children than women. We rarely hear of bestial crimes, especially sexual crimes, committed against children by women. Men are more likely than women to abandon children to whom they owe responsibility. In the general erosion of the sense of individual responsibility, often facilitated by the rationalizations about the misconceptions of the meaning of equality, children suffer most.

When I reflect on first and last things, I find myself believing that we value life and fear death too much. Unless we recognize that there are some things more valuable than life itself, life is not worth living. It may be puzzling but it is true: to be ready to die with dignity and courage not only enhances the quality of human life, sometimes it prolongs our life. When it does not, we may go down fighting in a good cause. But so long as we do not strike our own colors, so long as we resist with integrity and dignity, failure does not spell defeat.

M. Deborah Hyde-Rowan

b. 1949

In 1984, Dr. Deborah Hyde-Rowan, one of only two black female neurosurgeons in the United States, was honored by Esquire magazine as one of the "best of the new generation—those who exemplify in their professional lives the qualities of courage, originality, ingenuity, vision and selfless service."

Upon graduating with honors from Tougaloo College in her native Mississippi, she applied to graduate school at Case Western Reserve University in Cleveland, Ohio, but was rejected on the grounds that she would not be able to compete with students of that institution's caliber. She told an interviewer, "I assume they meant that because I had graduated from a black college, I couldn't be that good. I was discouraged, angry, and frustrated because I knew they were wrong." She then enrolled at Cleveland State University, where she earned a 4.0 grade point average and received an M.S. in biology in 1973. She again applied to Case Western Reserve—this time to medical school— and was accepted. As a resident at Case Western Reserve's Univer-

*sity hospitals she became the first woman to enroll in the hospital's
neurosurgery training program.*

*In 1982 she joined the Guthrie Clinic in Sayre, Pennsylvania, where
she now serves patients in rural Pennsylvania and New York and
performs about two hundred operations a year.*

I believe that divine intervention has guided my journey through life.
I am not implying predestation, for I do not believe that one's fate
is predestined. Rather, opportunities present themselves; how one deals
with those opportunities determines one's fate. I prefer to call my life
a series of divine accidents! I was conceived by and delivered unto a
woman who throughout my life has been the perfect mother and more.
I have been loved and provided for by a stepfather who treated me as
his own. I had a second set of parents—my maternal aunt and her
husband—who gave me tremendous support. Later in life, I ended up
in the same city with my biological father; we have developed a strong
bond. The greatest "accident" was to be raised by one of the most
remarkable women who ever existed—my grandmother. I was a
member of a strong, proud, intelligent, yet uneducated family. We
were rich with pride, love, and desires for higher goals, thus, our
meager finances represented but one obstacle to overcome.

My grandmother has been the most influential person in my life.
Articulate and dynamic, she became a leader in both church and community. I am convinced that had opportunities for furthering her education been available, she would have been a powerful force in our
society. Fortunately for me, she was not only my mentor but my
best friend. She constantly told me that I was somebody and could be
or do anything on this earth if I would only study hard and keep faith
in God. And more often than once she took me aside and said, "Please
remember your roots and be proud of them. And as you travel through
life and up that ladder of success, learn to walk with kings but never
lose the common touch."

Growing up in Mississippi, riding in the back of a bus, using water fountains and rest rooms marked "colored," entering the back door of restaurants and medical clinics, and contending with a society that tried to tell me that I was inferior, I never lost the feeling given to me by my family, and especially my grandmother, that I was someone special. Although "Mama" died shortly after I finished college, she continues to comfort, encourage, and inspire me.

Despite discrimination, racism, poverty, war, and famine, I believe an ubiquitous, omnipotent force orders the universe. Although I was raised in a strongly religious Baptist home, as a scientist I believe in evolution and do not accept some traditional doctrines. Nonetheless, a purely scientific approach to our creation is not acceptable to me! I believe that God will not condemn me for questioning and choosing to serve in my own way. I have been especially blessed in this life, and I believe that the abundance of blessings bestowed on me reflects God's way of using me as his instrument. I touch many lives directly and indirectly through my work as a neurosurgeon. My career has not only allowed me to learn from some of the "greatest scientific minds" of our age, but it has also given me the opportunity to walk into classrooms and inspire younger people who are still seeking.

No words can describe my satisfaction when I operate upon a patient and know that I have changed his life for the better or saved his life with God's help. And I have learned to deal with disappointments, suffering, death, and grief. In my profession there is often an infinitesimal margin for error. I always ask for God's blessings before entering the operating suite. When faced with a potentially life-threatening case, such as a tumor located in a critical area of the brain, I pray earnestly for the patient and God's guidance for myself. I call long distance to Mississippi and ask my mother to pray for us. Although I feel self-confident and technically capable, I always feel better if others are also praying for that particular patient.

Though exhausted, I am often exultant at the end of a long, demanding brain operation. I have spent many hours with the dissecting microscope in a "different world," oblivious to hunger, thirst, and the urge to urinate. During those long hours in "God's real territory," I am so caught up in a mission—to remove that tumor in the face of danger—that nothing else is important.

I often ask myself, "Why me?" Why was I guided into a career that demands life and death decisions? A career where the slip of my hand by just a millimeter can have devastating consequences?

As I think back on it, I had no conscious aspiration to become a physician. That career option had never been raised by my family, or by my counselors. But as a child I preferred science kits to dolls. And I remember begging for a set of World Book Encyclopedias, not an ordinary request to Santa Claus from a sixth grader. Although those books were expensive, somehow my wish was granted.

In high school, I did well in my courses, graduating as class valedictorian. But my favorite subject was always science. I majored in biology at Tougaloo College and went on to get a master's degree in biology at Cleveland State University. In both college and graduate school I was especially interested in the functioning of the nervous system.

I was actually planning to seek a doctorate in the sciences when I "accidentally" took part in a discussion with some other students planning to attend medical school. At that point I asked myself why had I not considered medicine as a career; it clearly appealed to me more than research and teaching. So I went to Case Western Reserve University School of Medicine. Studying the nervous system, dissecting the brain and spinal cord was exciting. During my second year I decided to become a neurologist.

As a third-year medical student rotating in General Surgery I fell in love with surgery. I never wanted to leave the operating room; if an interesting emergency case had to be operated on, I stayed in the hospital during my night off. I was ecstatic the first time I observed a neurological procedure. I quickly surmised that if I wanted to combine surgery and neurology, I should become a neurosurgeon. As a third-year student, I assisted in my first neurological operation on a young man with a subdural hematoma (a blood clot on the surface of the brain). From that moment, I was hooked for life. Divine intervention had "accidentally" led me to medical school; subsequent events led me directly to neurosurgery.

I was initially discouraged from entering a field that was clearly "man's domain." Given my persistence, academic achievements (including special honors in the General Surgery Clerkship, and election to the Alpha Omega Honorary Medical Society) as well as support from the neurological staff, I became the first woman, and first black, accepted into the neurosurgical training program at the University Hospitals of Cleveland, Ohio.

I thank God for blessing me with the ability to do my job. I give thanks for continued strength, compassion, humility, and sensitivity.

I accept my responsibility. My work is fulfilling and makes me feel that my contribution to the health of mankind will be my legacy.

I feel an obligation to serve as a role model for minorities, in particular blacks and women. But I hope I can be a role model for anyone interested in neurosurgery. It is physically and emotionally demanding, but tremendously rewarding.

In a poem by Will Allen Dromgoole, an old pilgrim, after crossing a deep and dangerous chasm, pauses in his journey to "build a bridge to span the tide." A fellow pilgrim wonders why the old man is building the bridge, telling him, "You never again will pass this way." The old man replies that the bridge will help those who follow to cross the chasm safely.

I hope I am a "bridge builder." I would like to feel that my influence will guide other people into the field of neurosurgery or medicine in general. I would like to feel that I can influence some young person to pursue a higher education in any chosen occupation. I have been influenced by wonderful bridge builders throughout my life who have guided me, instilled confidence, instilled racial and personal pride, and provided me with strength and perseverance. If I can accomplish this to some degree, then I, too, will have built a bridge to span the tide.

Petra K. Kelly
b. 1947

The co-founder of West Germany's newest political party, the ecological and countercultural Greens, is also its most vocal and visible driving force. Since March, 1983, she has been a member of the National Parliament and Speaker of the Green Parliamentary Group.

Although born in Bavaria, Ms. Kelly spent nine-and-a-half years in America after her parents divorced, and her mother married an American colonel. She studied at American University's prestigious School of International Service. Moved by the writings of Thoreau and Gandhi and by the activities of Rev. Martin Luther King, she participated in civil rights and antiwar demonstrations during the late 1960s. At the same time, she was a volunteer in the presidential campaign of Robert F. Kennedy. In 1970, she returned to Europe, obtaining her M.A. degree from the University of Amsterdam before joining the staff of the Economic and Social Committee of the European Economic Community (EEC) the following year. During the more than a decade she worked for the EEC she was concurrently engaged

in West Germany and in other foreign countries in ecological, wom-
en's rights, and peace activities. This culminated in the founding of
the Greens in 1979, when there seemed no way to influence govern-
mental policy from within an existing political party.

Since her emergence as an international figure, she has worked
tirelessly not only in West Germany, but throughout the world, in
the nonviolent struggle against all mass-destructive weapons, against
pollution of the environment, and for peace and human rights.

I have been most influenced by the examples of my seventy-nine-
year-old grandmother, my mother, and particularly my sister, who at
the age of ten died of cancer and radiation treatment. The life and
death of my sister, Grace Patricia, brought me directly into the various ecological and antinuclear peace movements of the early '70s.
Grace and the way she lived, smiling, loving, hoping, and enduring
pain, gave me all the guidance and inspiration I needed to continue
with my political, ecological, and feminist work.

I was raised until age thirteen by my grandmother, Omi. An anti-
fascist both prior to and during the time of Hitler, she has always
been a very courageous woman who, as a war widow, learned to live
without men supporting her. She took care of both my mother and
me during the hardest times. When I was six years old, she began
reading newspapers and news magazines to me, going through them,
page by page, explaining them in a way that was simple, yet most
precise. For her, it has always been quite clear that women must never
be discriminated against, and must always be allowed to have an interest in anything they desire. Since those early days as a child in
postwar Germany (with the exception of a ten-year separation during which I was in the United States), my grandmother has been at
my side: in the '70s and '80s during nonviolent demonstrations,
blockades, and antinuclear sit-ins. She has walked with me in the
streets of Munich and the streets of Carnsore, Ireland, protesting nuclear power plants and weapons, against police terror and the crimi-

nalization of pacifists. The way in which she has lived her life with such integrity, so honestly, so modestly, so courageously, has never left me; it gives me strength during times when I think I can't go on. She has watched the growth of the Green Party and been actively involved, supporting me daily in the four electoral campaigns—doing grass-roots work in wind and weather!

My mother, after an unhappy marriage and divorce in the same Catholic Bavarian town, has also set another example for me of integrity, courage, and independence. She needed no men to help her determine her life and her future. She derives her energies and her courageous attitudes from her mother, Omi. And then there was my sister, Grace Patricia, who died of eye cancer, which was possibly worsened through the radiation treatment used to try to halt its growth. My sister Grace has always pushed me in the right direction—during her life, and also since her departure from this world.

There is a strange, whole, and wholly mysterious interconnectedness between me and my sister in the other sphere of existence; I have felt completely attuned and committed and connected to her during my past life and feel this even more so now. I feel intuitively there is proof of life after death. When she died in 1970, one of the many millions of cancer patients and hostages of this radioactive atomic age, I vowed to dedicate my entire life to finding out why we have all become cancer patients and atomic hostages and why Hiroshima and Nagasaki are everywhere around us!

When times are rough and my soul and body are tired from all the battling and struggling for Green politics and all the trouble from the triple lives I must lead, at such times I always feel rejuvenated and strengthened by my sister Grace. I know she is watching me, guiding me somewhere all around me from transcendent spheres.

I have broken with the institution called Church, called Vatican, even though I was once a very devout Catholic. As a small girl I contemplated becoming a nun so I could pluck my guitar and sing to little black children somewhere in Africa, while trying to feed them and help them be healthy again. I broke my ties with that Catholic Church institution, with that patriarchal club of men dressed in black who determine how women all over the world should be subordinated, should be placed in categories below men . . . I broke with that Church because I am deeply religious and feel whole and equal to men and feel a need for feminist spirituality. I do not need an authoritarian male institution to help me look for my own inner truth and to search for gods and goddesses of cosmic energy and love-light.

I have found much wisdom in Eastern religions. I have also found it through contact and communication with my foster child, Nima, who lives in Northern India. I adopted her in the early 1970s. Since then I have been acquainting myself with Tantric and Buddhist beliefs as well as various other forms of religion, which all at their very heart seem to have the one truth that unites us: love. Buddha and Jesus Christ and many other spiritual men and women—they are all, in my belief, extremists of love, extremists of nonviolence, extremists of truth and courage.

In my days as a teenager and while growing into a young woman, I became enraged about the way in which women had been obliterated in the pages of history or in the pages of the Bible or other religious documents. Most women were subordinated, always dependent upon men for their own realization and value, always needing to seek men as their only path to fulfillment. I became very enraged at this and began reading Rosa Luxemburg's writings, particularly her diaries in prison. I began searching through biographies of Aleksandra Kollontai, George Sand, Emma Goldman, and Helen Keller and other women who have put a very special stamp on history, yet have been up to now ignored by male historians and male scholars. I set out to rediscover these brave women. I never had much respect for the Karl Marxes and Friedrich Engelses and all those other dogmatic macho men, theorizing and philosophizing about the working classes and capital and yet at the same time discriminating against their wives and children and leading the lives of "academic pashas," and being always rejuvenated by their wives and mistresses! They could not cook or clean or sew or take care of themselves. They always needed women for their most basic needs.

During my years of study in the United States from 1960 to 1970, I became very devoted and committed to the causes of minorities: the blacks who live in the South, the American Indians who mine uranium, the people who are not classified as WASPs, and who look toward Martin Luther King, Cesar Chavez, Dorothy Day, and others for guidance and nonviolent strength. During my years in the United States I began to learn there is another kind of power than the power of domination and oppression—there is the power of nonviolence, common to all, to be used by all and for all. *Power over* must be

replaced by *shared power*, by the power to do things, by the discovery
of our own strength as opposed to a passive receiving of power exercised by others, often in our name. In watching the struggles of the
black people in Mississippi, the Indian people, and the beginnings of
the American women's and anti-Vietnam movements, I realized that
we can find strength, confidence, and real power in working together
and practicing nonviolence. Essential to that idea is the belief that
each of us can do it, regardless of gender, color, class, age, or physical
abilities. And a basic principle of nonviolence is that one is not opposing the policeman or the soldier as a human being, but opposing
his uniform and his social role! We oppose that very system of domination and oppression that creates his job and the arms and guns he
must carry.

I also learned in the late 1960s that if we are trying to rid the world
of things as oppressive as nuclear weapons or poverty, we must also
rid the world of things such as sexism and racism and always look
carefully at their structural underpinning—which is essentially the
system of patriarchy. I see patriarchy as a system of male domination,
prevalent in both capitalist and socialist countries, oppressive to women
and restrictive to men. It is hierarchical like the Catholic church in
that men have more value, and far more social and economic power,
than women. And under a system of patriarchy women suffer, both
from oppressive structures and from individual men. I realized so very
clearly that in all economic and political areas there is sexual discrimination all over the world.

After my return from the United States and after some time of
study at the University of Amsterdam, I joined the European Economic Community, serving as an administrator for social/health policy at the Economic and Social Committee in Brussels. And there,
very bluntly, men are the center of a patriarchal bureaucracy, where
many structures of hierarchy and domination exist—like that of a
large country over a smaller country, strong economic class over a
weaker economic class, etc. Men's domination of women has remained and continues to remain a constant feature within every system of oppression. My twelve years at the EEC in Brussels and my
contact with women all over Europe, whether they be in Ireland or
Holland or France or Germany, have made it so clear that men's domination of women is basic to our world and is seen by most men and
by many women as part of "human nature." They think it is something that cannot be changed. But I have always believed that norms

of human behavior can and do change over the centuries and that these aspects can be changed, too. But because the oppression of women is so deeply embedded in all societies and in our psyches and because it is accepted as natural, it continues to remain virtually invisible, even to those working to change other sorts of injustice.

It has been the example of my grandmother, as well as my mother and my sister, that has shown me one simply cannot stop to analyze the structures of domination and suppression. One must practice "disobedience" in one's daily life, disobeying the systems of male domination.

What gives me faith in the future is the hope that many women will no longer accept the existing systems and styles of male politics. Women, whether they be at Greenham Common or Comiso or in Australia or in the Pacific Island of Belau, whether they be those women protecting the forest in the Himalayas or "Women for Peace" in East Germany or Russia—they have all been stirred to action by the complacent society that is unwilling to stop present and future atrocities. Now they will be motivated to take action on their own. But not only action primarily as mothers and carers and nurturers of the earth, but also action in playing leading roles in changing the world. We as women must begin to stand up and become elected to political and economic offices in countries of the world and change the policies and structures from those of *death* to those of *life* or we will all be exterminated. I do not mean that in doing this women should abrogate their positive feminist principles of loving, caring, showing emotions, nurturing, etc. When I am given the examples of Margaret Thatcher, Golda Meir, Indira Gandhi, and others, I can only answer that they have become just like men, better men—adapted fully to the male principles and values that have been priorities for thousands of years. I believe that each individual has both feminine and masculine values and qualities and that at the present time there is an imbalance of these values. We must always understand that we should not relieve men of their responsibility of transforming themselves, of developing caring human qualities and of becoming responsible for child care and housework and all other essential support work. We shall never be able to reclaim the earth if men and women do not end up sharing these tasks and unless men begin giving up their privileges. Children are not just the responsibility of their biological mothers.

I believe we must look back to the seventeenth century, at the scientific revolution that already contained the seed of today's oppressive technologies. We must trace the myths and metaphors associated with the conquest of nature and realize that there must be a radical reevaluation of masculine institutions and ideologies. Masculine technology and patriarchal values have already been applied in the concentration camps of Auschwitz, in Dresden, in My Lai, in Hiroshima, in Nagasaki, in Iran, in Vietnam, in Afghanistan, in so many, many parts of the world. And the ultimate result of this type of unchecked, terminal patriarchy will be ecological catastrophes or a nuclear or chemical holocaust.

An integral component of what I have learned in my past fourteen years of mobilizing against a "nuclear society" has been the fact that means and ends must be consistent, must be parallel. You cannot reach a good goal through bad means. You cannot reach justice by using injustice. The ecologically transformed world I long for cannot be built with the tools, the violence, and the value systems of the Old World. The road to peace can only be peace itself. We cannot abolish militarism through militarism.

We must ourselves refuse to build walls, tanks, bombs, and jails, for in the end it is all in our hands and our responsibility. During my stay in the United States, I was put in touch with the philosophies of wise Indians, among them Chief Seattle, who stated in 1854: "All things are connected like the blood which unites one family . . . whatever befalls the earth befalls the sons and daughters of the earth." I am in full agreement with the ecological philosophy behind these thoughts; everything is interrelated. Violence, oppression, and domination are also related. They are ways to keep the powerful powerful and the powerless powerless. The same type of racism that fuels war-making in Central America, for example, makes it also more difficult for the disadvantaged to find jobs, to get a decent education, or to acquire the basic necessities of life. The same strange respect for machismo that breeds war also encourages rape, pornography, the battery of women and children. There can be no peace while one race dominates the other or one people, one nation, one sex despises another.

Mahatma Gandhi said once that "non-violence is the greatest force humankind has ever been endowed with. And love has more force than a besieging army." Martin Luther King inspired me when he stated that the force of this power of love is physically passive but spiritually active—that "while the non-violent resister is passive in the sense that he is not physically aggressive towards his opponent, his mind and his emotions are constantly active, constantly seeking to persuade the opposition." Nonviolence is a spiritual weapon that can do what guns and armies only pretend to do—it can truly defend us.

I have come in my years of political struggle to realize that legal and moral rights are not always identical. At present we have a duty to disobey the law of destruction, the law of the bomb, the law of deterrence, and the law of militarism. The actions we take to stop the deployment of American missiles in our country or the deployment of Russian missiles in Eastern European countries is of a moral quality above and beyond the so-called law as we know it in our law books. Nuclear and other mass destructive arms create irreversibly new situations, leading us toward annihilation and reducing all chances for future survival. In this regard I am grateful that Henry David Thoreau wrote: "If however the law is so promulgated that it of necessity makes you an agent of injustices against another, then I say to you . . . break the law." The nonviolent measures we are pursuing are aimed at achieving disarmament, at detecting, removing, and counteracting existing forms of violence. The opponent is given an opportunity to reconsider, to change his behavior.

The words of Anne Frank, written at the age of thirteen, give me all the reasons to go on searching for methods of nonviolence and social defense in this nuclear age: "I still believe that people are good at heart." The ancient people knew that, as well as the aboriginal people and Indian people whom I have met on my travels throughout the world. Behind every life form there is a guardian spirit. An energy flame fuels the matrix of design. Reverence for all life is not only philosophy but also science.

In my quest to align the inner and outer conditions of our world and to make the political personal and the personal political, I go on looking for new strategies of creative civil disobedience against a system of militarism and oppression. And I search for nonmilitary forms of defense.

The SS-20s, the Pershing 2s, the Tridents, and the "Star Wars" weapons, they do not begin in factories; they begin in our minds, because we have been conditioned to think each other to death.

There is one thing we must all learn while struggling against the atomic age: the state is not absolute, and loyalty to the state cannot be absolute. The only loyalty we should have is that toward one another and that toward life. We must disregard ideologies and systems

and boundaries and borders and military alliances, for they have created the deadly illness called "missile envy." And perhaps the real
immediate harm from the atomic age is that it is killing us spiritually,
for something certainly has to be dead within us to be expending so
much of our financial and technical resources toward the creation of
bombs when over seventeen million children under five years of age
died last year of hunger and malnutrition. We have no other choice
than to change radically our situation and transform the missile tubes
of death into silos of life. Swords into plowshares!

In 1982, I appealed at the Greens' tribunal against first-strike and
mass destructive weapons in East and West: "We call upon women
everywhere, our sisters young and old, to recognize that our governments are constantly breaking the law. Governments are unable to
sustain and guarantee peace. The women from Greenham Common
formed a living chain, a chain of human beings, around a military
nuclear weapons base. We call upon women to form a chain around
the world and, further, not only to resist those that say that war is
inevitable, but to love only those men who are willing to speak out
against violence. And we invite all men who oppose violence to join
us in our cause for peace: we urge them to break out of their rigid
patriarchal institutions. I appeal to women not to let themselves become corrupted by male power. And we call upon people everywhere
to work for peace, to forget the quiet comfort of their homes, to leave
behind their fears and feeling of powerlessness, their privileges and
possessions and join us as active participants and co-workers for peace.
We all must work for the planetary consciousness that will ignite each
of us to work for an in-depth social and inner change. We must begin
to change ourselves before we can go on to change the world."

Elisabeth Kubler-Ross

b. 1926

The Swiss-born psychiatrist and writer has become a leading advocate of the Death Awareness Movement through her pioneering work in counseling terminally ill patients. On Death and Dying (1969), her best-selling account of a seminar she conducted on the process of dying, was instrumental in breaking the societal taboo on open discussion of death.

As a teenager at the end of World War II, she traveled through Europe helping the ravaged refugees. "It was there in the midst of suffering that I found my goal," she wrote later of the plans she made to become a doctor. She returned to Switzerland to study medicine. After her marriage to a neuropathologist, she emigrated to the United States, where she completed her training in psychiatry. In 1965, at the University of Chicago, where she was assistant professor of psychiatry, she began her studies on death that would later gain her fame.

In the years that have passed since Dr. Kubler-Ross' first emer-

gence as a national figure, her books, lectures, and workshops have benefited thousands over the world. Her training programs are now in place and, in many communities, support groups have been formed. In 1977, she founded a non-profit corporation called Shanti Nilaya (Home of Peace). In 1984, the Elisabeth Kubler-Ross Center was established in the Appalachian Mountains of Virginia, where a children's resource center is being constructed to enable disadvantaged children of all races and creeds to share the tenets of unconditional love—thus instilling at an early age, according to Dr. Kubler-Ross, "a loving and positive attitude to all that life has to offer."

I was raised in a rather typical Swiss Protestant family, and although we had religion as a compulsory school subject, it did little to contribute to the richness of my life. In fact, it left me disillusioned with religion, particularly the contrast between the preacher's incredible oratory in the pulpit and his lifestyle and behavior, especially with children. Nowadays, his children would be regarded as battered, as they often came to school unable to sit on the hardwood benches as a result of his frequent beatings. He often interrupted his morning prayer in the classroom to bash, beat, or otherwise physically abuse a child, only to return to his desk to complete the interrupted prayer.

My general impression was that pastors and preachers were not representing, and certainly not living, what Christ came to earth to teach. They were judgmental and critical rather than loving and caring, and so I dismissed the teaching of the church.

Both my father and mother repeatedly impressed on me the importance of what "is within and not without," and I tried to follow their teachings by practicing to "love thy fellow man as thyself." We fed the hungry, helped in the enormous refugee problem during World War II, and shared whatever we had with the needy.

Watching the Nazis shooting hundreds of refugees as they tried to cross the river into Switzerland, Warsaw being devastated and ruined, the tragedy of the ghetto people, and thousands disappearing in the concentration camps all over Europe—these were hardly images of practicing Christianity. Here and there we heard stories of Christian families who hid a Jewish child and risked their own lives in doing so, but they were rare and few. These, for me, were the heroes of the horrible war, rare rays of hope that there might actually be people who practiced what the Scriptures preached.

Decades later I would work with thousands of dying patients and learn what a genuine belief in a merciful God, a caring father, and Christ was able to do for people. I studied the reactions of young and old on their deathbed, people of all faiths and people who had no faith at all. I was impressed that all great religions basically teach the same thing: "Respect your neighbor and love them as you love yourself." I found that genuinely spiritual people had no fear of death. It did not matter what religion they belonged to. The same was true of authentic atheists. Those who had the biggest problems were those who were a little bit of one thing or another, but who had long given up practicing their original beliefs. They were often guilt-ridden, fearful of punishment after death and regretted not having paid more attention to matters of belief.

I met and worked with wonderful ministers, who actually cared and tried to practice what they preached from the pulpit, and slowly I began to develop a deep interest in religion and philosophy. I challenged the teachings of the church, I experimented, I read. But mainly I listened to the dying, who have for so long been my best teachers. I sat for hours with an old rabbi before he died. A fundamentalist Baptist woman shared her total faith with me and died as peacefully as a little child going to sleep. I observed the torment of a Unitarian minister who regretted having such a "pseudo intellectual belief" and who contemplated returning to his old religious background. All this led to my intensive study of ways to verify some of the Christian teachings of 2,000 years ago.

After half a century, my understanding of the human being in this world is simply that we are all children of the same God. We are in the most literal sense of the word brothers and sisters. The ultimate lesson all of us have to learn is UNCONDITIONAL LOVE, which includes not only others but ourselves as well. As long as we judge, label, criticize ourselves or others, as long as we fight and kill our fellow man, no matter who he is, we have not learned our lessons, and we should not consider ourselves religious men and women.

I believe that it is in the most literal sense true that we reap what we sow. Generosity, compassion, understanding, and love will plant seeds of the same kind and will, in times of need, return to us. On the other hand, seeds of intolerance, criticism, hate, and discrimination will equally return. All true benefits have to be earned and they are always mutual.

I believe that we are solely responsible for our choices, and we have to accept the consequences of every deed, word, and thought throughout our lifetime. Every thought and preparation for war will make the next war more probable. Every thought, word, or deed of love and peace will foster universal peace. We can change the world, but only by changing ourselves—by being aware of our actions in everyday life, by becoming masters of our spoken words, and being in control of our thoughts. If we make it our goal to live a life of compassion and unconditional love, then the world will indeed become a garden where all different kinds of flowers can bloom and grow.

It has been my life goal to contribute toward that fulfillment so that our children and our children's children can be proud of their forefathers (and mothers); and that they can learn to enjoy the gift of life, the miracle of nature, and the multitude of animals and plants created by God, who also created each of us, His own children.

I remember a Vietnam veteran who, in the midst of shooting children, pigs, and all moving obstacles in a rice paddy, ordered his gunner to stop the shooting. He discovered an old man being given some water by a little girl. As the two frightened people expected to be killed, a great sense of compassion made the American aware of the love between the old man and the little girl. He opened a can of peaches, and they all shared a simple meal together. It was after this incident that the soldier's life was changed, and his story has touched many lives and opened the hearts of some bitter men. This little light within exists in all of us. If we follow it and listen to our inner voices, our lives will be enriched immeasurably.

Origen, the Christian mystic of Alexandria, Egypt, persecuted for his "heretical" teaching 200 years after the birth of Christ, believed, as I do, that we are evaluated by our deeds. He taught that, depending on our growth and learning here on earth, we will be assigned to different places in the afterlife, with different groups of angels guiding us, all of whom try to teach us how to move on and to become more perfected in unconditional love.

Even the worst destructive persons, a Hitler, will be received with compassion and understanding at death. He will have to review all the horrors and the pain he has caused. He, too, will have a chance to purify himself, to learn and to grow, to make up for his misdeeds and to return to earth until he has learned not to follow the path of force, hate, and discrimination. As there are many stages of heaven, so there are many stages of hell. They are not for eternity, as time does not exist and nothing is forever. They are chances to see the consequences of our choices and to choose anew because free choice is the greatest gift God gives to his children.

It may take eons for some people to climb up the ladder, but no one is refused the opportunity to "return home," just as the prodigal son was welcomed eventually with open arms. This is what I call grace, and this forgiveness is the hope that sustains those who choose greed and selfishness over love and sharing.

To me, God is the creator of the universe, the true father of all living things. Most of us have misused the great gift he has given us, the gift of free choice. Now we are trying to make up for it, and all of us are on the path to learn and to practice what some of our great teachers have come on earth to show us as a living example (Buddha, Christ, etc.). Every so often, when man is on the verge of self-destruction and/or on the verge of losing the inner knowledge of our birthright, our origin, God has sent a man or woman to earth to teach us anew. If we follow the teachings of unconditional love and don't misuse them by planting fear and guilt, all of us can look forward to a long and exciting journey back home to the place where we began.

When I am working with dying patients, children as well as adults, my beliefs are not only strengthened and confirmed, but I can also help those who are afraid of a punitive, judgmental God. Parents of murdered children or those they have lost by accidents or illnesses can be assured that they will see their children again at the time of their own transition. My own research has confirmed this beyond a shadow of a doubt. Critically injured children, involved in a family accident and death of family members, often linger on for weeks and months before their actual death. When asked, shortly before they die, if they are able to share their experiences (during a coma, for example) with me, they all confirm that "It is okay, my mommy and Peter are already waiting for me." In all of the thirteen years of this research, I have never had a single child who mentioned someone still alive.

It is my belief that we should not impose our own beliefs onto others, but rather live an example of unconditional love. If my patients ask me about my research, I am naturally more than happy to share my knowledge with them, and it is up to them to accept those parts that are acceptable to them.

To practice the concept of unconditional love in my daily life, I have to become aware each time I react negatively to any one person, group of people, or situation. I have to work through my unfinished business, which results in negative reaction, and naturally correlate the origin of the trauma, thus becoming less and less critical, judgmental, and less and less reacting (rather than acting). The result is an ever-increasing positive energy, which allows me to work up to seventeen hours a day, seven days a week without the so-called burnout (which, in reality, does not exist)! The latter is a result of a lack of self-honesty, which reveals itself in negative-draining responses to others who push the "buttons" of our own unfinished business.

Once I can rid myself of all negativity, it becomes increasingly easier to make myself available to the neediest and to the most outcast people in my field of work. I can sit with parents whose children have been cruelly misused and murdered, with a single mother whose three out of five children have committed suicide, with abandoned children and toddlers who have AIDS. I don't shy away from helping any AIDS patient who feels rejected, judged, and blamed. This is probably one of the most difficult tests we face today: To help with compassion and understanding those men, women, and children with this disease, which has already taken its toll in recipients of blood transfusions, in three-year-old children of drug using mothers, and other innocent "bystanders."

I can pack a carry-on bag and fly to Juneau, Alaska, if a desperate family needs help, knowing that my expenses in money, time, and energy will be worthwhile if I can prepare them for death with the knowledge that we are provided whatever it is we need—as long as we do our services for mankind free-of-charge and practice, as best we can, unconditional love.

Harold Kushner

b. 1935

In 1981, when When Bad Things Happen to Good People was published, it vaulted to The New York Times best-seller list, where it
remained for over a year. Its author, Harold S. Kushner, was also
vaulted into sudden fame and has since devoted as much time and
energy to being an author and lecturer as to his duties of rabbi at
the conservative congregation of Temple Israel of Natick, Massachusetts, a position he has held since 1966. The book, an impassioned
attempt to understand God's role in tragedy, grew out of his own
attempt to come to grips with the illness and death of his fourteen-
year-old son.

The New York–born rabbi did his undergraduate work at Columbia
University and then attended the Jewish Theological Seminary, where
he was ordained in 1960. His interest in Hebrew literature culminated in his earning a doctorate in the subject from the seminary,
and led to postgraduate training at the Hebrew University in Jeru-

salem, the Harvard Divinity School, and a visiting lectureship in Jewish literature at Clark University.

Although before his best seller he had written two books—When Children Ask About God (1971) and Commanded to Live (1973)—it is When Bad Things Happen to Good People that struck the most responsive chord in people, people of all faiths, who seek to understand what it means when tragedy ravages the lives of the good.

My overarching sense of religious purpose rests on two cornerstones. From the Bible and my Jewish tradition, I learn that people are not born as human beings. They are only potentially human. The great challenge of our lives, and the one to which religion addresses itself, is to realize that potential, to become authentically human, to take a man (or woman) and make a *mensch* of him. (Konrad Lorenz made this point beautifully when he announced that science has discovered the missing link between the higher apes and human beings. It's us.) Religion tries to humanize us, not only by passing on to us the wisdom of the past, but by involving us in community. It gives us not only philosophy but biography, living examples of its truth, because it understands that most of us learn better from incarnations, from people who serve as models, than we do from abstractions.

The community of which we are a part shapes us in another sense as well. We act differently in the company of other people than we do when we are alone, and we act differently in the company of some people than we do in the company of others. We are decorous in church, boisterous at the football game, impatient in a traffic jam, because we tend to take on the coloration of the setting in which we find ourselves. (I once had the experience of going to see a funny movie on a weekday afternoon when there were only two other patrons in the entire theater. It made it harder to appreciate the movie.) Understanding that, religion tries to supply us with role models, saints and heroes, to pattern ourselves after, and tries to fashion a community of faith by whose values we will be shaped as we participate in it.

Religion helps us learn what is right by giving us models, live and historical, in the hope that we will respond to them by saying "I want to live like that and know the satisfaction and fulfillment they seem to know." But it helps us cope with one of the other major spiritual problems of life today, the problem of loneliness, by bringing together unconnected people and forging them into a unity, a single organism singing and praying before God.

In my Jewish background, there is no monastic tradition, no pattern of finding God by turning one's back on the sin-scarred world. Life is with people, and holiness is generated when people come together. As a congregational rabbi, I am bothered by those who take a condescending attitude toward organized religion and ritual, dismissing them as a pious neurosis, which only the benighted and superstitious take seriously. One does not attend church or synagogue at a stipulated hour because he believes God keeps office hours on Friday nights, Sunday mornings, and by appointment. We go to services and read prescribed words, not to find God but to find a congregation, to find other people who are in search of the same divine presence as we are. By coming together, singing together, reading the same words together, we overcome the isolation and solitude with which each of us ordinarily lives. We all become one and we create the moment in which God is present.

When people ask me "Where is God?" I tell them that I would rather rephrase the question to read, "When is God?" Asking where He is implies that God is an object located in a specific place, and if we could just find the right place, we would find God. I read the Second Commandment, prohibiting making a picture of God, as telling me that He is not an object. Asking "When is God?" gives us the idea that God can be anywhere, if the right things are happening. When people are loving, brave, truthful, charitable, God is present. He is not in the place; He is in the moment. Martin Buber, when asked, "Where is God Found?" would reply that when people act toward each other in a truly human fashion, God fills in the empty space between them. Like an electric arc between poles, God is not so much in either person as He is in the relationship that connects one to the other.

Being born Jewish, growing up in a tradition that stressed the horizontal dimension of religion, reaching out to people, more than the vertical, reaching up to God, one which located holiness in the community rather than in separating from the community, was one of the two factors that continues to shape my life. The other was the fourteen years I spent with our son Aaron, while he was living with, and ultimately dying of, progeria, the extremely rare, rapid-aging disease. The experience taught me something about the unfairness of life, and forced me to rethink much of what I had been taught about God's role in our lives and the reasons for being good. I have written about this in my book *When Bad Things Happen to Good People.* Compelled to choose between a powerful God who was not good, and a good God who was not all-powerful, I found the latter a more morally acceptable, more authentically religious alternative. Unable to understand how a God of love and justice could will such pain for an innocent child, I concluded that the tragedies of this world do not reflect God's will. They result from inexorable laws of nature and from the misuse of our human freedom. God does not send the tragedy; He sends the strength and faith to cope with tragedy, and He sends us friends to assure us that we do not grieve or cry alone.

I don't think I diminish God when I say that He does not control everything that happens in the world. I think that those people who attribute every heart attack, every malignant tumor, every flood, fire, and hurricane to God's will are the ones who diminish Him and offer us a God unworthy of worship.

But more importantly, the years I spent with Aaron taught me something about the ability of a fragile human soul to bear great burdens with astonishing grace, humor, and courage. Despite his appearance and physical limitations, Aaron went to school and was the top student in an academically competitive school. Rather than focusing constantly on his own problems, he was sensitive to the problems of others, because he knew how it felt to be hurt or left out. He was brave, he was funny, and he was lots of fun. We felt blessed that he was ours, albeit for too short a time.

I believe in miracles, but I believe only in big miracles, not little ones. Things like parting the Red Sea or making the sun stand still are not miracles for me; they are special effects. You don't have to be God to make them happen; Cecil B. DeMille and Steven Spielberg can do it as easily. Authentic miracles happen when weak people become strong, when timid people show courage, when selfish people turn generous. Only God can make that happen, liberating the potential for humanity, which is within each of us. I can believe in God, not because someone has proven it to me philosophically, but because I so often see ordinary people become capable of the most extraordinary accomplishments. For me, Aaron, though he died at fourteen, was such a miracle. Rather than cost me my faith, he restored it.

I determined to become a rabbi thirty years ago, when I was a nineteen-year-old college junior, largely because I wanted to teach people, and I saw the rabbinate as an effective way of doing that. (The Hebrew word *rabbi* means teacher.) I have since learned that what people want from their clergy is not preaching, but caring, the sense of a caring presence to symbolize God's caring presence. They want consolation, not information, reassurance of their worth rather than advice on how to be better. I still teach as much as I hoped to, but I teach differently now. I teach, not by lectures but by example. I lead people to believe in the reality of a loving, caring God, not by explicating the appropriate passages in Scripture, but by trying to be a loving, caring person in God's name. I suspect I do at least as much good by paying a mediocre hospital visit as I do by giving a superb Bible class.

When I was a young, inexperienced clergyman, people who had suffered misfortune would say to me, "Rabbi, why? Why would God let this happen to such a good person?" And I, in my naiveté, thought they were asking me a question about God. So I tried to answer their question by giving them some of the standard theological explanations of God's role in our suffering. When it was clear that they were not comforted by my words, I felt frustrated. Either my words were not well chosen or the people were too distracted by grief to listen and understand them. Now I know better. "Why me?" "Why did God do this to me?" are not questions about God. They are not questions at all. They are cries of pain and rage and cries for help. We help the person who asks "why?" not by explaining *why* but by easing his pain, holding his hand, validating his right to cry and feel angry, and telling him that we care about him. The person who says, "What did I ever do to deserve this?" does not want from us a list of the things he has done to deserve this. He wants the reassurance from us that we like him, feel bad for him, and do not believe he deserves his fate.

My sermons tend not to be explanations of complex theological ideas, because that would represent giving answers to questions nobody is asking. Neither are they analyses of how the government or the United Nations could run its affairs better. I rarely have a senator, congressman, or U.N. official present, and even if I did, it would be wrong to neglect 99 percent of the congregation to preach only to them. I learned many years ago that the best sermon is an answer to a question. I try therefore to begin, not with the Bible's or the tradition's answers, but with people's questions. To be an effective preacher, I not only have to know what the Bible commentators say, but where people hurt, where they are confused and perplexed. Once I have identified the question, there will almost always be an answer for it in the text.

My sermons tend to be psychological, not because I have abandoned religion for psychology, but because I believe that good religion is the care of souls, the effort to help people live happy human lives, even as good psychology is. In my sermons, I try to help people understand their behavior and the behavior of the people around them. Why do we have conflicts with our husbands, wives, children? Why, when we have succeeded in business, do we feel let down and depressed? And I try to show how the resources of the Bible and my religious tradition can help them to clarify what they want out of life and live as they would like to. I try to teach them to take pride in their Jewish heritage and the forms in which it has historically expressed itself. For me, it is a source of great pride that God chose the Jewish people to be a vehicle through which knowledge of Him and His will came to mankind. I read the Bible, the prophets, the psalms, not only as Holy Scripture, but as a family album, the story of how my great-great ancestors tried to articulate their encounter with God.

In recent years, I have come increasingly to appreciate the role of the irrational in religion. I have always been a very rational, intellectual person who was impatient with things I did not understand, things which did not make sense. Now I have come to understand that living and thinking rationally nourishes only the top two or three inches of my being, and leaves the rest of my soul starved. I suspect that the appeal of the charismatics and the cults in recent years reflects the souls of young people responding to this spiritually imbalanced diet. There has to be a place in our lives for ritual, for the drama and the magic of religion.

Does religion have the capacity to make people better, more honest, less cruel? Sometimes I think it does, and sometimes I wonder. I sometimes think that organized religion becomes important to a lot of confused people, people who have problems with issues of self-

worth and self-esteem. But that's all right, too. A church or synagogue that admitted only saints would be like a hospital that admitted only healthy people. It would be a lot easier to administer, but
I'm not sure that is what we are in business for.

But I think that religious institutions can enhance people's sense of
self-esteem and self-acceptance, and by doing that, reduce their psychological need to hate, to hurt, to envy. In fact, that may be one of
the most important things we do. It can introduce people to a God
who neutralizes the moral law of gravity and helps us rise higher.

My religion helps me to answer the two fundamental questions of
human life: Why am I alive? And why should I do what is right? I
have long ago left behind the idea that we should do right and avoid
sin so that God will reward and protect us. It would be nice if that
were true, but, alas, the world does not seem to work that way. I do
what is good for the satisfaction of knowing what it feels like to be
human. The selfish, dishonest person will never know that satisfaction. He will come to the end of his life having had the opportunity
to be authentically human and never having taken advantage of it.
For me that is the worst punishment I can imagine, even if he has no
idea what he is missing. It is far worse than being dipped in boiling
oil or tormented by little red figures with pitchforks.

And the greatest reward is to know that I have achieved the status
of *mensch*, that I have realized my potential humanity and helped
others in the process, that I have known love, honor, generosity, forgiveness, joy, both giving and receiving them. For me that is heaven
enough. I need no other.

Madeleine L'Engle
b. 1918

Right versus wrong, good versus evil; these, as well as other matters of conscience, are the unifying themes of Madeleine L'Engle's books. Blended with dollops of suspense and fantasy, her fiction has for thirty years been enjoyed by countless young readers. Her best-known novel, A Wrinkle in Time (1962), was the recipient of the prestigious Newbery Medal. In 1979, she received the American Book Award for A Swiftly Tilting Planet (1978).

Ms. L'Engle has been writing since her youth in New York City. After graduating from Smith College, she returned to her native city to work in theater. During the 1950s she devoted herself to raising children and writing. Since then she has seen over thirty books published, including some largely autobiographical poetry and nonfiction that speak of "the joys and conflicts in being a writer, wife, mother, and struggling human being in these late years of the twentieth century."

Her contribution to letters has been recognized by the bestowal of honorary degrees from such institutions as Miami University, Wheaton College, Wilson College, and the Berkeley Seminary at Yale University.

One of my earliest memories is of a night during a visit to my grandmother at her cottage on the dunes above a great, sandy beach. It must have been an unusually beautiful night for someone to have said, "Let's wake the baby and show her the stars."

The mosquito netting was untucked, I was picked up and carried out onto the beach, and there above me was the night sky, luminous with stars and the great flowing river of the Milky Way. I was too young to understand in any conscious way that this sight of the glory of creation was to set my way of looking at the universe, and at my small place in it.

I believe in an open universe, still being created, and that this is a purposeful, not an accidental universe. I share Einstein's affirmation that anyone who is not lost in rapturous awe at the power and glory of the mind behind the universe "is as good as a burnt out candle." I do not understand the belief of many people that God created the universe, and it was finished. I do not believe in a static universe. Complete, yes, but not finished! Recently I looked at my newborn grandson, complete and beautiful indeed, but anything but finished.

And so my faith is that our human calling is to continue with this ongoing creation, of stars, galaxies, the glory of the macrocosm; and with neutrinos, quanta, muons, the infinite complexity of the unbelievably tiny, the microcosm. What fascinates me most about the new physics is the understanding that everything is interdependent, in relationship. Nothing happens in isolation. No one can truthfully say, "It's my own business."

I came across a phrase in an article on astrophysics that means a great deal to me: *The butterfly effect.* This means that if a butterfly should come into my study and sit on my shoulder as I write, this effect would be felt in galaxies thousands of light years away; everything in the universe is that closely interconnected.

The writing of fiction is about connections, connections between people who break the connections, fragment themselves and others, and (it is hoped) remake connections.

I look at what is happening on our planet, and I see the breaking of connections, nation setting itself against nation, race against race, religion against religion, but I still feel hope that at least on an individual basis connections can be remade, must be remade if we are to survive as a planet.

Just a few days ago I returned from a trip, sponsored by the United States Information Agency, which took me first across Egypt, then Austria. With my actor husband I read scenes from my books, talked about writing (the techniques of storytelling are the same in any language, any culture), and felt a wonderful sense of connectedness with the varied people I met. I carried with me a small typewriter and the manuscript of the novel I am currently writing.

I wrote my first story when I was five, and I have been writing stories ever since, and it is the discipline of listening to the story and trying to hear it truthfully that helps me to live in an open, not a closed, universe. I do not think that I will ever reach a stage when I will say, "This is what I believe. Finished." What I believe is alive, like that baby, and therefore open to growth and development. What I write helps me to continue to grow, to endure growing pains, to be more fully alive. The work and the belief are not separable. I am sometimes asked if my faith influences my books. Surely it is the other way around. My books, as they emerge onto the page, influence what I believe.

Eileen Hohner

Ashley Montagu
b. 1905

The London-born anthropologist and writer has said that the principal interest of his life has been to inquire as to "what makes humans become the kind of people they become in all their great variety, and what can be done about remaking them into the kind of people who can make themselves into what a human being should be." The answer to that inquiry has taken the form of scores of books published over the last half-century, many of which have been on such sensitive subjects as race, the relations between sexes, child rearing, aggression, and sociobiology

After completing his undergraduate work in England, Montagu came to New York in 1927 to begin his graduate studies at Columbia University, where he eventually took his Ph.D. degree in anthropology. Over the years he has taught at New York University, the New School for Social Research, Rutgers University, where he was chairman of the department of anthropology, the University of California at Santa Barbara, and Princeton University. At the same time he was estab-

lishing himself as a teacher, he began his career as a published writer.
Both occupations peaked during the 1940s and 1950s, when Montagu
was perhaps the best-known anthropologist and one of the most pop-
ular university professors in the United States. It was also during
these decades when some of his most controversial books appeared,
including Man's Most Dangerous Myth: The Fallacy of Race *(1942),*
The Natural Superiority of Women *(1953),* On Being Human *(1953),*
The Direction of Human Development *(1955), and* Human Heredity
(1959).

Even though retired from teaching and in his eighties, Professor
Montagu has continued to write and to venture into controversy.

I was born in London, England, in 1905. I was an only child, and
lonely. Nevertheless, the world seemed to me to hold promise of never-
ending enchantment, over which, alas, adults, with few exceptions,
were engaged in casting clouds of confusion and incomprehensibility.
It seemed to me that adults had not the least conception of what it
was to be a child, and I often wondered whether they had ever been
children themselves. To judge from their behavior toward children it
seemed unlikely that they had ever belonged to that species. That
wonder was the beginning of my journey toward becoming an anthropologist. I wondered why people were so different: some warm
and loving, others cold and cruel, and all the variations in between.
As I grew older my curiosity extended to embrace differences, physical and behavioral, that characterized the many different peoples of
the earth, of whom, at the time, I had very limited knowledge—but
it was enough to pique my curiosity. What did all these differences
mean? How did they come about?

As a child I learned to live with my frustrations in a world of make-
believe and very early found magic casements open to me through
the world of books. By the age of ten I had already acquired a shelf
of books from the barrows and stalls of itinerant vendors. Then there
were many museums and galleries that sold books relating to their

collections, and which were marvelously inexpensive. I still have a number of these books, one, on Egyptology, inscribed in my hand as of February 1916. Blessed be the memory of these last dispensers of civilization. Thanks chiefly to my itinerant booksellers, I could range through the whole world of English literature and through realms of knowledge that I would not come upon until much later. Undoubtedly the key book in my development at this time was a publisher's discard owing to several omitted pages. This was Maurice Craig's *Psycholog-ical Medicine*. I did not know at the time that Craig was the most famous neuropsychiatrist in England. What attracted me to the book was first, that it was new, and then even more fascinatingly, the fact that it contained colored illustrations of nerve cells in various stages of development in a number of diseases and disorders. The book opened up a new world to me, and as I read it I began to understand how many of the questions that puzzled me about adult behavior might be answered. Years later, when I became a member of the medical sec-tion of the British Psychological Society, I met Maurice Craig and had the pleasure of telling him what a great influence his book had had upon me.

Interest in the brain led to the skull, which at first I was able to study only from illustrations. It was not possible for me to collect the skulls of fish and other animals, and certainly not human ones, until by great good chance a friend's father, knowing of my interest, pre-sented me with a human skull. This was a most interesting creature, for it had a slight, almost keel-like elevation running from front to back atop its head and was very dark in color—suggesting some an-tiquity. By the time I was fifteen I mustered up enough courage to take the skull, in a brown paper bag, to the Royal College of Sur-geons, where I knew the world's most famous physical anthropolo-gist, Sir Arthur Keith, was conservator. Arriving at the imposing building I was met in the portico by an even more imposing dignitary, a man in a blue, brass-buttoned uniform, who appeared at least nine feet tall, and who genially inquired what my presence betokened. I said I would like to see Sir Arthur Keith. He further inquired for what purpose. Whereupon I told him what I had in the brown paper bag, and that I would like Sir Arthur to explain its mysteries to me. Whereupon my genial porter retired and soon returned accompanied by a tall, benevolent, handsome man in his early fifties. Clad in his white lab coat, this was Sir Arthur Keith who, putting his arm round my shoulders, gently guided me into his laboratory, seated me, and treated me as if I were a learned colleague of not less stature than himself. After explaining the skull to me as what Thomas Henry Huxley had called "the Thames River-Bed type," Sir Arthur asked me about myself, and then extended to me the invitation to come and take advantage of the Hunterian Collection of skulls and other anatomical and anthropological materials over which he presided.

It can well be imagined what an effect this great man's civility to a young boy had. It is an effect that has had a tremendous influence upon me, especially in my relations with children and students.

I took full advantage of Sir Arthur's invitation and haunted the museum for years, in the process becoming a devoted student of my mentor, who was the kindest and gentlest of men. We kept in close touch until his death at eighty-nine in 1955.

Prior to my encounter with Keith, at about age nine, I saw in the window of a small shop the brightly colored cover of a magazine showing a black-bearded young man in a white lab coat seated at a bench on which there was a microscope and a variety of instruments, together with an assortment of ape and human skulls. I vividly recall gazing at this spellbinding scene and wondered how on earth anyone could achieve so blissful a state. Seventeen years later I became that young man, a professor of anatomy and anthropology, minus the beard. It was not for many years after that that I suddenly recalled the magazine cover, which I had completely forgotten.

Nine seems to have been a magical year in my life, for it was also at that age that I moved into the class in my elementary school where my teacher for the next four years was George Bidgood. It was from Mr. Bidgood that I learned the most important of all the lessons of my life: the nature and necessity of love. It was not that Mr. Bidgood, so far as I can recollect, ever uttered the word, nor do I think that any of us were ever aware of the fact that something remarkable was happening in his class. It was only years later that I understood what had occurred. Mr. Bidgood not only loved children, but considered it a privilege to be with them. He kept a notebook on each child, evaluating each one's aptitudes, personality, intellect, and other traits, each child being treated as a person and respected as such. He would call on parents to discuss their children with them, always with encouraging words, often suggesting that it would be a good thing if they could send their children to a better school in which their talents could bloom more fully.

At the university I had the good fortune to have similarly beneficent teachers from whom I learned what good human beings could really be like. At a later school I suffered the misfortune of an unloving teacher, and from him I learned, painfully, what an absence of love can do to damage and frustrate a child. My study of physical, biological, and cultural anthropology, of evolution, genetics, and psychoanalysis, dramatically served to point me in the direction of the basic behavioral needs, the most important of which is the need to love—not only to be loved, but also to love others.

The basic behavioral needs are essentially human needs, needs that correspond to basic physical needs (i.e., oxygen, food, liquid, sleep, rest, activity, etc.). Recognition of the nature of the basic behavioral needs is of fundamental importance, for they must be satisfied if the individual is to grow and develop as a healthy human being. By health I mean the ability to love, to work, to play, and to use one's mind as a fine instrument of precision. This has been the burden of a half dozen of my books.

My occupations as student, anatomist, biological and cultural anthropologist, social biologist, and above all, teacher, have all been directed toward helping others understand the nature of human nature, how humans came to be the way they are, and what can be done about making ourselves over into what we are designed to be—healthy human beings. As a teacher my purpose has been to help my students to perceive education not as something that leads to a way of making a living, but rather as a way of life; to learn, not to become learned persons, but learning persons, to wonder, to think critically, to question the obvious, to be experimental-minded, curious, imaginative, and much else, all the days of one's life.

I count myself fortunate that of all the many sources from which I have learned, and the unusually broad interests I have cultivated, I have been able to perceive and understand relationships, which, as a generalist, I so seldom observe among specialists. As a lifelong student of our species I know that humankind's speciality is nonspecialization. Indeed, our speciality as a species is versatility, for we are the most educable, adaptive, and generalized of all creatures. We are designed to be, programmed to be, generalized learners. Understanding this, it saddens me to see the trend toward narrow specialization casting its gray shadow over the so-called educational system. As I see it, it is not an educational system that we have in the cubistically dilapidated world in which we live, but an instructional system, training in techniques and skills, mainly in the three "r's" (reading, 'riting,

'rithmetic), while the most important of all the "r's" (human relationships, love) is largely uncared for. Education, as I conceive it, means
to nourish and to cause to grow and develop the unique potentialities
with which every human is endowed. That is the original meaning of
the word from which the term is derived, namely, *educare*, only too
often confused with *educere*, which means to draw out, a very different thing. *Educare* means to nourish and to cause to grow the basic
behavioral needs. *Educere* means to draw out whatever the particular
"educator" feels should be established.

Just as we are designed to grow and develop in all those physical
traits with which we are born, so we are also designed to grow and
develop in all those behavioral traits with which the child is born. We
are the only creatures who are born with the capacity to develop those
childlike traits, but unlike the physical traits, the basic behavioral traits
must receive a prolonged training from the child's socializers. We are
all born with the capacity to speak, but we would never develop the
ability to speak unless we were repeatedly spoken to. So it is with all
other behavioral needs. To mention some of the behavioral needs:

The need for love	Experimental-mindedness
Friendship	Explorativeness
Sensitivity	Playfulness
To think soundly	Imagination
To learn	Creativity
To work	Flexibility
Curiosity	

These basic behavioral needs constitute the inborn, genetically based
value system of the human organism. They tell us what the organism
requires in order to grow and develop as a healthy human being. We
do not at present understand or recognize these needs and in our
ignorance we deform and attenuate them. What years of investigation
and study have taught me is that every human is at birth designed to
be a generalist, who grows and develops all the days of his life in
those childlike (not in the adult-produced childish) traits with which
we are all endowed. This means not to grow into the adults we are
forced to become, but to continue to grow and develop our childlike
traits to the optimum. Adults at the present sorry state of our evolutionary history are, in the civilized world, nothing more or less than
deteriorated babies; and that, as I see it, largely accounts for the peril
in which the civilized world is in today. To me these are not theories
but demonstrable facts. Yet most scientists, especially in the behav-

ioral sciences, seem to be unaware of them. They appear to be locked into a view of human nature that almost totally disables them from perceiving the facts for what they are.

I do not believe in absolute truths. I believe that theories are golden guesses to the full round of truth. I believe that theories as well as facts are subject to testing, and that one should never become so enamored of a theory or a fact that it renders one insensible to the evidences that tend to falsify it. A scientist believes in proof without certainty, other people believe in certainty without proof. My beliefs have been arrived at primarily by the scientific method of verification and falsification. Consequently, I have learned to take the meaning of a word to be the action it produces, and through my daily conduct I have tried to relate warmly and creatively to my fellow human beings. I believe that love is demonstrative, and in a society of untouchables, such as we have become in the Anglo-Saxon speaking world, I have made it a point to unashamedly embrace people whenever I was sure that they would not be embarrassed by or misunderstand my message. I have done this with many of my students of all ages and have enabled them to hug others as easily as I have embraced them. My book on the subject, *Touching: The Human Significance of the Skin*, astonishingly enough, was the first of its kind and has gratifyingly had some influence in the Western World.

Human nature is plastic, malleable, educable, adaptive, and capable of change. I believe that no matter who made one what one has become, and however inadequate a human being one may be, that doesn't relieve one for a moment from the responsibility of making oneself over into what one ought to be: a warm human being capable of love, work, play, and critically sound thinking. I further believe that such an accomplishment is within the capacity of everyone who is honestly willing to make himself so. Such easy evasions as "You can't change human nature," "The leopard cannot change its spots," and the like, through the whole calendar of myths, belong to another era. Today we know that human nature isn't something that is fixed and inexorable, the equivalent of fate or predestination, but something that is eminently malleable, and while it is true that the leopard cannot change its spots, we can certainly change ours, if only we are willing to devote ourselves to the task.

I think this is a wonderfully hopeful discovery, a discovery open to each one of us to make for ourselves, a self-discovery, the rediscovery of our authentic selves: to learn to flourish and fulfill ourselves, to live as if to live and love were one.

Helen Miljakovich

Jules Olitski
b. 1922

The Russian-born painter is probably best known for his "color field" paintings of the 1960s, achieved by the technique of spraying paint directly onto unprimed canvas. He continues to enjoy an international reputation; his work is included in many major museums and significant collections in the United States and abroad. He is also a sculptor of note: an exhibition of his sculptures at the Metropolitan Museum in New York City earned him the distinction of becoming the first living American artist to be given a one-man show at that venerable institution. Mr. Olitski has not only created art, but has taught it as well at Bennington College and at New York University, where he earned his Master of Fine Arts degree in 1955.

He has written that the events that shaped him, "some welcomed, others endured," have been: "decision to be an artist, made upon the death of my grandmother; art studies at the National Academy of Design; life in the U.S. Army; living in Paris on the GI Bill; first marriage and first child; second marriage and second child; dozen

years of teaching in colleges and universities; third marriage." A re-
juvenating event occurred in 1984 after he entered a rehabilitation
treatment center for alcoholism. He left it with, he has written, "a
new life of health, sobriety, and, I feel, spiritual awakening." Since
then he has been able to do his creative work with "a sense of joy,
excitement, hope and a good measure of awe. I can hardly imagine a
happier life than mine at this moment."

Wonder is sacred. It's what we begin with: childlike wonder, like seeing
for the first time clouds swiftly moving across the moon. The sight
leaves me chilled and wide-eyed still. One of my earliest memories,
even before I learned to walk, is of being in the country and seeing
smoke rise above a pile of burning leaves—and inhaling the wonderful fragrance of it all. To this day the sight and smell of burning
leaves stops me in my tracks. I am almost overcome by a feeling of
great joy, as if something loved and long, long gone had returned.

I've heard it said that a man never grows old if he keeps his childhood alive in memory. Maybe yes, maybe no; but surely he is done
for if he loses all sense of wonder.

Many years ago, when I was eleven, I was reading late at night in
the kitchen of our house in Patchogue, Long Island. I was eating a
pear, cutting each slice with a knife. Raising the knife to my lips, I
would take the slice from the blade. At one point my lips came away
empty. Where was the slice of pear? The knife blade was clean. I
looked in my lap, on the floor, between the pages of the book; no
slice of pear to be seen. Wonder of wonders. God had eaten my slice
of pear!

The book I was reading and had been reading night after night
while my parents and brothers slept was the Old Testament. Somehow I had found my way to that book so full of wonders. I say somehow, because I had had no religious instruction—neither at home nor
at school. Nonetheless, my belief in the God of the Old Testament
was absolute. I dreamed of becoming a rabbi when I grew up. Natu-

rally, at the age of eleven I considered myself abundantly qualified as far as goodness, righteousness, and wisdom were concerned. All I needed was a command of Hebrew and a Yeshiva diploma. All the same, from the age of four, I had also dreamed of growing up big and strong so that I could successfully commit murder: first my stepfather, after him my older stepbrother, and then, more than likely, the stepbrother my age. As to my poor dear mother—she had always remained mute while I was being bullied; only her eyes would speak: anxiously consoling and imploring—I never could quite decide what to do about her.

The evil I experienced in the cold bosom of my family was really of a low level: petty, sadistic acts accompanied by mocking laughter, jeers, or just callous indifference. Day in, day out, I was told I looked like a freak, had the mind of an idiot, and would die in the gutter if not in the electric chair. For a time, my mind numbed. I was left back in the second grade.

To understand the impact upon me of what was taking place in the kitchen that night, and my reaction upon the later reappearance of the slice of pear, I must backtrack further. I was born in the city of Snovsk in the U.S.S.R., a few months after my father, a commissar, had been tried by the state and executed in that city. My mother, grandmother, and I came to the U.S.A., and while my mother worked in a sweatshop to support us, my grandmother took care of me. When I was three and a half my mother remarried: a widower with two sons. At a stroke, it seemed, warmth, love, and tenderness were replaced by cold, unrelenting malevolence. Where to turn for help? Each night I fantasized that my father was not dead: he wandered the earth searching for me; he would rescue me from my hell. He never came. In time I yielded up my hope, though in a sense, not entirely. God was watching. I had come to believe in the all-powerful, all-knowing and all-seeing God of my ancestors. A just God. When He got around to it He'd smite my enemies; they'd wish they'd never been born.

At the time, 1933 or thereabout, an evil, so horrible as to be beyond a child's comprehension, was making itself known to the world. I had a newspaper delivery route. Every now and then in a short paragraph on a back page of the newspaper, I read some words, rumors usually, that spoke of Jews being persecuted in Germany: beatings, disappearances, concentration camps, death camps. Was it possible? Something told me it was all too true. Why was everyone silent? Silence, at home, in the school, in our town—just a handful of words in a newspaper every now and then. Where was the good FDR, so beloved by the Jews? And God, the God of us all, surely He would not turn His face away from such a *schrecklichkeit.*

Oh, I believed! God was with me. He had eaten a slice of my pear. I had never felt such joy as at that moment; the kitchen had become a radiant and holy place. I was in a state of bliss, at least for a minute or more, until I came to my senses. What a poor host I was being! Quick, offer Him another slice. I turned the knife to make the cut, and *there,* clinging to the blade's underside, was the missing slice of pear! Stunned, I wondered, had it been there all along? No, impossible for me to have missed seeing it. No, I had been betrayed! God had tricked me. Like a cunning, cruel stepfather, God had made me play the fool. I raised a fist and shouted: I won't believe in you anymore!

Paul's words come to mind: "When I was a child, I spake as a child, I understood as a child, I thought as a child; but when I became a man, I put away childish things.

"For now we see through a glass, darkly. . . ."

Does God exist? My childish faith had not survived its first blow. And swiftly came horrors piled one upon the other: Hitler's and Stalin's and horrors that seem to come without end.

I long ago stopped believing in the God of my ancestors, but if He exists, this great and awful God who can look with equanimity or a tolerant smile upon horrors unspeakable—if He does exist, then I must not look upon His face.

I am convinced it was the love of my grandmother, a love given without stint and with no strings attached, that helped me survive with some degree of sanity those dreadful years of childhood. My grief at her death was to affect me most powerfully. My decision to become an artist was made as she was lowered into her grave.

Her death came at a time when I was in my last year of high school. My art teacher, a dear, good man, had taken me under his wing and was urging me to become a high-school art teacher like himself. The idea of securing my future in this way was tempting. How else could I make a living? I knew I had some talent for drawing and painting, but it never occurred to me, even in fantasy, that I could ever make a living as an artist, or, for that matter, in any other line of work. I had so little confidence in myself. Even the idea of pursuing a teaching career was scary. But I was taken (literally) by the hand by my teacher and introduced to his professor friends at New

York University as a prospective student. This was the closest I got to becoming a high-school art teacher.

When I decided to become an artist, I didn't know what making art really meant. Yes, I clearly had the talent. Even as a very young child I could draw accurately from the model. Since a talent for painting became evident during my high-school years, I wanted to continue the kind of work I felt suited for and in which I took considerable pleasure and satisfaction. But, I think what I most wanted in becoming an artist was to live a life utterly different from the kind of lives I saw being lived by my parents and their circle. Their lives seemed barren, without joy or purpose apart from getting rich. (How harshly I judged them! Youthful arrogance and dumbness.) I, to the contrary, would live a *really* meaningful life. At any rate, I told myself, I would be doing the kind of work I loved.

I tried not to think about my future. All I wanted out of art school was to learn to paint in the manner of the Old Masters and, who knows, maybe I could paint portraits to earn my living. This did happen. I went to art schools; I learned some Old Master techniques; I even had a brief career as a portrait painter. But it was to be ten years after the New York art schools before I had my first taste of what making art was about. It all began as one hell of an identity crisis.

1949. I was living in Paris, studying art on the GI Bill. I was away from family, friends, and my country. I spoke no French. But one afternoon many things suddenly seemed to come together, enough to make me question myself. What does the art I make have to do with me? Is it enough to make the kind of art I make? It seemed as if I had learned, from the art schools and museums and the art I saw in art galleries, to speak, as it were, in many voices—where was *my* voice? Had I a voice? How to find out? Surely this meant somehow connecting with the child I had once been. Was the child still alive? How to find out? I must look inside myself. But how? My eyes would have to be covered. If I couldn't look out, my vision would be forced inward. I squeezed out gobs of color from tubes of oil paint onto a wide plank of wood. That would be my palette. Brushes were placed close to hand where I could feel for them, as needed. A canvas was supported on a chair in front of me. I wrapped a towel around my head. I felt the tip of my brush sink into paint; I had a rough idea of where each color was, but I couldn't be sure. Was I in the yellow or orange? No matter. My brush found the canvas and moved on it. Another brush, another color, another brush, another color, another,

another, another . . . I have no idea how long I worked before I peeked. Five minutes? An hour? I had to see!

What I saw were daubs of bright, flat colors that looked slap-dab rough and startlingly alive. I forgot everything: who I was, the child, Grandma in her grave, everything but this crazy, alive-looking thing. A lot of raw canvas was still showing. Back to the blindfold and back to work. Except that it wasn't work. It was more like a child *playing*: completely playful and completely serious, both at the same time.

I painted blindfolded for I don't know how many months—in any case until I felt strong enough in myself that I could allow the work to take its course; to develop in time, I hoped, into good works of art. Through an odd, unanticipated route I had found my way into flat, bright, colored abstract painting. At a stroke the devices and techniques I had learned in the art schools were gone, as if I'd never gone to school. Before Paris, I had painted in the styles of certain Renaissance masters. I had also done work while under the influence of the Impressionists, Post-Impressionists, Nabis, Fauves, and Cubists. Though the "blindfold" paintings were not truly *realized* works of art, they were, I believe, my first true works. They had come out of play, and to me, at least, they looked alive. The kind of play I mean is serious play, inspired play, where imagination, intelligence, intuition, and experience all together and at once reconstruct reality into a vision (a unique vision, if we're talking about great works) of order and harmony.

In time, the methods and techniques I'd abandoned, such as underpainting, modeling, half-tones, impasto, chiaroscuro, tinting, glazing, and so forth found their way back into my work. Nothing is ever lost altogether, or so it seems.

Very well, the child spoke. A beginning. But a beginning, even an auspicious one, is not enough, does not take us very far. Now we must find out who we are as all the while external reality presses, testing us . . . we must find what we believe so that we may live in accord with our beliefs.

In *Poetry and Reality*, Goethe writes: "However much a man searches heaven and earth, the present and the future, for his higher destiny, he remains the victim of a perennial vacillation, of an external influence which perpetually troubles him until, once and for all, he makes up his mind to declare that right is that which accords with him."

In looking back, tracing how some of my beliefs got formed, I see

I was fortunate from the start, in that there was always someone or something to endure, to go up against, to survive.

Obscurity and hard times are useful if they don't last forever and if they don't leave you crazy and suicidal. Because I could get no one interested in my work, and no one was watching (and try as I might, I could not get a one-man show; no art dealer was interested enough to take a chance), I felt I had nothing to lose. I could practice my art without much concern for the world and none for my face in it—the ideal situation for a young artist. I could fool around, try anything out. If I played the fool, no matter. I was unseen, and alone.

But I am leaving out the truth, the truth I almost dare not tell. Shaking my fist at God, that long ago night, by no means erased my belief that some kind of reality existed apart from the one I could see and touch. At times I had sensed a nearby presence. God who seeth? A higher Power? I don't know. A presence not necessarily Divine, but presence enough to convince me, as Hamlet puts it:

"There are more things in heaven and earth, Horatio, than are dreamt of in your philosophy."

I think of the time I looked in a mirror and saw a face, not mine. It was at a time I felt beset by problems: my marriage going sour, a job I minded going to, my frustration at not being able to get my work seen, agonizing over a troubled child, and guilt, lots of guilt.

I happened to catch a side glimpse of someone as I passed a hall mirror—but who? I stopped short. Was that me? I went back and looked. The more I looked, the more convinced I became: I was seeing someone else—granted, someone who looked like me, but wasn't me. Ghost of my father? I didn't think so. The eyes seemed ageless; they were without a trace of human feeling, certainly no pity or compassion . . . indeed, without any comprehension of my concerns; what were they saying? I stared and stared. I saw an image in his eyes: a long, long line of small gray ponies, without saddles or reins, ridden by men bundled in gray furs, hunched forward against a blinding snowstorm, moving ever so slowly across an unending plain. A half hour must have passed before I said, "You've come to tell me something. What?"

"You are not your concerns. Your concerns are not you." That's all he said. When I got back to the mirror after pouring myself a drink, all I saw was me.

Why resurrect my mirror spirit and put him in a book where he can be used against me by my enemies and make my friends embarrassed for me? Well, I'm damned if I know why. It's not as if I believe I have some special destiny and the image in the mirror came to remind me of it. Indeed the sense I have of my own destiny is merely of something unfolding and inevitable, something like the inevitability that the moment my mother-in-law arrives at our door for a visit, the plumbing will overflow.

Maybe what I'm trying to get at is that my belief in some power outside of myself was there all along, but it was a belief that had little or no effect; it was of no use to me. But every now and then, though all too infrequently, while painting away in my studio, an event would occur that I couldn't explain, and which I called inspiration. It would feel as if I were being given over to something, to a force, working through me. Afterward, I never could remember the sequence of events. It was as if without knowing how or why, I had stepped from one level of consciousness into another and this other was powerfully charged with concentrated energy. All I needed to do was let it happen. When it did happen, that particular painting always appeared to me not only as singular, but also as an opening into new territory.

As we all know, inspiration, like love, can't be induced. If we are fortunate, it will happen, falling upon us like a gift from the gods. If we are very fortunate, it will happen more than once. The only thing I could hope for was that I would be at work when the miracle came about; so I worked all the time. And then some seven or eight years ago I came upon this sentence by Ralph Waldo Emerson: "Do the thing and you will have the power." I didn't know, and still don't, its exact meaning, but the words had for me a power in themselves, an incantatory power. It was as if, simply by saying the words and in that instant taking hold of the work, I had also taken hold of the power. Now here was a power I could induce. And what's more, the experience was similar to that which I had called inspiration. I believe I had tapped into some universal power. My experience is far from unique. Creative workers in many occupations and professions have experienced a communion with a divine source. It is maybe what Matisse had in mind when he asked himself if he believed in God and answered, yes, when at work.

Paul Klee wrote of " . . . works which are indications of the work of God," and of the artist as "merely a channel." And "Genesis eternal! Chosen are those artists who penetrate to the region of that secret place where primeval power nurtures all evolution."

Any further need I might have had for an open sesame into power

was given me by William James: " . . . give up the feeling of responsibility, let go your hold, resign the care of your destiny to higher
powers, be genuinely indifferent as to what becomes of it all . . . a
greater self is there."

There is something of a paradox in all this. In order to be most
truly myself, I must give myself up. In effect, it's winning through
surrendering. I've come to believe that this power I can surrender to
in my studio is indeed a higher power. I don't know its natural shape,
nor do I need know it. Enough that I have found my way to it. What
remains is to bring the power into all areas of my existence so that,
in communing with the power, it may work on me as I believe it does
on my art. Play, aliveness, openness, inquisitiveness, giving oneself,
and all the rest are what being human should be about.

I believe in a Creator. My belief may well be simple-minded. It
goes like this: Since creation exists, there had to be a Creator. We are
told by astronomers and astrophysicists that creation continues. So I
assume the Creator is still around. (It pleases me to imagine the Creator on some new and distant planet creating an utterly new gazelle.)
"To me," says Isaac Bashevis Singer, "the most wonderful miracle is
what Spinoza called the natural order of things. To me causality is
more than a category of pure reason; it is the essence of creation."
Of course, nothing can be proven about the existence of the Creator,
one way or another. I can have no certainty, only belief.

I believe the Creator simply provided the creation. We have everything from which we choose: good, evil, everything. I am what I do.
Behind another's conscience I cannot hide.

Jim Wright

Fazlur Rahman

b. 1919

Born in undivided India, in what is now Pakistan, educated there and at Oxford University, Fazlur Rahman has traveled, taught, and lectured in many parts of the world. The author of some of the classic works on Islam, Dr. Rahman has been characterized as "one of the most learned and acute of modern Islamic thinkers," as "an outstanding intellect, an immensely erudite scholar straddling traditional and modern learning," and "one of the clearest and wisest Islamic thinkers in the world today." Over a long and often controversial career, Dr. Rahman's combination of learning and commitment has almost single-handedly made Islam comprehensible and respected in circles that in the past have tended to dismiss Muslim scholarship.

During the regime of Ayub Khan in Pakistan (1962–68), Dr. Rahman headed the Islamic Research Institute charged with carrying out the religio-ideological policies of the government. This rare opportunity for a scholar to bring religious reform to a developing country through modernized Islamic thinking was caught in a political web

that ultimately resulted in the Institute's forcing Dr. Rahman to re-
sign the directorship. Since that time, while serving as professor of
Islamic thought in the Department of Near Eastern Languages and
Civilizations at the University of Chicago, he has tried to disseminate
his ideas through numerous articles and books, including Major Themes
of the Quran *(1979) and, most recently,* Islam and Modernity *(1982).*

   Dr. Rahman has written that over the last decade or so there is
"some reason to believe that an increasing number of educated Mus-
lims are accepting my line of thought . . . the reason being that
traditionalism is unworkable in practice and some solution on mod-
ern Islamic lines is requisite."

I was born into a Muslim family that was deeply religious. We practiced Islamic rites of prayer, fasting, etc., with meticulous regularity.
By my tenth birthday, I could recite the entire Quran from memory.

   My mother and father had a decisive influence in the shaping of
my character and earliest beliefs. From my mother I was taught the
virtues of truthfulness, mercy, steadfastness, and, above all, love. My
father was a religious scholar educated in traditional Islamic thought.
Unlike most traditional Islamic scholars of that time, who regarded
modern education as a poison both for faith and morality, my father
was convinced that Islam had to face modernity both as a challenge
and an opportunity. I have shared this same belief with my father to
this very day.

   In 1933, we moved from our ancestral home in what is now north-
west Pakistan to Lahore, which was called the "City of Gardens and
Colleges." There I went to a modern college, while at home my father
put me through the traditional course of Islamic study he had under-
gone at the Deoband Seminary in northern India.

   After I went to England, where I studied for my doctorate at Oxford and then taught at the University of Durham, a conflict between
my modern and traditional educations was activated. From the later
forties to the mid-fifties I experienced an acute skepticism brought

about by the study of philosophy. It shattered my traditional beliefs.

In 1956, I wrote a book entitled *Prophecy in Islam,* in which I discussed the head-on collision between the views of traditional Islamic theologians and those of Muslim philosophers who derived their theories on the nature of religion from the precepts of Greek philosophy. The philosophers were intellectually clever, excelling in subtlety of argument, but their God remained a bloodless principle—a mere intellectual construct, lacking both power and compassion. Although intellectually less skillful, the theologians were nevertheless instinctively aware that the God of religion was a full-blooded, living reality who responded to prayers, guided men individually and collectively, and intervened in history: "He speaks and acts," as Ibn Taimaya so poignantly put it.

Convinced that the Muslim philosophers were headed in the wrong direction, I was "reborn" with a new impulse to understand Islam. But where was that Islam? Had I not studied it with my father? But then my father had transmitted to me a fourteen-century-old tradition, and my skepticism had been directed at certain important aspects of that tradition. I then realized that although Muslims claim their beliefs, law, and spirituality are "based upon the Quran," the scripture embodying the revelation of the Prophet Muhammad (570–632), the Quran was never taught by itself in any seat of traditional learning, but always with the aid of commentaries. A study of the Quran itself, together with the life of the Prophet, enabled me to gain fresh insight into its meaning and purpose, making it possible for me to reevaluate my tradition.

Soon thereafter, I came to believe that while traditions are valuable for living religions in that they provide matrices for the creative activity of great minds and spirits, they are also entities that ipso facto isolate that tradition from the rest of humanity. Consequently, I am of the belief that all religious traditions need constant revitalization and reform.

The Quran insists that divine guidance has come to all peoples and that it is not the exclusive possession of any single community. It definitely regards mutually exclusive and mutually confronting religions as a form of polytheism. It sternly rejects Jewish electionism and also castigates Christians for laying proprietary claims on truth. At the same time, it tells Muslims that if they turn their backs upon the divine message, "God will bring another people who will not be like you." Muslims are therefore required to believe in the totality of divine guidance and "in any book God may have revealed"—not just the Quran and other Semitically revealed books. Early in its career, however, the Muslim community was led to declare itself infallible!

The entire fabric of my belief rests upon the Quranic teaching. Now, the Quran is not a treatise about God. The God of the Quran is not something to be proved but to be "discovered." Why is there this plenitude of being rather than pure nothingness? This fundamental question needs a decisive answer. But although Allah (God) is considered necessary and mentioned well over 2,500 times in the Quran (let alone other equivalents of the divine name), its central aim is directed toward guiding the affairs of mankind. The Quran's theme, first and last, is man's conduct, both individual and collective. Belief in God is absolutely essential, of course, but not in order to entice us to pry into His nature, but in order to save and develop the integrity of the human personality: "Do not be like those who forgot God, and eventually God caused them to forget themselves." The God of the Quran intervenes between "man and his own heart," and also between man and man, for "There is no meeting of three but that God is the fourth, nor of five but that he is the sixth, nor yet of less or more that God is there."

Islam means "to be safe, integral, whole" through accepting God's law. One who accepts God's law is a Muslim. The Quran calls all nature "Muslim" because nature obeys the law of God ingrained in it. Thanks to this, nature is one huge, well-knit system—a cosmos, not a chaos. But while nature is automatically Muslim, God was not content with nature's Islam and created man to be Muslim by choice— to be the unique locus of responsibility, and God's assistant on earth. The Quran's recurrent theme is that "man has not yet fulfilled this trust," the trust of moral responsibility. Humanity still needs to become a human cosmos rather than a chaos.

This trust cannot be discharged by isolated good individuals, no matter how virtuous their intentions. Certainly, the locus for a fully developed consciousness of responsibility is the individual, but the task of assisting God falls upon humanity as a whole. It was for this purpose that the "Muslim Community" was set up by the Quran to "remove corruption from the earth and reform its affairs," to "commend good and prohibit evil," to establish a social order on a viable ethical basis.

My whole statement up to now culminates in the following point: one God—one Humanity. This is the invitation with which the Quran started in 610 and with which it ended in 632. While it protested against the polytheism of the Meccan Arabs, it protested equally passionately against the grave socioeconomic unevenness in the corrupt, commercial Meccan marketplace. The Quran made a sustained effort to lift the downtrodden segments of society—have-nots, orphans, women, and slaves. It abolished all distinctions based on ethnicity, color, etc.: "We have made you into different nations and tribes only for the purpose of reference; otherwise the best of you in the sight of God is the one with the most sense of responsibility."

The above task of reforming the earth has obviously not been fulfilled by historic Islam. As a result of the astonishingly swift conquests in early Islam, so many slaves and slave-women swarmed into Muslim cities that the Quran's policy of sociopolitical programs was inhibited. Further, the Quranic vision of establishing a moral social order was submerged under the tide of a mixture of cultures that imposed itself on Islam. The community expanded rapidly but at a great cost. This is not to say that the history of Islam has been a total failure, for Muslims built a civilization, which in its heyday was truly remarkable. Under the Muslim aegis (particularly in Spain and the Middle East) Muslims, Christians, Jews, Zoroastrians, and others cooperated to create an intellectual culture in science and philosophy, literature, and medicine, that was brilliant, international, and interfaith. Moses Maimonides, for example, of whom every educated Jew is proud, was court physician to Saladin, the Muslim adversary of the crusader Richard the Lion-Hearted. There are innumerable other examples.

Nevertheless, I passionately believe that we Muslims owe it to ourselves and to the world to resurrect the Quranic vision from the debris of history, for in the Quran the real and the ideal coalesce. I contributed my part to this when I was in Pakistan (1961–68) at the invitation of the President, Ayub Khan. I was in charge of the Islamic Research Institute, established by him to advise the government on religious policies that would be true to the principles of Islam, interpreted by us for application in the changing context of the modern world. At the time, Pakistan was desperately poor, so poverty was its primary moral problem. To remedy this situation, wealth had to be created, which could then be distributed fairly throughout the populace. Accordingly, I strongly advised the government and the society at large, on Islamic bases, to do just that. This meant large-scale introduction of modern technology—technology imported from the West.

But the West itself, in the process of developing its technology and accompanying knowledge, has come dangerously close to sweeping aside human and moral values. Under the impact of pure technology, man's vision becomes so myopic that he lives from day to day and loses sight of the "morrow," to use the word of the Quran, and hence his deeds "lose all weight" and meaning. His priorities become warped and distorted. He first manufactures atomic weapons and piles them up and only then thinks of the consequences. He flies to the moon while the affairs of the earth become ever more complicated and dangerously intractable. As the Persian poet Firdausi said:

Have you managed the affairs of the earth so well that you've got yourself involved with the heavens?

I therefore warned the Pakistani government and people against the pitfalls of pure technology while emphasizing the necessity of its adoption through our advice, publications, and lectures.

The stiffest resistance I faced was from religious conservatives, and it centered mainly on the question of the rights of women and the reform of family law. Throughout medieval Islamic development, women's rights have been steadily encroached upon. A woman could not even exercise the right of divorce, which the Quran had granted her from the first day. I believe that the current feminist movements in the West cannot be a model for Muslim women, and I also believe that this Western phenomenon is a severe reaction against the medieval condition of the Western woman, who was decidedly worse off than her Muslim counterpart. Yet it is undeniable that the Muslim woman has been suffering from severe disabilities, verging on oppression. The situation still needs urgent improvement. I wholeheartedly defended and supported the progressive law promulgated by the Ayub Khan government in 1961 streamlining and reforming Muslim family law.

As a cumulative effect of these and other similar controversies, large-scale uproar and disturbances broke out against my views in the summer of 1968. I resigned in September of that year; the Ayub Khan government fell six months later. Since 1969, I have been writing books and articles trying to disseminate the Quranic message from the University of Chicago, where I am professor of Islamic thought. During these past fifteen years, the views defended by me and like-minded persons have exerted visible influence on an increasing number of Muslim intellectuals in several countries. Most recently (summer 1985) I have visited Indonesia, at the invitation of the government of that country, to assess the situation of Islam there and have tendered advice particularly on the reform of higher Islamic education, which seeks to confront modernity in a more creative manner. At the same time, conservative Islam has become the official policy of governments in Iran, Pakistan, and the Sudan. Islam at present stands radically polarized and is in unmistakable ferment and transition.

. Medieval conservatism cannot, however, supply genuine and effective answers to today's problems. It appears largely to be a reaction against Western colonialism. I am therefore confident of the eventual success of the pure Islam of the Quran, which is fresh, promising, and progressive. It will take a few years and considerable effort, however, for the current obscurantism to be laid to rest in its grave. During the ensuing years of my life the bulk of my activity will be directed toward the realization of this end.

Elliot L. Richardson

b. 1920

It is ironic that Elliot Richardson is best remembered not so much for what he did, but for what he refused to do while Attorney General during the waning days of the Nixon Administration: fire Archibald Cox as the Watergate special prosecutor. Yet the liberal Republican from Massachusetts has one of the most distinguished political careers in America. He has held four different Cabinet positions: Attorney General; Secretary of Defense; Secretary of Health, Education and Welfare; and Secretary of Commerce. He has also served as Under-Secretary of State, Ambassador to England, and Ambassador-at-Large for the Law of the Sea.

Like the rest of his family, he attended Harvard College. After serving in World War II, where he took part in the landing at Normandy and received a Bronze Star and two Purple Hearts, he returned to Harvard Law School. After several years in the private practice of law, he entered public life in 1957 when President Eisenhower appointed him Assistant Secretary for Legislation in the De-

*partment of Health, Education and Welfare. He was later elected
Lieutenant Governor and Attorney General of Massachusetts.*

*Elliot Richardson has also held many nongovernmental posts, in-
cluding trustee of Radcliffe College and member of the Board of
Overseers of Harvard College. He is a member of the Council on
Foreign Relations, a fellow of the American Academy of Arts and
Sciences, and a fellow of the American Bar Association.*

Samuel Johnson was wrong. If anywhere is paved with good intentions, it is heaven, not hell.

This, in essence, was the message of a sermon by the Bishop of
Exeter I heard in Exeter Cathedral on Easter Sunday, 1944. Intoned
rather than spoken so that it would carry to the farthest reaches of
the cathedral's cavernous, bomb-scarred nave, the sermon made an
enormous impression on me. It has ever since reverberated in my
memory.

The bishop's text was taken from the Gospel according to John:
"Gather up the fragments that remain, that nothing be lost." Every
human undertaking, however noble, however inspired, is bound to
disappoint our highest hopes. Not just the accomplishment, then, but
the aim, the concept, the aspiration, is of value. The most precious of
human attainments are those that, though imperfect, have stretched
our capacities to their utmost limits. These are the fragments that
must be gathered up and cherished. Pieces of an unimaginable whole
hurled into the unknown, the thrust of their trajectories reaches out
toward . . . God, I think.

Aspiring, creating, procreating—striving to be and become all we
are capable of being and becoming—each of us seeks to be identified
with something of enduring value. Each of us feels entitled to a measure of dignity and respect. But we are not alone: other people are
also real; other people affirm the same values. To understand this
fully—to grasp it not just with our intellects but with our imagina-
tions—is to understand that we share mutual claims and obligations.

Still, our first duty is to ourselves. If we do not feed ourselves, dress ourselves, support ourselves, we selfishly impose burdens on others. How, then, can the claims of self be reconciled with the claims of others? This question once troubled me deeply. An answer that has ever since seemed to me sufficient came to me one day during my senior year at Harvard. I was working on an honors thesis in philosophy and had come to a point at which it seemed necessary to try to think through the meaning of "self."

At a perplexing stage in this effort, I had to get outdoors. The recollection of that slaty, late-winter afternoon, with its wet wind, is still vivid. Walking beside the Charles River and thinking hard as I walked, I suddenly understood that no person's identity can be fully defined except in terms of others: family, friends, teachers, fellow workers, other members of the same community and the same heritage. Each unique inviolable self exists in the midst of a web of interconnecting relationships with other people. To be a complete person is to be a part of others and to share a part of them. This is what we mean by love. This is why giving is natural. If it were not for our physical separateness, we would more clearly perceive our psychic interdependence.

But if our obligations to ourselves include obligations to others, what is the extent of those obligations—and to whom are they owed? At least part of the answer, I believe, lies in what I call the principle of proximity (or remoteness). It is both a precept and a fact. Our obligations, not just to refrain from harming others but to help those in need, should—and do—run most strongly to those who are closest to us and grow weaker in proportion to emotional distance. A widening series of concentric circles starts with the family and goes on to the neighborhood, the larger community, and the nation. At its farthest reach, whether of distance or time, the moral bond is most attenuated, but still there. It embraces the whole world. Every other human being, including those not yet born, has some claim on me—and I on them. And, in proportion to their proximity, those in greatest need have the strongest claim on my help.

Moral obligation is thus implicit in self-fulfillment, and freedom to choose is implicit in both. Each is an end in itself; none, however, is imaginable except in association with the other two. This is why the freedom to exercise control over our lives is inseparably linked to our sense of worth. It is also why it is important to us to be able to influence the external forces that affect our lives. Because government is one of these forces, we want to be able to control what government does to us and for us. This was the impetus for and remains the purpose of the democratic process.

It follows that the more pervasive the regulatory role of government becomes, the more essential it is that we the people should have a voice in the decisions of government. It is in our capacity as citizens that we exercise such a voice. Indeed, the very possibility of representative democracy imposes on us a measure of responsibility toward its successful working. Those to whom we, their fellow citizens, delegate authority are accountable to us for what they do. We retain both the power and the duty to hold them to account. That is why, in a free society, citizenship is always the highest office. We may or may not fully discharge the obligations of this office, but we can shed them only by renouncing citizenship itself.

I believe that the duty to participate is a moral imperative. For me this conviction is more nearly religious than philosophical. Philosophies are endlessly arguable. Religions are not arguable at all. To my way of thinking, the need to exercise choice, to feel capable of exerting an impact on the events that affect our lives, to influence the flow of things around us rather than merely to be influenced by them— the need for a sense of autonomy, in short—is unarguable.

From these beliefs it also follows that the goal of civilized society is to develop and replicate the conditions under which each of us is free to fulfill his or her potential in security and peace. That is why we need law. Beginning with the tribe and expanding outward to the fiefdom, the municipality, and the sovereign state, the progress of civilization is marked by the extension of the rule of law. A beginning—but only a beginning—has been made in extending it to the global community.

As a wise American lawyer once observed, the history of civilization is the history of myriads of solved conflicts. The survival of civilization will depend on preventing their escalation. Given the prospect that the detonation of even a small fraction of the superpowers' nuclear arsenals will precipitate nuclear winter, the world needs not just arms control but far more adequate means of reconciling competing claims and keeping the peace.

These are the beliefs that orient my actions. Their origins go back to my earliest years. The effort to give them practical effect has been woven into my whole life.

Brought up in a family of doctors who were also professors of medicine or surgery, I learned from their example something about the meaning of service. To be fully alive is to be fully employed; unused, we rust. And yet I must have wanted a role more suspenseful and less familiar than the practice of medicine. As early as my graduation from college, I responded to the yearbook's question about my intended vocation with the single word *politics*. There, I was sure, lay the best possible avenue toward being of service in the cause of things I believed in.

Politics, government, and law have dominated my vocational life ever since. The culmination was my nearly four years as head of the U.S. Delegation to the Third United Nations Conference on the Law of the Sea. An extraordinarily complex and difficult assignment, it was in many ways the most demanding—and most rewarding—of the many I've had. The conference was charged with creating legal principles and institutions governing more than two-thirds of the earth's surface. All human concerns with the oceans—fisheries, pollution control, marine scientific research, freedom of navigation and over-flight, deep-seabed mining, the exploitation of oil and gas in the continental margin—were within its province. Although the United States did not in the end sign the treaty that emerged from the conference, that was only because of what President Reagan viewed as serious defects in the deep-seabed mining regime; the administration has endorsed the other nineteen-twentieths of the treaty. It has been subscribed to, meanwhile, by 159 other signatories.

A belief in the importance of working toward a more stable world order has always been a part of my feeling about politics and law. As a boy I knew more about the players in the League of Nations than I knew about those in the National League; at college, before World War II, I took a course on the League of Nations; at law school, after the war, I got my best grade in the school's first course in international organizations. Now that I have gone back to the practice of law, my principal outside commitment is to the United Nations Association of the United States of America. And within the UNA-USA, my main goal is to involve more people in thinking about better ways of coping with the intractable problems that defy solutions by any single nation or group of nations.

The experience of government service has, for me, been a deeply rewarding way of seeking to create fragments worth gathering up. I have found great satisfaction in trying to serve the public interest as best I could discern it. The effort has confirmed my conviction that the key to individual completeness lies in giving and sharing. I feel lucky to have so often been called upon to do my utmost in causes whose outcome has meant so much to so many.

As one of those whom H. L. Mencken called "the chronic hopers and optimists of the world," my instinct is to trust people. I try to inspire them to rise to their best selves. Though I may be aware of petty motives in myself or others, I do not accept their primacy. That, perhaps, is one reason why I have never viewed politics as a dirty business. I see it, rather, as an activity whose role is to strike a creative balance between liberty and equality and between individuality and community. Thus perceived, politics is the most difficult of the arts and the noblest of the professions.

Benjamin Spock
b. 1903

"You know more than you think you do." So begins one of the most influential books ever published in the United States, Baby and Child Care. Since the first edition appeared in 1946, it has gone on to become the most successful book ever written in this country and has enabled its author, Benjamin Spock, more than any other individual of his time, to reshape the process by which human beings are reared in America.

Dr. Spock attended Yale University, where he was a member of the crew that won a gold medal in the 1924 Olympic Games, before taking his M.D. degree at Columbia University's College of Physicians and Surgeons. After completing his residency in both pediatrics and psychiatry, he began practicing as a pediatrician in New York City. In 1947, he moved to Minnesota to teach psychiatry at the University of Minnesota and serve as a psychiatric consultant to the Mayo Clinic. He was professor of child development at the University of Pittsburgh from 1951 to 1955, when he joined the faculty of

Western Reserve University in Cleveland, Ohio, as professor of child development.

In 1967, he retired to devote all his energy to the campaign against the war in Vietnam. He was found guilty in 1968 of "conspiracy" to foment draft resistance; the conviction was overturned the following year. In 1972, he was an alternative candidate for the presidency of the United States. Since then, he has devoted much of his time to the cause of nuclear disarmament and continues to find himself jailed from time to time for "disrupting the peace."

I got my most basic beliefs—in the sense of unthinking attitudes rather than rational credos—from my stern, moralistic, unyielding mother. She wasn't all grim, though. She had a great sense of humor, was a hilarious mimic, and was as invariably charming to outsiders as she was severe with her children. Her scorn was withering. When during World War I my parents decided that, to help conserve wool, I should wear one of my father's cast-off suits, almost black, floppy, cuffless, the exact opposite of what youths were wearing, I cried out, "Everybody at school will laugh at me." My mother said fiercely, "You ought to be ashamed of yourself for worrying about what people will think. Don't you know that it doesn't matter what people think as long as you know you are right." Of course at age fifteen, when peer pressure is enormous, I didn't believe her. Nevertheless, I got some comfort from her words fifty years later when I found myself indicted for my opposition to the Vietnam War.

My mother was totally devoted to her children. She particularly loved and enjoyed babies because, I think, she didn't have to watch them suspiciously to squelch any signs of evil (especially sexual) or rebelliousness, as she did when they were a little older. Basically, she was deeply moved by the trustfulness, the lovingness, the eagerness, the idealism of children. Every year at the Easter ceremony at Sunday school, when the small children carrying lighted candles led the march, my mother's face would turn red as a tomato, and tears would stream down her cheeks. We Spock children hardly dared look at her because all of us would then weep, too, sensing that this symbolized the positive bond between us. Of her six children, five went into child psychology or school teaching.

Like my parents, I have never been a regular church member or churchgoer. It doesn't seem plausible to me that there is the kind of God who watches over human affairs, listens to prayers, and tries to guide people to follow His precepts—there is just too much misery and cruelty around for that. On the other hand, I respect and envy the people who get inspiration from their religions.

I am deeply impressed by the potentialities of human beings—to love generously, to dedicate themselves to causes, to be loyal and honest, to forgive, to create beauty in all the arts and to appreciate them, to make experiments and discoveries. What wonderful creatures! Yet, of course, humans can also be cruel, vengeful, ungrateful, deceitful, and greedy. Child psychiatry tells us that our good and evil traits come mainly from the way we were treated as children and from the examples we had in our parents.

When I entered medical school, I did not have any broad vision of contributing to a better world through preventative pediatrics and child psychiatry. I just thought in terms of helping my share of patients. I worked as a counselor in a small home for crippled children during my undergraduate summers and gradually came to the decision that I'd like to be a children's doctor. This choice must have been strongly influenced subconsciously by my having been the oldest child of a mother who devoted her life to children, for the oldest is apt to make a particularly close identification with parents and to go into one of the so-called "helping professions." I changed diapers, gave bottles, and rocked the baby carriage for my sisters and brother.

During my pediatric residency, I got the idea that I should have some kind of psychological training in order to give mothers sound advice. (No doubt this idea came in part from a feeling that there must be easier, more pleasant ways to rear children than my mother's rather tyrannical discipline.) But I found there was no such training designed for pediatricians. So, for lack of anything better, I took a year's residency in psychiatry. Taking care of adults with schizophrenia and manic-depressive psychosis gave me not one glimpse of how to answer mothers' questions about thumb sucking and nail biting, but I did come to realize that the staff members who found meaning in the patients' actions and speech were the psychoanalysts. So the following year (1933), as I started pediatric practice, I also started part-time psychoanalytic training. I gave my own analysis during evening seminars twice a week for five years, and I also gave the analysis of a patient under supervision. This gave me much valuable background theory about emotional development in children, but it still gave me no answers for mothers. And there were no people for me to ask. No other pediatricians had taken the training I had. Child psychiatrists and child analysts were preoccupied with the treatment of major neuroses, not with the common problems of feeding and toilet-training. Every day in the office I gave the best advice I could figure out, on the basis of theory. Then, on the baby's next visit, I would eagerly ask the mother how the advice had worked out. It was a slow, anxious process.

After five years of pediatric practice, an editor from Doubleday came to my office to ask me to write a book for parents. This was not because I was known. In fact, I was unknown and having great difficulty making a living for my wife and first child in those Depression days. But any publisher making inquiries in New York's medical schools would find that I was the only pediatrician with psychiatric and psychoanalytic training. Without hesitation I said, "I don't know enough." After five more years of practice, in 1943, an editor from Pocket Books came to my office. He said jokingly, and without much logic, that the book they wanted would not need to be very good because, at twenty-five cents a copy, they could sell tens of thousands. Now I felt more confident about my advice. The prospect of helping tens of thousands of families appealed to the do-gooder in me.

Baby and Child Care sold three-quarters of a million copies during its first year. It appealed to parents not only because it encouraged respect and kindliness toward children but because, unlike previous books, which tended to be condescending and authoritarian, it bent over backward to be friendly toward parents. A typical fan letter would say, "It sounds as if you are talking to me and as if you think I'm a sensible person."

The new approach of the book and its popularity promptly brought invitations to join various research and teaching centers. For four years, I worked at the Rochester (Minnesota) Child Health Project which, supported by the Mayo Clinic, was trying to develop a preventive program in physical and emotional health for all the children of the town. Next I organized a program in child psychiatry and child development at the University of Pittsburgh Medical School. The last twelve years of my teaching career were at Western Reserve Medical School in Cleveland, where the curriculum was being revolutionized. Each first-year student was given the responsibility of being the medical contact between one family with a new baby and the medical center. It was an effort, very successful, to prevent the depersonalization of the future physician. Depersonalization occurs so often in the traditional curriculum where the student takes only laboratory courses for the first two formative years. I had wanted for many years to participate in such an experiment, believing that two keys to excellence in all medical education are giving students responsibility, and encouraging them to focus on their emotional relationship with the people they are training to deal with.

I reached retirement age at Western Reserve in 1967. But back in the late 1950s, I had received two invitations to join the National Committee for a Sane Nuclear Policy. At that time it was primarily concerned with the need for a nuclear test ban treaty with the Soviet Union. I had declined because I knew nothing about radiation and because I wanted to be a reassurer of parents, not an alarmer. Nevertheless, I was approached a third time, in 1962, and my conscience was touched. I had to admit that if we didn't have a treaty, while more and more nations tested more and more weapons, more and more children around the world would die of cancer and leukemia or be born with physical and mental defects. It was a pediatric issue. I joined the National Committee for a Sane Nuclear Policy and became a spokesman for the disarmament movement. I also fought against our government's increasing involvement in Vietnam—arms, money, and "military advisors." In 1964, I was asked by Lyndon Johnson's campaign committee to support the President on radio and television because he had declared that he would not send Americans to fight in an Asian war. I agreed readily; and I did enough so that Johnson called me a couple of days after the election to thank me and added, "Dr. Spock, I hope I prove worthy of your trust." He waited only three months to prove that by bombing North Vietnam and starting the buildup of fighting troops that eventually reached half a million men, he didn't deserve the trust of anyone who voted for him as a peace candidate. I was alarmed and outraged at Johnson's betrayal, and I quadrupled my antiwar activities.

So, on retirement in 1967, I went from being a professor to being a full-time political activist. When I was not on vacation, I was on the road six days a week, speaking mainly at universities and colleges, at the invitation of the undergraduates. I often made five appearances a day.

It was soul satisfying to be expressing my deepest convictions about peace and justice to audiences ready to agree. The students who came, and particularly the members of the committee who had invited me and escorted me, were not only interested in ending the war, they were also interested in such issues as civil rights, reform of the university, an end to imperialism, and a lessening of both materialism and competitiveness. I learned from them and I was inspired by them, especially when they spoke of the desirability of going to work in the spirit of cooperation and brotherly love instead of dog-eat-dog competition, of living simply instead of ostentatiously.

In 1968, much to my surprise, I found myself, along with four other people including the chaplain of Yale University, William Sloane Coffin, indicted by Johnson's Department of Justice on the charge of conspiracy to counsel, aid, and abet resistance to the military draft. We were tried, convicted, and sentenced to two years in jail. We were not allowed by the judge to present our defense: that the war in Vietnam was unconstitutional, illegal, a crime against the peace, and full of war crimes; and that, according to the Nuremberg principle, anyone holding these views is not only permitted but obligated to refuse to obey orders in such a war. The indictment and trial were intended to intimidate us and other opponents of the war. But its effect on me was to intensify my indignation. (The Court of Appeals reversed the decision a year later.)

At first, as an excessively law-abiding person, I shuddered at the thought of civil disobedience. Nevertheless, with the example of others, especially the Berrigan brothers, I got up my courage and found that while it was uncomfortable to spend a night in jail, it was not humiliating or lethal. So I spent several other nights in jail. It certainly paid off in media attention.

In those eight years of speaking in colleges and feeling the warmth and approval of the students, my personality became much more outgoing and affectionate. Instead of picking my words cautiously, I learned to say what was in my head—or in my heart—and it made more sense. I changed my politics and came to see that political activity is an essential part in the solution of our problems.

It was by becoming involved in opposition to the war in Vietnam that I became convinced that the United States is an imperialist nation, that our government responds to the desires of industry more than to the needs of our people (because industry pays most of the election bills), and that the Democratic party fails us almost as much as the Republican. So I became a socialist and helped to organize the People's party in 1971 out of a dozen small local independent parties. At the conventions every conceivable liberal and radical point of view on every issue was argued vehemently. This was educational for me. I was nominated for President in 1972 and for Vice-President in 1976.

Though there was evidence that gradually more citizens, congressmen, and senators were coming into opposition to the Vietnam War, there was also enough backsliding to keep us frustrated. Then suddenly, unexpectedly, Johnson withdrew as a candidate in 1968. It seemed like a great victory for us. Unfortunately, he insisted that Humphrey continue the war policy that had ruined his own presidency, and Humphrey obeyed. And, also unfortunately, Nixon, who won the election on his pledge to find a quick and honorable ending, found neither a quick nor an honorable solution.

It was a blow to me that, when American troops were finally withdrawn in 1973, young Americans stopped protesting against anything, for I had hoped that a permanent shift toward idealism had occurred. For a couple of years I comforted myself that they were only waiting for a suitable cause and for inspiring leadership. But the retreat toward a preoccupation with grades and a good job continued.

For several years my only invitations to speak came from university departments of child development and child welfare organizations. Then came the protests against nuclear power into which I entered with conviction. The election of Ronald Reagan in 1980, with his frightening beliefs in rapid and endless escalation of the arms race, in the "winnability" of nuclear war, and in the USSR as being "the source of all evil in the world," caused the disarmament movement to become active again. I eagerly participated in it.

I still believe that humanity is potentially loving, idealistic, and creative, but also potentially vicious, that what makes the difference is how children are raised and how societies are led. Perhaps our species' ingenuity that produced nuclear weapons is incompatible with our species' readiness to believe that it is always the other nation that harbors all the aggression. Perhaps we are doomed to extinction like the dinosaurs, as no longer adaptive. But I will continue to work for peace and justice and love until I keel over or am annihilated with all the rest.

Edward Teller
b. 1908

The physicist with the famous beetle brow and the deep voice with accents of his native Hungary achieved fame in the years following World War II for his contributions to quantum mechanics and hydrogen bomb technology. In recent decades he has become known to a generation for his staunch advocacy of United States defense policy.

Dr. Teller immigrated to the United States in 1935, taught for several years, and then joined the Manhattan Project in the development of the first atomic bomb. In 1949, after spending three years at the University of Chicago, he became assistant director of Los Alamos Scientific Laboratory. In the fifties he was associated with the new Lawrence Livermore Laboratory in California, becoming its associate director in 1960, the same year that saw his return to academic life as a university professor at the nearby University of California in Berkeley; he held both positions until his retirement in 1975. Since that time he has been a senior research fellow at the Hoover Insti-

tution and a consultant at Livermore Laboratory. He has served on the General Advisory Committee of the United States Atomic Energy Commission and the White House Science Council.

Though still a controversial figure to many—in particular those involved in peace and disarmament movements—Dr. Teller has nevertheless been widely and variously honored for his work. The numerous awards and honorary degrees bestowed upon him include the National Medal of Science, the Enrico Fermi Medal, and the Albert Einstein Award. His interest in the peaceful uses of nuclear energy has been expressed in such books as Nuclear Energy in the Developing World *(1977) and* Energy From Heaven and Earth *(1979).*

I like activity. In fact, I believe that there is no other way in which to enjoy life in a consistent manner.

I hate doubt, and yet I am certain that doubt is the only way to approach anything worth believing in.

I believe in good. It is an ephemeral and elusive quality. It is the center of my beliefs, but it cannot be strengthened by talking about it.

I believe in evil. It is the property of all those who are certain of truth. Despair and fanaticism, historically sources of incredible destructiveness, are only differing manifestations of evil.

I believe in excellence. It is a basic need of every human soul. All of us can be excellent because, fortunately, we are exceedingly diverse in our ambitions and talents.

I consider life a miracle. My desire for logical consistency rebels against miracles. Yet I cannot, nor would I, deny the miracle of life.

I know that an understanding of life may require an even greater miracle than the creation of life itself. Yet miracles can only be recognized when they happen. Wishing for them does little good. I am forced to reject the present explanations of life, on scientific, religious, or any other grounds. Obviously, I do not claim to understand life. I can only attempt to remain responsive in a flexible manner to its various manifestations.

To be alive implies complication, and the most complex of all systems are those composed of aggregates of human beings. I believe that some laws are necessary for people to live together. These laws contribute most when they are few and carefully thought out.

The life of the spirit is made possible only by the knowledge of imperfection. To perceive imperfection in others is easy but sometimes mistaken. To recognize imperfection in oneself is obviously difficult, but this ability is the important part of one's relationship to perfection. It is difficult for imperfection to serve as the basis of collaboration between people. Yet, as the story of the democracies shows, acknowledged imperfection can be a remarkably solid foundation for human cooperation.

I am a Jew. Throughout the years I was growing up, Hungary had a great deal of anti-Semitic feeling. Much Jewish philosophy was criticized, and as a high school student, I asked my grandfather why Jews taught "an eye for an eye."

My grandfather pointed out, "The law in question does not command one to respond to an injury. It is better not to seek revenge. But this law says that one must never take more than an eye for an eye or a tooth for a tooth. Anger is a human response, and not everyone can be a saint. The man who has just had his tooth knocked out may be very angry. However, the teaching forbids ever returning more damage than was received. And this everyone can obey." A law that cannot be obeyed by most of us humans is no law.

I also remember an instruction from my father who was a lawyer. When I was a child, he taught me a Latin sentence that he said was the basis of all good laws and good government: *audiatur et altera pars*, let the other side be heard. I believe that my father's statement was correct. Concerted human action—which is called politics—is full of immense, far-reaching tragedies that have damaged the lives of everyone on the planet. Most would have been avoided had this instruction been commonly heeded.

I was born in Hungary. I knew when I was young that Hungary would fall victim either to fascism or communism. I did not know that my homeland would fall victim to both.

I have spent the longest part of my life in the United States, the land of imperfection. I immeasurably prefer it to Hungary's neighbor,

Russia, the land of age-old belief in perfection. With minor short-lived exceptions, doubt has never been permissible there. The dictatorial imposition of "truth" has led and continues to lead to incredible cruelties.

In my early youth toward the beginning of the century, the following distinctions were used to characterize four nations:

In England, everything is permitted except a few things that are forbidden.

In Prussia, everything is forbidden except a few things that are permitted.

In Austria-Hungary (where I lived), everything that is forbidden is permitted.

In Russia, everything that is not forbidden is obligatory.

During my lifetime, little in this regard has changed in the last-named country. I am grateful that I have been able to live where my beliefs and actions could be consonant.

The life of the spirit, although it is less visible than the physical world, is even more actual. Here are some examples:

Three years before I was born, the theory of relativity was published. This set in motion a radical change in the physical sciences. The development of quantum mechanics during my young years changed the scientific description of the world from one of mechanical determinism to one in which even the behavior of atoms could not be completely predicted. Atoms were found to be, in some respects, as unpredictable as we imagine ourselves to be.

This understanding of the nature of the world is in harmony with my beliefs. Paradoxes are very real. A single perspective seldom provides reliable understanding. The most permanently pleasurable experiences of my youth consisted of getting acquainted with these unexpected insights.

Whether my beliefs spring from these ideas or are independent of them, I cannot say. In both the physical and the social world, the perception that complementary, seemingly contradictory visions must be acknowledged in order to approach a real solution seems to be borne out with extraordinary consistency.

For years, I worked on science for the reward of understanding, and I nurtured and enjoyed the greater reward of friendships that arise from the common pursuit of understanding. But by the end of the 1930s, science could no longer be separated from technology and from all the problems and solutions that flow from technology. Eventually, this led to conflict over whether it is permissible to pursue understanding beyond the limits where understanding has only predictable and desirable consequences.

Reaching a decision on this question caused painful, difficult doubts. Later events have continued to reinforce the decision that I reached: the possibilities inherent in the laws of nature must be pursued to their resolution. Self-imposed ignorance is even less likely to have predictable, desirable consequences.

I believe that no limits are set to human knowledge; that knowledge leads to power; that power, when it is equally shared among large numbers of people, can be used to benefit everyone. To believe more seems to me foolish; to believe less seems cowardly.

The one great conflict in my life arose when I was in my early forties. The question was whether a hydrogen bomb should be built. The view I held gained political ascendancy, and I played a significant role in the scientific effort that produced the first thermonuclear reaction on earth.

My action was motivated by a firm belief that we must not recoil from knowledge and its fruits. It was also motivated by my opinion that the Russians would proceed with this development regardless of whether we progressed or held back. My guess was verified as correct by a Soviet success almost simultaneous to ours and by Andrei Sakharov's statement in 1974 that the Soviet project began in the summer of 1948, more than a year before work was authorized in the United States.

In the country of imperfection, I believe that knowledge can be used for positive purposes. I believe that the strength that has flowed from the pursuit of knowledge has helped doubt and imperfection to survive in the face of those so certain of truth that for them no other values can exist.

Because of my beliefs in action, I have obtained what I did not desire and lost one of my great joys. I gained a dubious form of fame. Once, on a television show, seconds before the end of the broadcast, an unexpected question was put to me: "How do you want to be remembered?" My prompt and honest answer was and remains: "I do not want to be remembered." As a result of acting on my beliefs, I lost what I wished to retain: friendly fellowship with many of my fellow scientists. The merits of the friendships I retained with people who do not quarrel over a belief lead me to suspect that I may have gained in friendship more than I lost.

While the price has not been small, I suspect that it has been a lesser cost than having to acknowledge that I lacked sufficient courage to speak my beliefs honestly. With one exception in 1945, I have not denied my beliefs and understandings. I continue to regret that at that time I allowed myself to be dissuaded from supporting and circulating a petition asking President Truman to demonstrate the atomic bomb, by exploding it harmlessly high above Tokyo, before using the bomb. As it turned out, a demonstration probably would have been sufficient to end the war. Had that occurred, today we would be more reasonable and secure.

I detest pride, but I still tend to be proud of one accomplishment. I helped start a laboratory that continues to work on the one worthwhile contemporary issue: the prolongation of the insecure freedom that is the hallmark of Western civilization. In the last few years, my young friends, the scientists in the Lawrence Livermore National Laboratory, have concentrated their work on developing protective defenses against nuclear weapons. I could have no greater satisfaction in my life than that belief and action would meet in this enterprise, so sorely needed to produce increased security and a greater opportunity for peace.

I firmly believe that each of us has a duty to live and eventually has the right to die. I believe that death is an end more nearly perfect than the deepest sleep. This is not in contradiction to Jewish tenets. They do not postulate death as the beginning of perfect happiness. I believe, as I wrote in my diary when I was a sixteen-year-old in Hungary, that without death, life would be unbearable.

I believe that people use logic painfully and sparingly. Logic in humans seems a paradox to me. It is both a perversity and one of the most precious human gifts. It is a perversity because it is rare and painful. It is a gift because of its consequences—for example, the brilliance of mathematics.

Logic is the link between physical and spiritual life, and its use makes both possible. Without logic, all spiritual life would resemble chaos. Nevertheless, in our actions, and even in our thoughts, we are guided much less by logic than by our much more ancient biological processes.

I believe that the preservation of peace and the improvement of the lot of all people requires faith in the rationality of human beings. If we have this faith and pursue understanding, we have at least the possibility of success. Total security has never been available to anyone. To expect it is unrealistic; to imagine that it can exist is to invite disaster.

I believe that the most important aim for humanity at present is to avoid war, dictatorship, and their awful consequences. Survival is not simply the fact that some people will continue to live on earth. That much I consider a certainty for the foreseeable future. Survival of humanity must also include the survival of human dignity.

I believe that no endeavor that is worthwhile is simple in prospect. If it is right, it will be simple in retrospect. Belief in action will accomplish that which does not exist but which in the future will be taken for granted.

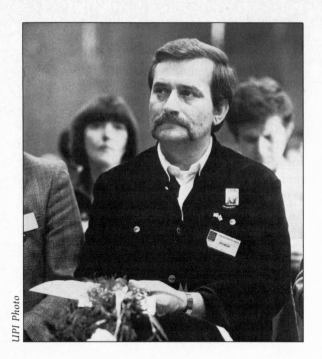

UPI Photo

Lech Walesa
b. 1943

"The heart and soul of Poland's battle with a corrupt Communist regime" and "an international symbol of the struggle for freedom and dignity" were the phrases used by Time *magazine to introduce Lech Walesa, their Man of the Year for 1981. A year earlier, he was an unknown electrician working in the shipyards of the gray Baltic seaport of Gdansk. A year later, he would be the recipient of the Nobel Peace Prize. In the span of time between, he founded the Solidarity labor union, spent almost a year in detention, and taught the world a lesson in courage.*

A staunch Roman Catholic who takes daily communion, he believes he has a God-given mission of leadership to fulfill. A man of the working class who defiantly claimed that he never read a serious book in his life, his inspirational speeches, spoken in rough, often ungrammatical, Polish demonstrate his knack for reducing complex issues to simple words and images intelligible to the common man and woman.

Since the state banned Solidarity under martial law, Walesa has been officially described as a "private person." However, unlike other private persons, he is followed everywhere he goes by the police. He was not permitted to travel to Oslo to hear the Norwegian Nobel Committee characterize him as "an exponent of the active longing for peace and freedom which exists unconquered in all the peoples of the world." Despite the restrictions and danger, he has no intention of fleeing Poland. It is there he intends to continue the struggle.

Faith is the sole meaning of my life. I am not a devotee, but if I did not believe in the Creator and in all that we profess in our Christian credo, then all that I am would be meaningless and pointless. I would be nothing. All that I do I do because I have faith. That does not mean that I am a saint; just as every human, I make mistakes, many mistakes.

People often ask me: What do you really believe? What is the basis of your faith and what are your deepest convictions? Who is God to you? I was brought into the faith like every child. I suckled it with my mother's milk. Yet I was often a delinquent worshiper in my youth. I pondered upon God's existence and looked for signs to confirm Him, but faith did not grow in me until life grew harder. The more difficult my path became, the closer I came to the faith.

Faith provides me with breathing space, with a respite. Agnostics think my faith provides me with an excuse not to accept responsibility for final outcomes, while religious people think that the presence of someone above assists me, allows me to pray and ponder. As for myself, I simply believe in Providence. I believe that I am here to execute the verdicts of Providence. This is precisely why I can accomplish significantly more than if I were just Lech Walesa, without God directing my fate. It's good to have the awareness of that great force outside us and above us directing our lives. It's somewhat hard for me to understand agnostics. In my opinion, no one is without some kind of faith. I think that everyone, in his or her own way, believes in something. Of course, the hierarchy of values may differ. Each person's belief and, accordingly, faith, is a little bit different, just as each one of us is different and goes through various, distinct experiences.

Of all the people around me when I grew up, my mother was the most religious. She was religious in an honest, down to earth, wise way. From her I inherited the Cult of the Holy Mother.* She looked upon the Holy Mother as her own model. Her greatest longing was to get to Czestochowa, although she never succeeded.† But I have made this dream of hers come true in my own life; often, you can find me on the Jasna Gora. You might say that the Cult of the Holy Mother is innate in me.

I would have accomplished nothing if I did not have faith. At the same time, I know that there can be no certainties in matters concerning God. If God had given us that, equipped us with the ability to answer all our spiritual questions, we would have lost our free will. Yet the faith, the belief in God, is also the choice of our will. This is the reason why all my doubts and reflections—different, at different stages of my life, and multidirectional—have led me to conclude that a human being who is by definition limited in time, cannot grasp and perceive something that is infinite. We humans are born into this world and die without having much to say about it. Therefore, if God, the highest power, is limitless, then human beings, limited by the nature of their dimensions, are incapable of penetrating and understanding God's mysteries.

I therefore think it's best to build one's convictions by focusing on small issues. If our goal is to comprehend the mysteries of heaven and hell, let's first try to understand the essence of our basic duties as humans. By following these duties and our own sense of human dignity, we'll gain an understanding of reward and punishment in proper time. Now it is my turn to explain to each of my children, when the time arrives, who is God. I will say to them that God is someone who wants the child to try to do good and to act in accordance with honesty and truth. I will also tell my children to keep in

---

*The Poles worship the Holy Mother, literally the Mother of God, rather than the Virgin Mary.

†The town of Czestochowa is famous for the ancient icon of "The Holy Mother of Czestochowa," said to be endowed with miraculous healing powers. The church and the adjacent monastery containing this icon are located just outside the town, on a mountain called Jasna Gora, "The Bright Mountain."

mind that God will always see them and that no one can deceive that being that we call God.

I have met many priests, bishops, and even the Pope. Through these encounters, and through my participation in the life of my people, in their religion and faith, I have come to see how very much each of them is needed just where they are. Sometimes a person is put to a greater advantage, sometimes to a lesser; some have more talents, some less. On my path, I have encountered some wonderful, brave, great people who astounded me with their deductive powers. I have also met people less gifted, yet each and every one of them is necessary in their own position. It is not just me who needs these people. It is our cause as a whole, all our nation, who needs these people, their gifts and talents.

Sometimes I think of a priest who, many years ago, predicted that if I did not change my ways I would spend my life in prison. He was my religion teacher, and up to this day I do not know whether or not he was right. He taught me in the first few grades of grammar school and kept track of my development. He was aware of my hypersensitivity to truth, my desire to have it revealed no matter what the price may be. If I believed that something was one way and not another, I'd always do all that I could to have the truth surface, no matter who was hiding it or trying to obscure it. I wasn't obstinant once someone would prove me wrong, but if there was no such proof, then I would demand an acknowledgment that I was right—and would always proclaim so loudly. That is the kind of incident that transpired between that priest and myself. I had always respected him deeply, and still do, even though he is no longer alive. Once in his class, when I was right, I became stubborn and insisted that he admit that in front of my classmates. Maybe he was short on time, or maybe he didn't want to voice that truth out loud, but years later he admitted to me that I was right and once again repeated to me that people like myself end up in prison. Therefore, I think that my character was and still is a little bit warped whenever truth is at stake; it's something I just won't compromise, no matter what.

And yet, one should try to select moments that are appropriate for seeking or exposing the truth. One should consider: maybe not today, maybe tomorrow, maybe under different circumstances. Even today, it is hard for me to accept this. I wish that truth, no matter what the circumstances, could be revealed and righted in the public consciousness as fast as possible. Maybe that is a flaw in my character. And lately I wonder more and more if perhaps that priest wasn't right, especially now that I have spent time in prison. Perhaps I shouldn't have insisted on the truth right then and there. Maybe I should have approached him during the break and made myself content with a private acknowledgment that I was right, just between the two of us, whispered, so to speak, into my ear. Perhaps I should have weighed and considered what impact this small revelation of truth would have upon the rest of my classmates. Would they be indifferent? Would it have a good or evil influence on them? Certainly it would have been wrong if it led to someone's unjust humiliation. And yet I believe that the truth liberates more often than it does not.

After the events that led to the emergence of Solidarity in August 1980, as I grew progressively more popular, photographers began to take pictures of me in very private, personal situations—for example, during prayer or while taking the sacraments. But I got used to this visibility. It no longer bothers me. I am able to concentrate on those things that are most important to me at any particular moment. When in church, I am focused on God; during interviews, on the things I tell reporters; in the dockyard, upon the accumulator cart that I must repair. I am not playing a role. I go to the church to pray. It is totally unimportant to me if there are cameras clicking and lights flashing.

Many times, people have accused me of putting my faith on display. Others accuse me of misusing the rosary. But this is not so. Never have I done it for show, to please the public eye. Fate itself placed me in situations in which I could not have acted any differently than I did. Look, for example, at the rosary that was put on my neck during the first Sacred Mass of the strike. Some woman put it there. I couldn't have taken it off; as a matter of fact, it never occurred to me. Apparently, its true place was on my neck. Something similar happened in the final stage of the strike. A group of pilgrims from Gdansk, upon their return from Jasna Gora, brought me a button with the image of the Holy Mother, a button that was specially sanctified and blessed by Cardinal Wyszynski. They pinned this button on my lapel. I couldn't possibly remove it either. First of all, being religious, I didn't want to remove the Holy Mother. Secondly, all this was happening in public. The removal of this kind of sacred object in public would have been perceived as the denial of a symbol that is particularly dear to all Poles. I do not see this event as an indication that I must always wear this little sign. But I simply could not take it off. From that time on the increased trust of the people can be dated. I had no influence on these events—I was but a tool to help them materialize—and therefore both the Holy Mother and the rosary carry a symbolic value for me. I am glad that somebody put me into such circumstances, but I also know that I could not have acted any differently.

There are many matters I cannot comprehend, perhaps was not meant to comprehend. For example, people who knew me prior to the events of August 1980 remember well that I was incapable of saying anything in public. My tongue used to outrun my mind. I was unable to keep track of the words I said. I would always speak before I thought and was therefore a poor public speaker. Come August, things changed. I don't know how it happened. The agnostics would probably interpret it as necessity, as something I was forced to do by the flow of events. But it was from that moment that I started to speak publicly, and from that moment that I have been able to speak publicly—if there is a need—in any situation. Something occurred, which I do not comprehend.

Still other things remain mysterious. Precisely four years before the tragic death of Father Jerzy Popieluszko, Father Tischner expressed the following idea during his sermon in the Wawel Cathedral: *

> What is the meaning of this old and yet new word "solidarity"? What is its call and challenge? What memories does it bring up? In order to give a more precise definition of the word "solidarity" we should probably turn to the gospel and search there for its source. Saint Paul speaks of its meaning as "carrying each other's burdens and in so doing you will fulfill God's word and live by it." What does it mean to be in Solidarity? It means to carry your fellow's burden. No man is an island. We are all united, even when we do not know it. We are connected by the land, we are connected by flesh and blood, by our work and by language. Yet we're not always aware of these ties. When solidarity is born the consciousness awakens, the speech and the word arise; then all that was concealed becomes visible. Our interconnectedness becomes all obvious. This is the time when one man carries upon his shoulders his fellow's burden. Solidarity speaks, calls, shouts, summons, makes sacrifices. That is when the other's burden often becomes more heavy than one's own.

* Wawal is the traditional seat and palace of the Polish monarchs.

In December 1984, Father Popieluszko died. His was the death of a martyr. If one could say that someone had the gift of saintliness, they would say it about him. In spite of all his organizational abilities, in spite of the depth and keenness of his mind, he did not really care about himself. He handed down to us the wisdom of the faith, which he had implemented into action and into the sacrifice of his own life. During his funeral, I unknowingly referred to the same issues spoken four years earlier at Wawal. Here is what I wrote:

> The victim of this crime pleads, demands, binds. The victim of this crime pleads and demands for today, pleads, demands, and binds us for tomorrow. According to the teaching, and following all that he had preached, we know today: he pleads and he demands that we bring forth all that has remained from his own lesson.

When I was writing up the text of this farewell to Father Popieluszko, a time when the burden of his death was truly greater than our own, I had no recollection of the things said in Wawal. The words of farewell I have just mentioned came to me at the last moment; I added them on to the already finished text. I do not know how it happened. Today, I am truly amazed by the way they resonate with each other. This episode reinforces my conviction that there are things and matters in this world that the human mind cannot fully comprehend.

I have never signed a private contract with the Lord. I didn't do it in September 1980, when I assumed the responsibilities of Solidarity's chairman, nor did I do it in December 1981, when I was confined to my quarters. Naturally, like any religious person, I would like to fulfill that which is written in my lot; even more than that, I'd like to be able to read my lot. That's what I pray for. That's what I want to be able to do. And yet I know that I make mistakes, that I read poorly and realize things awkwardly.

I am convinced that my faith had a powerful impact upon me during the time of my confinement. My belief in Providence, in its logic, was strengthened then. I have faith in the superior force that reigns over all this. If something doesn't work out for me, it only means that I must be either too weak or too simple-minded or that it had to be that way because of the superior force. Deep religious belief, deep faith, eliminates fear. If it were my fate to be deported, I couldn't have changed the roadmap of my life. This does not imply that I should put my head underneath a tram or become careless. My duty is to try to solve problems, avoiding whatever is unnecessary. If then, in spite of all attempts, things do not turn out as I hope, it only means that that is exactly the way it was supposed to be. This is my philosophy of life.

I can never be certain that I won't make some major error, that my belief and faith will shelter me from that. I am not at all convinced that what I do today will be considered good or worthwhile in one hundred years or even tomorrow. Maybe the order will reverse and what we see today as bad will be considered excellent in the future. God, our Lord, distinguishes each one of us from all the others; he assigned a task for every person. I fall into this category, too, but I do not believe that I was chosen for some special reason. I am too small, too much a nothing, to even begin to suspect that I am a man of Providence.

During the first national congress of Solidarity, a holy Mass was conducted every morning in the hall of congress. I'm not sure if everyone understood what was going on in there, especially the foreign reporters. But for us the goal was clear: through prayer, we sought to keep in mind the moral and spiritual principles upon which the congress was founded. And the congress held up well under the many threats and obstacles because we were closely linked by basic values. The basic closeness and connectedness kept us from making major errors. We had to have a lot of valor and discretion in order to conduct the congress properly, in order to avoid being split up and consequently crushed. Were this basic moral and spiritual component absent, had we not daily contemplated, pondered our higher purposes, exercised self-restraint, things would have been very bad indeed. This is why everything had to be just as it was. Still, we made several errors, a thing practically inevitable in our crash course in Democracy. But we stayed with the principles that were brought up during our morning masses. We carried in our minds the things we spoke of in the morning, and did our best to act accordingly. As for myself, the prayer kept me grounded and in focus; it gave me strength and kept me from losing my common sense. The same held true for others. It could not have been otherwise. Had we not obtained such things from prayer, I do not know what the situation would be today. I cannot even imagine it.

If you look back now at the congress, at the short time we had from August 1980 until the time when we were wiped out, you will see how quickly we were learning. We wanted very much to act in good will and in wisdom (at least the majority of us did). The outcome was the way it was and probably could not have been better. Naturally, if we were better prepared, then things would have been different (but I don't like discussing what-ifs). Yet already today I see that our consciousness is changing. We continue to learn in more difficult situations, and are still learning fast.

This doesn't mean that everything is already just fine. Our personal individual morality, our social morality, all still leave much to be desired. The same holds true regarding leading our lives according to the values we believe in. Yet it is hard to demand and to expect an overnight change in our society after it has been programmed and directed in certain ways for over forty years. It is hard to expect that every person would instantaneously become a human being in the full sense of the word, and society become a society in the full sense. We need continuous reflections on ourselves; we need examples, including negative examples, in order to draw conclusions for the lesson. In many interviews I have tried to point out that no one will go far if one won't stop every so often, look behind, see what one leaves behind; are these by any chance just smoldering ruins? Even a mason has to stop and look behind, to see what he has built; is his wall straight or is it bent and crooked? All of us, as individuals, as a society, as well as Solidarity, need this kind of pondering and reflection. What are we constructing? How do we influence our surroundings? What are we leaving around us? Everyone needs this kind of reflection, even in the weekly rhythm of life. Sunday plays a major role in this weekly rhythm—a day for balancing with oneself and God. This involves not just personal matters, but also the life of the family and society. If this could be instituted, many people would not commit as many mistakes as they actually do. Much could be rectified. We should do something to convert Sunday into a special day, a day for clearing the accounts of life, for thinking things over, for turning from an ill-chosen path.

The actual transformation of our convictions and beliefs into action is a difficult path. The thing that lies at the foundation of positive change, the way I see it, is service to a fellow human being. We made some mistakes with our union and they cannot be undone. But there is precisely one error that we did not make; we adopted a position of service and reminded many people what the basis and essence of such an attitude is. And this is still the way things are. I am in service. I attempt to be in service to all those who need it. I will be in service to them as long as they want it. This is the basic principle and essence of my mandate as chairman of Solidarity.

Rob Lewine

Irving Wallace
b. 1916

Having sold almost two hundred million books, Irving Wallace is one of the most widely read contemporary authors in the world. After many journeyman years writing for magazines and films, and a few moderately successful books of nonfiction, Mr. Wallace produced The Chapman Report *in 1960, a novel dealing with the impact of a sex survey on the lives of suburban women. It became the turning point of his career, catapulting him from an existence marked with struggle to a life characterized by, in his words, "complete financial independence so that I could continue to write books for the rest of my life."*

Since then, Mr. Wallace has enjoyed enormous popularity; his novels, their brief titles characteristically beginning with "The," include The Prize *(1962),* The Plot *(1967),* The Word *(1972), and* The Miracle *(1984). In between novels, he has continued to write nonfiction as well as edit with his children, David and Amy, such successful books as* The People's Almanac *(1975) and* The Book of Lists *(1977).*

Over the years the gripping and complex plots and the timely and

provocative themes that characterize the books of Irving Wallace have
varied widely. Nevertheless, the body of the work is directly linked
to what he has identified as "my desire to listen, to let imagination
run wild, and then to write." He loves to tell stories, to create people
and worlds half real, half imaginary, adding that "even if I could not
earn a penny from my writing, I would earn my livelihood at some-
thing else and continue to write at night."

I am a writer, mainly of novels, but also of biography and oddments
of history. Most authors believe that a novel should entertain, not
instruct. But I am one of those contemporary authors who, more often
than not, prefer to make a social statement in their story, to dramatize some belief that they hold dear, even hold passionately.

Central to my working life has been my strong belief in the power
of the written word, the importance of words to modify, persuade,
move, enlighten. As a youth, I was affected by the writings of Sten-
dhal, Tolstoy, Maugham. In turn, I have sought to affect others in
the same way—and sometimes have been gratified to learn, through
readers' written responses to such books as *The Three Sirens, The*
Man, The Seven Minutes, that my words have communicated useful
ideas and stimulated useful thoughts, thus influencing other people.

Believing, as I do, in honesty and openness in all sexual matters—
as one possibility of making life healthier and happier, and human
relationships better—I wrote *The Chapman Report,* which was published in 1960. As a result, I went through three major criminal ob-
scenity trials in West Germany and Italy, but was vindicated in each,
reinforcing my belief that justice does sometimes prevail.

I wrote *The Prize* to reveal something I hold true—the fallibility of
human institutions. But there was more. Since I believe that humans
should strive to fulfill their potentials and to achieve their goals, I
tried to reflect these feelings when my hero in this novel visits the
graves of two great poets in the Protestant cemetery in Rome and
reflects before the shaft marking Keats's burial site:

"Shelley and Keats. That day Craig felt an affinity for them, felt a sense of history as had they, felt that he was not one of the faceless of the world, the nonentities of time who come, stay briefly, and are blown away . . . forgotten and unremembered as the flying sands on a windswept beach. He, too, would leave a shaft on earth that would stand as long as men stood or could incline their heads before it. That day, in Rome, he knew strength and purpose, and he was filled with his uniqueness and his mission."

I wrote *The Three Sirens* about a fictional utopia in the South Seas to share my belief that other societies, foreign to us, less sophisticated, might have much to offer the west in the areas of child-rearing, love-making, law (even propounding my belief that our present jury system is inadequate, and that jurors should be trained and be members of a profession of their own).

I wrote *The Man* to dramatize the evils of racism. I made a black politician accidently become president of the United States to fill an unexpired term. At one point my fictional president tells a press conference:

"If a newborn child has a dominant gene that will cause the production of excessive melanin, a dark pigment, he will be black on the outside. If he has an unseeable gene that produces hardly any melanin, he will be some shade of white. And so what a Negro is comes down to no more than a slight shake and blend of genes, like tiny dice rolling out of the past, and when the shake is done, one goes before the world as a black-skinned individual or a white-skinned one, and that's it for life. And because of this luck of genes, a man or woman comes forth a Negro, a human being labeled for the rest of his days as inferior."

Just as I made a statement about peace and nuclear disarmament in *The Plot*, I wrote about my belief in freedom of expression and against censorship in *The Seven Minutes*. Aside from believing that those who choose to avoid reading, seeing, or hearing what they find objectionable should in some way be protected, I do not believe in any kind of overall censorship. After all, as Juvenal wondered, "Who shall stand guard to the guards themselves?" It was George Bernard Shaw who reminded us that the ultimate in censorship is assassination. It was Stanislaus Lec who assured us that burning stakes do not lighten the darkness. At the end of *The Seven Minutes*, I have my protagonist, defense attorney Mike Barrett, speak his thoughts—and my own—about what is or is not obscene in our lives:

"The real fight to be fought is not against writings about sexual intercourse or the use of four-letter words, but against obscenities like calling a black man 'nigger' or labeling a person you disagree with 'commie.' What is truly obscene is clubbing or persecuting a man because he is different from you or has different ideas, or forcing young boys to murder other young boys in distant countries in the name of self-defense, or as one preacher stated it, seeing 'a fully clothed man twitching and writhing as the shock of electricity applied by our state prison officials burns through his body.' What is really obscene is teaching students lies, promoting hypocrisy and dishonesty with a wink, making material goals a way of life, ignoring poverty in a land of plenty, condoning injustice and inequality while paying lip service to the Flag, the Founding Fathers, and the Constitution. Those are the obscenities that concern me."

Basically, I still stand behind that statement made in 1969, but with perhaps one modification. Fifteen years ago, I was totally against capital punishment. Today, I am ambivalent. I still hold that capital punishment is inhumane, but I think murder is also inhumane, and I can imagine certain circumstances where I might agree that an offender should suffer an eye for an eye.

I believe that man and woman, and all things living on planet earth, are not unique to our solar system. Possibly intelligent life may exist only on planet earth in our galaxy. But we know that there are countless galaxies, beyond our reach, and in these I believe there are numerous planets with intelligent forms of life, exceeding our own or lesser than ours, some that evolved ahead of our form of life (and may even have reached extinction) and others still in early forms of dynamic evolution.

I believe that we on planet earth, with the proliferation of nuclear weapons, are toying with extinction in the foreseeable future. No matter how much we freeze their production, no matter how much we disarm, the doomsday weapons will continue to exist. Once invented, they cannot be uninvented. I believe our options for survival depend on a continuity of sane and sensitive leadership in the leading nations on earth, or on scientific discoveries that will render nuclear weaponry useless, or on the establishment of a One World government (which I suspect is an unlikely reality).

I believe that people are born unequal, due to accidents of intelligence, physique, position, or place. People simply cannot be born and live as equals. Nevertheless, I do believe in equal opportunities for all, and this can be achieved.

After observing and reading about all the systems on earth by which

humans have governed one another, I believe that the system of cap-
italistic democracy or free enterprise as practiced in the United States
and Great Britain (ignoring the cosmetics of its monarchy) is to date
the best system possible. It is terribly imperfect, but the best seen so
far. Ideally, I would prefer a system employing individual incentive,
perhaps limited capitalism, with solid protection for less fortunate
persons in the areas of health, education, housing, sustenance. Or
perhaps a limited socialism would be better. I believe in individual
freedom circumscribed by laws subject to change and improvement. I
believe with William Allen White that liberty is the only thing you
cannot have—unless you are willing to give it to others.

I believe that human beings must band together to preserve the
beauties and benefits of nature and to sustain all forms of animal life.
I believe in the extended family as a means of making the young
more secure and ensuring that the old are treated with respect. I believe in laughter, in companionship, and above all in love, in the magic
and warmth of giving and receiving love.

I believe with Santayana that humans should know and be attentive
to their history in order to avoid repeating the mistakes of the past
and to progress. I believe in the goodness of most men and women,
despite the sufferings perpetrated by the criminal, the psychotic, and
the misfits of the species. I believe that certain human beings have
served as milestones in the story of human growth. I believe in personalities and achievements (while I am aware of the shortcomings
and frailties) of numerous historical figures, including some favorites
of mine like Socrates, Voltaire, Lincoln, Shelley, Tolstoy, Thoreau,
Freud, Frederick Douglass, Nehru, Kagawa, Upton Sinclair, Eleanor
Roosevelt.

Having said all this, it may be surprising to many readers that my
hopes and actions are in no way sustained by a belief in a personal
God or a transcendent principle. Like most of us, of course, I would
like to believe that my life has meaning in the history of the universe
and that there is a plan to it in which I have a part, but I simply am
unable to hold this view with rational dignity. In short, I believe in
nothingness. I believe that we came from nowhere, by some means
beyond our ability to understand. I believe that we go nowhere. I've
found my real sustenance through my work as a writer, through my
own family, and through my belief in elevating the condition of the
entire human family on earth. I believe that we are meant to make
the most of our time on earth—whether seeking survival, achieve-

ment, pleasure—and procreate to be sure that others of our species also have their turn on this wonderful planet.

Oh, I do believe that in the scheme of things there are mysteries—seemingly miraculous happenings, seeming wonders—which may or may never be explained. I do not believe that these happenings have to do with some superintelligent invisible force.

Despite my skepticism in this area, I am fascinated by organized religion and like to write seriously and evenhandedly about it, as I attempted to do in two of my novels, *The Word* and *The Miracle*. I am fascinated by all the evasive actions humans take against despair.

Yes, all that I believe is part of my life as a writer. But it is also part of my daily life, when I am not writing. I try to act out what I believe each and every day, yet it is almost impossible to do so completely. While I believe in total honesty with others, I cannot always be entirely honest with everyone, and must resort to some white lies in order not to hurt those I perceive to be vulnerable or weak. While I believe in sexual freedom, I had to overcome inhibitions incurred during my early years because I was a captive of my upbringing. As a result of that struggle, I attempted to preach what I had not always been able to practice to my son and daughter, and by my lights they have come out wonderfully well. While I believe in fairness and decency in all business matters, I am sure that I have rationalized cutting a few corners here and there. Nevertheless, at the core, I try to behave as I believe. I believe in thoughtfulness, kindness, courtesy, optimism. I believe in these virtues, but I'm afraid I don't always succeed in embodying them. But I try.

Have I been inconsistent in some of my beliefs? Possibly. But why not? It was Emerson who told us that consistency is the hobgoblin of little minds.

I probably would not have written this set of beliefs at twenty-seven or at thirty-seven, but now I am sixty-seven and this is what I believe.

Colin Wilson
b. 1931

At the age of twenty-four, with the publication of The Outsider (1956), this self-educated son of an English factory worker achieved instant and brilliant literary success. The Outsider set out to create a new and, what Wilson termed, "optimistic existentialism." In subsequent books he has explored various methods of achieving this visionary state, a state he has come to believe is a harbinger of evolutionary change. The books, which have been published in over fourteen languages, include scores of nonfiction works on philosophy, literature, parapsychology, music, and the occult, and more than a dozen novels and plays.

His work over the last thirty years has earned him a reputation as one of his country's most versatile and provocative writers. He has taken time from his writing to teach, including visiting professorships at the University of Washington and at Rutgers University.

He has said that his deepest interest is religion and his deepest

*need, to create his own religion. With his prodigious energy and for-
midable intellect, he seems amply equipped for this task.*

When I was about fourteen, I came upon a book called *I Believe*, a
symposium with contributions by Einstein, H. G. Wells, Lin Yutang,
and other well-known figures. It excited me tremendously—particularly the beginning of Wells's essay, in which he pointed out that we
change every cell in our bodies every seven years, and that therefore
the "self" of seven years ago is simply not the same person. One
Saturday afternoon I settled down with a lined notebook and began
to write down my own credo. I can now remember very little of it.
But looking at other essays I wrote at the time, I can reconstruct what
it probably said: Human beings seem to have an extraordinary capacity for being deluded by their emotions, so their "convictions" are
usually a mass of unexamined prejudices. Anyone who really wants
to get at the truth of things has to begin by dissecting every conviction about which he feels any strong emotion: patriotism, religion,
aggregate loyalties, personal loyalties, family ties, strong personal at-
tachments. And if he does that with total honesty, he would probably
be left in a kind of emotional desert. As I expressed it later: "Truth
is about as useful to human beings as bookcases would be to cows."

For several years I wrestled with a sense of total meaninglessness.
If I had read Sartre at the time, I would have agreed that "Man is a
useless passion." Yet it gradually began to dawn on me that I was
making a mistake in equating feeling and emotion. A feeling can often
be a direct, intuitive insight. There were the days when a sense of
excitement and anticipation would "snowball" until it seemed self-
evident that the universe was infinitely fascinating, and that boredom
and doubt were an illusion. The problem was that the insight had
always vanished by the following morning, and the sense of futility
was back. But at least I could see the essence of the problem quite
clearly. *Which was true?*—the feeling of futility—*vanitatum vani-
tas*—or the sense of infinite potentiality? When I read my favorite

romantic writers—Shelley, Hoffmann, Beddoes, Kleist, Yeats—I could see that they had confronted precisely the same problem: the moments of vision and ecstasy, then the rude awakening, and the descent back into the triviality of everyday life. Beddoes and Kleist had decided that the triviality had the last word, and that it would be better to commit suicide. I also decided to commit suicide one day when I was almost seventeen. I went to a night class in analytical chemistry with the intention of drinking potassium cyanide. As I reached for the bottle, I had a sudden clear vision of a horrible pain in my stomach, and I knew with total certainty that suicide was a stupidity. It was as if I had turned into two people: a self-pitying little idiot called Colin Wilson, and the real *me*, Colin Wilson, seemed such an irritating nonentity that I felt it could hardly matter if he killed himself. The trouble was that he would be killing *me* too. I experienced a kind of magnificent, overwhelming cheerfulness, and for the next few days I ceased to feel bored and frustrated.

So the answer to that basic question—the question Carlyle expressed as Eternal Yes or Eternal No—was Yes. Life was *not* basically trivial and futile. The affirmative vision was deeper and truer than the sense of futility. But that still left an equally difficult question: How could one *maintain* that affirmative vision?

It was, at least, the right question to ask. I looked for the answer in writers who had committed themselves to a thoroughgoing optimism or pessimism. The optimists included Goethe, Shaw, Chesterton, and Wells; the pessimists: Leopardi, James Thomson, Andreyev, and Artsybashev. A few major figures, like Tolstoy and Dostoevsky, had created masterpieces out of the conflict between the two. Dostoevsky seemed to me the greatest of all. I attempted my own analysis of the problem in a novel called *Ritual in the Dark*, but while that was being read by an obliging friend, the novelist Angus Wilson, I decided to write a critical book about the problem. *The Outsider* was sketched out on Christmas Day, 1954, a symbolic day for me, for I had always been fascinated by the sense of joy and affirmation a child experiences at Christmas. I was lucky. The book was accepted by the first publisher to whom I submitted an outline and specimen chapter. When it appeared a year later, it was an instant success and quite suddenly solved the problem that had occupied most of my attention until then: how to make a living?

The Outsider was a study in optimists and pessimists. It began with writers like Sartre, Camus, and the disillusioned Wells of *Mind at the*

End of Its Tether, proceeded to those who had attempted to struggle beyond pessimism—Hesse, Nietzsche, Dostoevsky (who, inevitably, had two chapters to himself)—and ended with figures who had achieved some kind of affirmation: William Blake, George Fox, Ramakrishna, Gurdjieff. The basic theme of the book was that the pessimists usually arrived at their negative conclusions by including some purely personal element—more often than not, self-pity—in their analysis. The result was the nineteenth-century cult of death worship, or the cult of failure in modern writers like Graham Greene and Samuel Beckett.

It was my fundamental conviction that this *is* a problem that is susceptible to intellectual analysis. In other words: Does life have a purpose, or is it basically meaningless? Is it of the same order as: Can we determine the internal constitution of the stars? I was aware that philosophers like Ayer and Ryle regarded it as a pseudo-question. They seemed to me merely short-sighted. Their type of philosophical analysis was based on the kind of scientific materialism that was popular in the nineteenth century and that was expressed most clearly in La Mettrie's *Man the Machine.* If man is *not* fundamentally a machine, a creature who can be explained entirely in mechanical and biological terms, then all forms of positivism are built on foundations of sand. Among modern philosophers, it seemed clear to me that Merleau-Ponty had refuted the mechanical view as decisively as Charles Renouvier refuted it in the nineteenth century. (It was Renouvier who saved William James from his crisis of despair with the formulation: "Free will is demonstrated by my ability to choose to think about one thing rather than another.")

In my second book, *Religion and the Rebel,* I tried to express the conclusions I drew from these assumptions in the following manner. Science began as an attempt to apply reason to the subject that seems most remote from man himself: the stars. Physics drew closer to the human reality; so did chemistry (alchemy). Biology and zoology came closer still. But in its early days, in the late eighteenth and early nineteenth century, psychology was not regarded as a science so much as a branch of philosophy or even theology. (Alexander Bain combined them in his *Mental and Moral Science.*) Only in the closing years of the nineteenth century did psychology begin to look like a science. The same thing applies to psychical research. The Society for Psychical Research was started by a group of thinkers who asked whether the study of paranormal phenomena might provide an answer to "the riddle of the Universe." Even half a century later, it looked as if that hope was totally unfounded. It was not until the late 1930s that psychical research began to look like a real science. Like psychology, it seemed *too* close to the existential reality of our experience. Yet with determined effort, we have, so to speak, succeeded in getting it at the end of our microscopes.

In the 1840s, Kierkegaard raised the basic existential question: "Where am I? Who am I? How did I come to be here? . . . Why was I not consulted? Where is the manager? I would like to see him." But according to Kierkegaard, there was no way in which this question could be scientifically examined; an "existential system" is impossible—except to God. Yet Kierkegaard contradicted himself by trying to subject the existential question to intellectual analysis. My own conviction that the "life question" could be subjected to the scientific methodology arose from my observation that the moments of "affirmative vision" always seemed to bring precisely the same insight, the sense of grasping the same *psychological reality*. It was like looking down on a city from the air and seeing the same pattern of streets. The problem was simply this: to try to achieve these "bird's eye states" as often as possible, and to use each one as an opportunity to try to sketch a small part of a street map.

It was, then, basically a problem of a search for a *method* of achieving the "bird's eye moments." Almost without exception, the mystics had insisted that it cannot be done—that they are ineffable. In 1958, I received a letter from an American professor of psychology, Abraham Maslow, who told me that his own psychology was based on the study of what he called "the peak experience"—those moments of sudden bubbling happiness. But Maslow also told me that he felt the "peak experiences" cannot be achieved at will; they come and go as they please, and any attempt to induce them is bound to be a failure.

Yet Maslow, like Kierkegaard, contradicted himself in one important respect. He said that when he talked to his students about PEs (peak experiences), they not only began to recall PEs they had experienced in the past but hardly noticed at the time (for we are inclined to take happiness for granted) but as soon as they began to think and talk about PEs, they began having them all the time. So thinking and talking about them was one method of inducing the "bird's eye moments."

Why are they so difficult to achieve? My own answer was as follows: We all possess a kind of subconscious valet who does things for us. So I learn to type, or to drive a car, or to speak a foreign language, painfully and slowly. Then this robot-valet takes over and does the job much more quickly and efficiently than I could do it consciously. The trouble with this robot is that he is too damned efficient. He not only does the things I want him to do, but also the things I would much prefer to do myself. Like a thermostat, he tends to "cut in" when I am tired. I hear a piece of music that moves me deeply; but the twentieth time I hear it, the robot is listening *for* me and spoils all the fun. I go for a country walk; but it is the robot that hears the birds and sees the clouds. I note that I have even caught him making love to my wife.

It is the robot who stands in the way of PEs. We cannot dispense with him entirely, or we would be like newborn babes facing the world. Nevertheless, we *can* set the thermostat higher, so that he doesn't "cut in" so often. This was the essence of the method of George Gurdjieff, who forced his pupils to make greater and greater efforts. When I am bored, I tend to withdraw my effort voluntarily. And I am always withdrawing—quite unconsciously—from the reality around me, like someone recoiling from a bad smell. In effect, Gurdjieff taught his students to "smell" reality continually, to lean over and sniff it deeply, as if smelling a rare variety of rose. The kind of meditation taught by the Buddha and the *Bhagavad Gita* is again an attempt to keep the mind focused unwaveringly instead of switching it on and off erratically from moment to moment.

The next major clue came when I became acquainted with "split-brain physiology," and the discovery by Sperry and Gazzaniga that we apparently have two people living in our heads, in the left and right cerebral hemispheres. One split-brain patient tried to pull up his fly with one hand and undo it with the other; another tried to hit his wife with one hand while the other hand held it back. We have two people in our heads. The "left" is a scientist, the "right" is an artist. And the person you call "you" is the scientist. The artist is somehow out-of-touch with personal consciousness. So Mozart said tunes were always walking into his head fully fledged—he meant out of the right brain and into the left, where "he" lived. We are all, to some extent, split-brain patients.

This I saw as one of my most important steps forward. As a writer, it had been clear to me from early on that this split-brain business was *my* problem. When I was in a good mood, the intuitions and insights came up in a flood, and I tried to turn them into words and get them down on paper. I often felt I had succeeded magnificently.

But when I looked again the next morning, the insight had evaporated; the words had squashed it flat. Nevertheless, I kept on trying, and eventually I learned how to catch the insight without squashing it. And on some occasions, my left brain would catch the insights so neatly that the right began to get excited, and its approval would encourage the left. Then suddenly the two halves would be working together in magnificent cooperation, like two lumberjacks at either end of a double-handed saw. These are the states we call "inspiration."

Early in the nineteenth century, the philosopher Johann Fichte made the same observation: that a philosopher can feel a total nonentity when he is sitting in his armchair brooding on the nature of reality. But the moment he launches himself into *action*, something seems to harden inside him; the alienation vanishes and he feels "real." In terms of the right-left analysis (which, I must emphasize, is offered only as a working model, not as a physiological description), he had become stranded in his left-brain identity. Launching into action woke up the other lumberjack. We only feel "real" when the lumberjacks are working together. Sartre may have been wrong about many things, but he was right when he said the philosopher must make a commitment that allows him to *act*.

Certain writers and artists have always understood this intuitively—for example, D. H. Lawrence, Henry Miller, and most of that "Beat Generation" who derived from Miller. Yet, it seems to me, they all made one major mistake. They felt that the answer lies in breaking the monopoly of the left-brain identity by deliberately withdrawing into the realm of intuition—often with the help of pot or psychedelic drugs. Voltaire perceived the fallacy involved here when he pulled Rousseau's leg about wanting to move in with the cows and eat grass. Left-brain consciousness may entrap us in boredom and alienation, but we developed it for a reason: to be able to focus *precisely* on problems—like a watchmaker peering through his eyeglass—and make the correct diagnosis. The answer does not lie in returning to the broader and less demanding right-brain awareness of our Neolithic ancestors. Left-brain awareness tends to slow us down because its narrowness—its "worm's eye view"—leads to discouragement and loss of direction. The direction can be regained by the peak experience, the "bird's eye view." But there is also a left-brain solution. If I can use the "bird's eye moments" to draw a map, then I shall eventually be able to navigate my way around the city with as much confidence as if I could achieve PEs at a moment's notice. In fact, I may eventually develop so much sense of direction that I can reconstitute the "bird's eye view" in my mind's eye, and see the city from the air while walking on the ground, so to speak. This is an ability that the psychologist Pierre Janet labeled "the reality function" *(fonction du réel)*, and which I have called "Faculty X."

When this faculty is operative—as it is in me for brief periods— the question of the connection between belief and action disappears. They blend into a unity. For me, the problem—and the daily task— is how to get the faculty to operate all the time.

Edward O. Wilson

b. 1929

As an adolescent, Edward O. Wilson decided that he would pursue his interest in ants and other social insects and become an entomologist. After earning his B.S. and M.S. degrees from the University of Alabama, he entered the doctoral program in biology at Harvard, where he contributed to the "new systematics," which combined principles of evolutionary theory with the methodologies of scientific classifications. In 1958, he joined the Harvard faculty, becoming professor of Zoology in 1964, and the Frank B. Baird, Jr., Professor of Science in 1976. Since 1973, he has also held the position of curator of Entomology at Harvard's Museum of Comparative Zoology.

Drawing mainly on his own work on biogeography and population biology, Dr. Wilson published The Insect Societies *in 1971, a definitive and comprehensive treatment of social insects. He soon extended the approach he had used in studying insects to the social behavior of other organisms in another monumental book,* Sociobiology: The New Synthesis *(1975). Its publication unleashed a storm of contro-*

versy, largely due to his belief that biological principles underlying the structure of societies in other animals are applicable to the social behavior of humans. Professor Wilson drew fire from academicians who resented his intrusion into the social sciences and by scientists who contended that cultural and environmental forces alone shape man's behavior; still others charged him with encouraging racism.

While attempting to reassure his critics that he only saw "maybe 10 percent of human behavior as genetic and 90 percent as environmental," he vehemently protested the attempted suppression of a scientific theory simply because it could be distorted for political ends. His insistence on the freedom to study nature and to confront the implications of scientific findings, however unorthodox, contributed to his decision to write On Human Nature *(1978), a work he claimed to be not of science, but about science. The provocative and gracefully written volume was awarded the Pulitzer Prize for general nonfiction in 1979. In* Biophilia *(1984), Dr. Wilson argues that despite some outward evidence to the contrary, humans are genetically programmed to love all living things.*

My beliefs, by which I mean my view of how the world works from the top down, originated from an unusual blend of religious and scientific experience. I was raised as a fundamentalist Baptist in Alabama and Florida during the thirties and forties. At fifteen, I accepted Jesus Christ and was officially born again at a baptismal service by being tipped backward under the water. I remember vividly the moment I decided on this action. It came, as it has for so many others before and after me, at a revival meeting. A tenor was singing a deeply moving hymn, the back-country equivalent of Haydn and cathedral organs:

> *Were you there, when they crucified my Lord?*
> *Were you there, when they nailed him to the cross?*
> *Oh, sometimes it causes me to tremble . . . tremble . . .*

I loved the power of the evangelical songs and services. I can still remember the sequence of events of that remarkable day: opening hymns by the choir, followed by prayers, the reading of a biblical passage by the preacher, the exegesis (lightened with a funny anecdote or two), and then the climactic moment toward which the service had been pointed all along—conversion. With all standing and the choir singing, the preacher called for those yet to be saved to come forward down the aisles to declare for Christ. As our faces were lifted and tears filled our eyes, the preacher intoned the hymn's counterpoint in a soft-breaking chant: "Won't you come? Jesus is calling. Won't you come?"

It so happened that I was listening to a second call at the same time. Partly because I was an only child, introverted by nature, growing up in small towns close to the woods and shoreline, I developed an intense early interest in biology. I was thrilled by the teeming life around me, by frogs, snakes, fish, and the seemingly endless variety of plants and insects in the southern habitats. By the time I entered the University of Alabama at the age of seventeen, I was a devoted entomologist with a large personal collection of insects, dreaming of a life in science. Very soon I encountered the formal disciplines of genetics and evolutionary theory. I came upon a hard truth: I saw that all I had learned and hoped to accomplish in natural history studies made sense only from the vantage of scientific materialism. Very little of it could be fitted into the fundamentalist view of the world in which I had been indoctrinated.

When an overheated vessel is plunged into cold water, it will crack or be tempered. I felt I had to choose the path of scientific materialism to make sense of the real world as it now appeared to me in vivid detail. I chose to learn as a scientist, but I never forgot the power of religion. I never lost respect for the sincere feelings of my fellow southerners, however different from my own. Not long ago I attended a small service given at Harvard University by Martin Luther King, Sr., months before his final illness. As the sermon and spirituals rolled me back forty years, the tears returned. Somehow the allegiance seemed compatible with the intellect.

Today, I would call myself a scientific humanist, someone who believes in humility toward other people but not toward the gods. (Religionists are for the most part oriented the other way around.) A scientific humanist in turn is someone who suggests that everything in the universe has a material basis. And that means *everything*, including the mind and all its spiritual products. I think it probable that mankind evolved without external direction. We are responsible to ourselves alone, and this condition imposes on us both more personal freedom and a heavier obligation toward one another and life on earth than is usual for systems relying on divine guidance. I also believe that the only way we will ever really find out about our place in nature is through scientific research. It will not resemble the creation myths of traditional religions.

Rash words, you might say, arrogant. The ancient Greeks called it *hubris,* a punishable affront to the gods, but I think that we ought to push science and the philosophy of materialism to their limit and not worry about the gods. I am respectful toward, but not impressed by, those who claim to draw strength from sources outside humanity. I believe religion and ideology are products of the mind, and that they can be profitably studied as such. In fact, they are best understood as material phenomena. What have we to lose? Who can reasonably fault humanity for displaying intellectual courage, or doubt that the best in human beings is yet to come? Let us see how high we can fly before the sun melts the wax in our wings.

Humanism is in the spirit of Prometheus, who raised human beings from the animals and tried to set them free. Mysticism and piety could appropriately take as their patroness Pandora, who merely transferred what the gods chose to offer. Scientific humanism implies that the material content of a human being is awesome in its own right. Consider the genetic content of a single cell. If the DNA in the forty-six chromosomes were to be fully stretched out, it would reach about a meter, half the height of a tall man. But the material would be invisible, because the double helix of DNA is a super-thin giant molecule. If the double helix were now enlarged until it were as thick as a piece of wrapping string, and hence easily seen by the naked eye, it would stretch over a thousand miles—say, from New York to some point past Kansas City. By walking from one end to the other, read-ing off fifty or so nucleotides to the inch, you could acquire roughly one billion bits of information, whereas one bit is the amount needed to know whether a tossed coin comes up heads or tails. If that much information were then translated into English prose (two bits to a letter) and printed in letters as large as those on this page, the script would just about fill all fifteen editions of the *Encyclopaedia Britannica* published since 1768.

That is merely the blueprint. One of the final products built from

the molecular instructions is the human brain, by far the most veri-
fiably complex structure in the universe. It comprises about 100 billion neurons, each of which makes hundreds of thousands of connections with other neurons. The microscopic anatomy and computing
power of this organ has scarcely been mapped. The honeybee, a creature one-millionth our size and with a brain composed of a relatively
modest million nerve cells, is able to perform more than fifty very
different instinctive acts, from the building of waxen combs to communication by the performance of waggle dances. It can also memo-
rize the location of five different flower beds and the hours of the day
in which each bed comes into fullest bloom. If an insect can accomplish that much with a brain the size of a sugar grain, it should not
be thought scandalous that human beings can speak, dream, and experience soaring emotions without divine instructions.

Of course most people, even if they accept a material basis of the
mind, still think that the human brain could not have arisen on its
own. They make an assumption older than philosophy itself, that a
product of high quality implies a craftsman of equal or higher quality.
Thus the mere existence of a human being implies the existence of
God. But the whole thrust of modern biology points in the opposite
direction. So far as can be determined, life consists of the action of
molecules (immensely complex molecules, to be sure) and is obedient
to the same laws of physics and chemistry that govern the nonliving
world. Once the genetic code and operational proteins are put in place
within a favorable environment, tissues and organs assemble themselves. Evolution proceeds for the most part by natural selection, a
blind but creative process that directs change millions of times faster
than any conceivable randomization of molecules. The history of the
earth has spanned enough time—4.5 billion years—for simple organisms to originate from nonliving molecules and to proliferate into the
higher manifestations of life, including the thousand miles of genetic
information, the one-pound brain, and the passionate religious faiths
that define the human species.

Humanity came this way alone. Evolving populations of pre-humans
diverged from the line leading to chimpanzees (with whom we still
hold about 98 percent of genes in common) five to ten million years
ago and commenced the steep climb to its present state two million
years ago. We know few details of the final ascent, and we have only
begun to study the interaction between genetics and culture that pow-
ered it. Nevertheless, from what is understood of the general princi-

ples of evolution, two million years was time enough to produce the complex architecture that differentiates the human brain from that of the animal. A natural creation of humanity is more plausible than a supernatural creation.

The autonomous origin of mankind is the linchpin of scientific humanism. Yet most scientists have tacitly agreed to stand clear of the subject. In particular they avoid the most interesting of all human traits: religion. Like the 1493 papal decree that divided the world into Spanish and Portuguese dominions, they accept a line of inquiry that places religion on one side and science on the other. They do so because the linchpin of religion is *feeling*. How rewarding it is to suspend further doubt, to belong to something greater than the self, larger than humanity! How tempting it is not to scrutinize those feelings too closely!

There is a strong counterargument to the separation of science and religion. Whether or not it is correct makes, quite literally, all the difference in the world. It goes as follows: Religion presides over consecration, adult initiation, marriage, and the other rites of passage, and sees you through the dark hours. Faith is woven from powerful emotions and is virtually built into the emotive centers of the brain. It promotes strength, survival, the ability to put DNA into the next generation. The DNA thus favored prescribes brains capable of such faith. Religion is ultimately a product of evolution by natural selection. Above all, these feelings bind us to family and to the tribe. They gain added power by being sacralized, in other words reinforced by a supposed divine power presiding over the welfare of the tribe. Our brains are programmed to this extent: morality is unconsciously shaped to create new rationalizations for the consecration of the group, the proselytizing role of altruism, and the defense of territory. Human behavior, including the capacities for emotional response that drive and guide it, is the circuitous route by which human genetic material has been and will be kept intact. We are religious to survive; we surrender to the tribe and its sacred rites in a gamble for both personal and genetic immortality.

In reaching this position (tentatively: it is after all only a theory), I have departed from most other humanists in stressing that the predisposition to religious belief is the most complex and powerful drive in the human mind, an innate and possibly irreplaceable part of human nature. But this does not mean that any particular religious code enjoys a divine sanction. Not all who claim such a sanction go so far

as to assert that their religion is superior. But there are those who
do, and they press their belief with self-righteous fanaticism. Ayatol-
lah Khomeini, for example, recommended killing infidels as "a sur-
gical operation commanded by God" and religious (actually tribal) war
as "a blessing for the world." This form of bigotry normally comes
in softer forms with an aim to protect co-tribalists, proselytize unbelievers, and encourage conformity. No Christian ever became a saint
by promoting Hinduism.

The idea that something outside our brain is in charge of human
destiny is emotionally rewarding and worked marvelously well during
the heyday of tribes and chiefdoms, when communal self-delusion
gave a competitive advantage over other cultures. The need today, if
the humanist explanation is correct, is to understand the material origin of the religious drive and direct it back to humanity without
losing its ability to give power and joy to the human mind. At the
close of *On Human Nature* I suggested that the Promethean spirit of
science can liberate man by giving him a more secure knowledge of
his own meaning.

My interest in the objective study of human nature was aroused in
a roundabout way. Since my greatest ambition was to be an entomologist, I began my career by specializing in the biology of ants.
While an undergraduate at the University of Alabama, I conducted
some successful research on these insects. As a result I was invited to
enter the doctoral program at Harvard in 1951. I joined the faculty in
1956 and have been there ever since. Over the years, my studies expanded to include the social life of all kinds of insects, which I set out
to explain by means of modern genetic and evolutionary biology. In
1971, I published *The Insect Societies*, the first book in my "sociobiology trilogy." I then began a still broader survey of the entire
animal kingdom, producing *Sociobiology: The New Synthesis* in 1975.
The central purpose of the new discipline, to which this work contributed, was to explain all forms of social behavior as the outcome of
biological evolution. My book met with good reviews and grew into
that relative rarity, an academic best seller. It also received a good
deal of criticism and has been the focus of continuing controversy
ever since, because I suggested that much of human behavior is under
the control of genes. I argued that the core of human nature, including not only the ability to create language and culture but also our
drives and the predisposition to learn certain ideas, is prescribed by

genes that were assembled in stepwise fashion over millions of years. In *On Human Nature* (1978), I explored the consequences of this updated version of materialism for religion and moral reasoning.

Yeats once said that to quarrel with yourself produces poetry; to quarrel with others, rhetoric. For more than thirty years I have struggled inwardly to explain evolution by natural selection, which I consider demonstrably true and the only rational explanation for the diversity of life on earth. I have tried to avoid quarreling with those who believe otherwise.

Every person constructs his life around a belief system. Mine has led me increasingly to environmentalism, which I try to promote by means of writing, by service on committees and boards devoted to environmental issues, and, as much as an introverted personality allows, by activism on behalf of particular threatened species and habitats. My attention has turned increasingly to the moist forests of the tropics, where the great majority of the ten million or more species live. Because these remarkable habitats are being reduced at the rate of about one percent a year, thousands and possibly even millions of species could be lost during the next half century. Each species is a wonder unto itself, worthy of a lifetime of study and contemplation. The native fauna and flora of each country are part of its national heritage, as important as its art and history. I am convinced that they will come to be valued far more by our descendants than they are by us, and that we will someday be blessed for every species we save as we pass through the current bottleneck of environmental impoverishment.

It is further true that the chief problems of the developing countries are ultimately biological in origin. Overpopulation, disease, soil depletion, and habitat destruction are at the base of their tumultuous political and social change. These difficulties cannot be solved merely by industrialization or a change in ideology. A better existence can only come from crops sowed on the land and a redemption of the environment. Hence, I feel doubly committed to help save these threatened tropical environments.

I suppose that my life illustrates the observation by Albert Camus that a man's work is nothing but "the slow trek to rediscover, through the detours of art, those two or three great and simple images in whose presence his heart first opened." The confluence of my concerns has become the study of life in all its manifestations, from the evolution and preservation of organic diversity to the origin of human nature. I am convinced that to act on these beliefs, to pursue humanism through a search for material knowledge with due respect for the beliefs and feelings of others, is a decent way to conduct a life.

Pat York

Michael York

b. 1942

Michael York is the internationally known actor. He was born in 1942 in England. He found an early love for the theatre and was a member of Britain's National Youth Theatre. He is a graduate of Oxford University, where he majored in English and also appeared in numerous theatrical productions. He made his professional debut the traditional way "in rep" and went on to appear with the National Theatre Company. His first film was Zefirelli's The Taming of the Shrew *and he has subsequently made over thirty others, including* Cabaret, The Three Musketeers, *and* Logan's Run. *He has also appeared on Broadway and in regional theatre and in many TV productions, including "Jesus of Nazareth" and, more recently, "Space."*

Fundamentally, I believe that one has a responsibility to organize one's life so that it embellishes society. Altruistic concern with whales or disadvantaged people is pointless if one's own affairs are disorganized and morally unfocused. But how? How are we to live in a world where moral standards are constantly shifting? Nationalism has proved a false god. Colonialism is discredited and imperialism suspect. The most obscure cults and religions are no longer practiced in the remoteness of some mountain or jungle, but are the stuff of Western ashrams and television documentaries. The family as an organic unit has lost its homogeneity. In the babble of prevailing doctrines is there one still small voice that can be clearly heard?

A quotation of George Bernard Shaw's comes to mind, one that made a strong impression on me at an early age. I submitted it, in fact, in a children's competition organized by an English newspaper for the "best New Year's resolution." The prize was a dinner, dance, and overnight stay at a prestigious London hotel. I proved to be the winner, and as I luxuriated in the unaccustomed splendor of my award, I vowed whenever possible to live up to Shaw's maxim: "Without good manners human society becomes intolerable and impossible."

Being brought up as an English schoolboy meant that I learned to raise my cap and observe the niceties of polite society. With my accent slowly conforming to what was then considered acceptable in our class-conscious society, I was more a snob than a model of the English gentleman I aspired to be. And yet that paragon—the gentleman— had quite definitely existed. In his most nearly perfect realization, he was the envy of the world—a compendium of courage, wisdom, humility, daring, and kindness. Perhaps in our changing times this quintessence of civilization has gone the way of the dinosaurs. Yet despite all the snobbery and stupidity that have besmirched the name of the gentleman, I still believe that the observance of his finer qualities has a positive benefit for us all.

You will notice that in my definition of the gentleman, I omitted any reference to religion. I did so reluctantly, however, because religion has been a great civilizing force. But as much as I admire some of the social by-products of organized religion, I believe that spiritual life is far too extraordinary to be cramped within the confines of rules. I was brought up in the state religion of England; one honored both the old God and the new Queen, which at the time seemed a sensible distribution of allegiance. But now that I live and work all over the world, I look for wider spiritual horizons.

As a boy I sang in the church choir. It kept me off the streets and even provided me with welcome pocket money. After a while, and especially during the emotional intensity of adolescence, I came to love all the dramatic associations of the choir—the robes, the sun-struck glass, the fuming incense, the ritual, and the ceremony. Indeed it infused in me a kind of aesthetic confusion. Since then, whenever I am deeply moved by music or drama, I am reminded of that time in my life and that side of my nature that aspires to the ecstasy, radiance, and passion of godly perfection.

But this same fervor has a darker side. Too often inflamed into fanaticism, and bred with intolerance, it has brought forth its terrifying progeny: war. Peter Ustinov once remarked to me that "we are united by our doubts and divided by our convictions." Indeed, I would love the establishment of a Doubters Church (although I regret the negative connotation) where each man could enjoy, not unthinking dogmatic solidarity, but a union of souls seeking paths to enlightenment. As a child, I resisted being confirmed in the faith in which I had been baptized because I wanted this step, when and if it came, to be vitally meaningful: the willing and joyful acceptance of a formula for living that had been weighed in the balance of real experience.

A Doubters political party would probably lead to anarchy. Unlike the spiritual realm, the physical world has to be organized and fed, educated, reprimanded, and encouraged. Conviction becomes the wellspring of action, and leaders are rarely drawn from the ranks of the irresolute. Amidst whatever political coercion, one condition remains fundamental and inviolate: the freedom of thought and speech. As one who trades in borrowed thoughts and mimicked actions, fettered only by the constraints of taste and style, I am especially aware and appreciative of this basic freedom. Where it is denied, for whatever reason, tyranny prevails. As William Pitt observed, "Necessity is the plea for every infringement of human freedom. It is the argument of tyrants; it is the creed of slaves."

As an actor, I appropriate other people's thoughts and words and often, by a process of spiritual osmosis, this rag-bag of assorted phil-osophical scraps is absorbed into my own being. "This above all to thine own self be true" is probably the best and the most difficult advice to follow. For an actor it seems an almost impossible task. Where is the true face behind the multiplicity of masks? I have al-ways tried, whether playing a lover or a lunatic, to find some essential truth of character with which an audience could identify, so that the essence of the piece was honorably served. One is reminded of Ham-let's advice to the players: "The purpose of playing, whose end, both at the first and now, was and is, to hold, as 'twere, the mirror up to nature."

I value my profession most when a work of drama has the power to shake and shape public opinion. I think of the television film *The Day After*, about a nuclear attack on America, that forced a reluctant world to ponder the unthinkable. In my own experience, I remember a young woman visiting backstage after a Broadway performance of *Bent*. She told me that her mother was a near victim of the Holocaust, and prior to seeing my play she was unable to speak about her expe-riences. Upon seeing *Bent,* she was now able for the first time to recount and relate these experiences to her daughter. In my profes-sion, such moments are rare, yet unforgettable. Since then, more by coincidence than design, I have portrayed several people whose lives were inflamed by war. I have been involved in the re-creation of scenes of horror and moments of terror—the victimization of an entire race and the brutalization of both victim and victor. I have been there in the *Umschlagplatz* as trainloads of Jews were taken on the one-way journey to the camps. I have herded with refugees in the streets and have been beaten into subjection. In costume and make-up I have borne witness, not just as an actor, but for a whole generation.

Now that we have this extraordinary gift of television and film, this electronic mirror to hold up to nature, we must not squander it. It is a potent instrument of renewal, reformation, and life-affirming laughter. The sound of a packed theater laughing helplessly—sharing joy and raising spirits in moments of delighted complicity—is perhaps one of the most irresistible sounds that man has yet devised. The ability to make an audience laugh is certainly one of the most precious gifts that an actor can have; it is a philanthropic service and a giant boost for the ego! And certainly we all yearn for laughter to keep up our spirits in this stressful world. Byron's sardonic comment, "And if I laugh at any mortal thing/'Tis that I may not weep," may be too severe. Yet we have to be reminded that the sublime coexists with the ridiculous. The success of, nay the need for, wartime comic reviews, for example, demonstrates the urgent necessity for all of us to find comfort by emulating that Miltonic image of "laughter holding both its sides," even as the world is torn apart.

Perhaps the most daunting aspect of my work is its essential public nature: I become a role model, cast in scenarios over which I have little control. And herein lies an enormous responsibility. The screen image has a totemistic strength. It is no accident that the present chief politician of the free world is a former screen actor. And actors are employed by other countries for purposes of propaganda. Despite this manipulative offshoot of the acting profession, I still feel a responsibility to behave in such a way as to bring honor to my profession. That is why I consider the actors' acceptance of any kind of public office, the headlining of some charitable cause, even the writing of an essay like this one, to be not just a remarkable privilege, but an obligation to be fulfilled with all possible probity.

My work is essentially free-lance. Eschewing contracts and long-term engagements, I go from one engagement to the other. There is no continuity of environment or colleagues, no guarantee of success or opportunity. I am in the hands of a capricious destiny. Because of this, I am more than usually reliant upon the encouragement and support of friends. Living as I do as an alien in foreign lands, I am indebted to every one of my friends who has shared his or her time and trust with me. I hope that, if required, I would have the courage to emulate E. M. Forster's astonishing wartime resolution that he would rather betray his country than his friends.

There would be no hesitation or moral dilemma in the case of my greatest friend. She is my wife, Pat. She has shaped and uplifted my life from the moment I first met her that April day in London almost twenty years ago. We have rarely been apart since then. This is partly because we resolved to be together in a life that was both by choice and by profession peripatetic. I am a strong believer in the positive power of proximity and in the efficacy of vows and troths, and in the sharing alike of obligations and rewards. We have also shared a wealth of experience both pleasurable and painful. We have together marveled at some of the world's more extraordinary sights and have dipped into its cornucopia of earthly delights.

Edith Wharton once remarked that there are two ways of spreading light: to be the candle or the mirror that reflects it. I know that Pat and I have illuminated and mirrored each other's joys and have helped one another to laugh our fears into insignificance. Loneliness is an experience I would have to use an actor's skill to fabricate, for, in reality, despite the differences and misunderstandings, the checks and balances that are an inevitable part of marriage, I have never been without the encouragement and comfort that this committed companionship provides. Moreover, Pat is the most positive person that I know, and I can think of no one who better illustrates the power of this affirmative attitude than she. She sees life in terms of potentiality; she has taught me that "no" is the unacceptable answer. Nowhere has her belief in action been better illustrated than at the beginning of our relationship. We were in India, where I was making a film, when she fell ill and almost died. She fought to live and by sheer determination refused to give in to death. While her life was hanging in the balance, the grave Rajasthani doctors who were treating her told me simply that "She is in God's hands now." I believed it then and I believe it now. A power shapes our destinies, however much we convince ourselves we are free.

I believe that life is too extraordinary a privilege to compromise or waste, especially a comfortable life such as my own. At this midpoint, I would like to acknowledge this good fortune and even attempt to repay it. This perhaps can best be achieved by using the remaining years to complement the preceding ones, minimizing the mistakes and consolidating and confirming the achievements. I am convinced that the actor and the drama are essential to the well-being of our complex society. Isolated and exposed within proscenium or film-frame, humanity can be seen in all its paradoxical attitudes—an object of ridicule and admiration. But also, if our function is correctly fulfilled, an object of compassion, too. Indeed, "What a piece of work is man!"